ART AND HISTORY
ROME
and the VATICAN

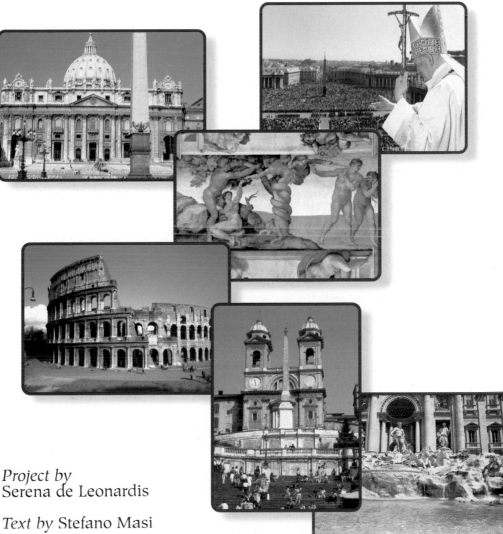

Project by
Serena de Leonardis

Text by Stefano Masi

BONECHI

CONTENTS

The city within the Aurelian walls has been
divided into 25 areas.
The corresponding chapters describe all the churches
and the palaces, the ancient monuments, the museums, and the
galleries in each area.

ART AND HISTORY - ROME AND THE VATICAN

© Copyright
by Casa Editrice Bonechi - Firenze - Italia
E-mail: bonechi@bonechi.it - Internet: www.bonechi.it

Publication created and designed by
Casa Editrice Bonechi
Editorial management: Serena de Leonardis
Picture research: Stefano Masi, Giovannella
Masini
Graphic design and layout: Serena de
Leonardis
Cover: Manuela Ranfagni
Make-up: Vanni Berti
Editing: Anna Baldini, Cristiana Berti
City and monument illustrations by
Stefano Benini

Text by Stefano Masi
Translation by Paula Boomsliter.
The chapters 'The Esquiline', 'The Aventine', 'The Oppian Hill',
'Piazza Esedra and the Umbertine Quarters', 'The Janiculum',
'Piazza di Spagna', and 'The Via Appia Antica'
were translated by Richard Dunbar.

Arte e Storia - Roma - n° 4 - Pubblicazione Periodica Trimestrale - Autorizzazione del
Tribunale di Firenze n° 3873 del 4/8/1989 - Direttore Responsabile: Giovanna Magi

Printed in Italy by
Centro Stampa Editoriale Bonechi - Sesto Fiorentino

PHOTOGRAPHY ACKNOWLEDGMENTS

The majority of the photographs are property of the Casa
Editrice Bonechi Archives. They were taken by
Marco Banti, Gaetano Barone, Marco Bonechi, Emanuela
Crimini, Gianni Dagli Orti, Serena de Leonardis, Paolo
Giambone, Nicola Grifoni, Stefano Masi, MSA, Andrea
Pistolesi, Gustavo Tomsich, Cesare Tonini, Michele
Tonini, Arnaldo Vescovo.

Other photographs were provided by

Foto Archivio Fabbrica di San Pietro in Vaticano:
pages 14, 15, 17, 18 above, 19, 20, 21 left.
Gaetano Barone: pages 23, 35.
Gianni Dagli Orti: pages 72 below right, 73 below
left, 96 below right, 116 above right and center, 123
below, 172 center, left, 173 center right, 183 below.
Foto Musei Vaticani:
pages 2, 26, 31 below;
page 38 below (P. Abbrescia);
pages 27/30, 31 above, 32, 33 below, 34 (A. Bracchetti, P. Zigrossi);
page 38 above (T. Okamura);
pages 33 above, 41 (P. Zigrossi).
Photographic Service of "L'Osservatore Romano" (Arturo Mari):
pages 7 below, 42.
Foto Pont. Comm. Arch. Sacra: page 189.
Scala - Istituto Fotografico Editoriale: pages 39, 40, 73 above, 138.
Giuliano Valsecchi: page 156 above.

The publisher apologizes for any unintentional omissions. We would be
pleased to include any appropriate acknowledgments of which we are
informed in subsequent editions of this publication.

ISBN 88-476-0178-9

* * *

INTRODUCTION

THE CITY THROUGH THE CENTURIES

*T*he history of a city like Rome is for all practical purposes the history of the world - and for this reason it is all but impossible, in a brief introduction, to succeed in delineating anything like an even essential chronology. More thorough information has been included in the paragraphs introducing the single districts, when it seemed fitting to provide a more exhaustive outline of the history of the area and the evolution of the urban fabric in relation to the single monuments and works of art that qualify each. It is nevertheless indispensable that we provide those basic historical, artistic and general cultural coordinates that defined the environments in which the major development initiatives took place; those points which can help to shed light on the pluri-millenarian and obviously complex process of evolution of a metropolis like Rome, from the date of its legendary foundation in 753 BC to the two-thousandth year of Christian history, which elected as its capital the city on the Tiber, and in particular the Vatican.

One possible 'reading' of Rome may proceed through analysis of its dual nature as **capital of the ancient world** and **capital of Christendom**, each of which roles profoundly influenced the city's development as they alternated, or better interacted and succeeded the one the other over the course of the centuries. The essence of a city like Rome lies precisely in the progressive stratification of successive urban entities, each informed by different criteria and different functional requirements; that is, by overlapping ordering principles that were the fruits of different epochs and cultures but that nevertheless all aimed (and aim) at proclaiming Rome caput mundi, guiding light of Western civilization, holy city, and symbol of the history of mankind.

The head of the colossal statue of the emperor Costantine. Capitoline Museums.

city extended to embrace nuclei of Italic populations living on the surrounding hills: the Sabines, who occupied the **Quirinal** and the **Viminal**, the Latins, who lived on the **Aventine**, and other communities on the **Esquiline** and the **Caelian** hills. When unification was achieved, a seventh hill, the **Campidoglio**, on which as tradition has it Romulus had offered his hospitality to all these peoples at the **Asylum Romuli**, was chosen as the acropolis: on it stood the Capitoline Arx and the Temple of Jupiter Optimus Maximus, the patron god of the city.

The city later spread out into the flatter area demarcated by the Palatine, the Oppian and the Quirinal hills, where the **Roman Forum** rose, and into that area that from the Campidoglio faced the Tiber and the Tiber Island, where instead the Forum Boarium and the Forum Holitorium were built. These forums were more markedly trade-oriented, since the area was near the Portus Tiberinus, the river port that played such an important role in the economic life of Rome.

When the age of monarchy (6th century BC), in which seven kings succeeded one another, was drawing to its end, the city was provided with a defensive circle. The so-called **Servian Walls**, traditionally attributed to king Servius Tullius, were actually built in about the 4th century BC during the republican age, a period of great economic prosperity for the city. Well-being later increased, above all following the Punic and the civil wars, and the urban fabric consequently stretched to include the previously uninhabited Campus Martius, a vast flat area between the Tiber and the crown of hills from the Campidoglio to the Pincio. The look of the city also changed, thanks to construction of new public buildings in marble and travertine, including the great basilicas of the Forum, temples, patrician palaces, and villas - but also sprawling 'low-income' neighborhoods.

Expansion continued into the successive centuries, and was given a strong stimulus in the first century BC by Caesar, who enlarged the Roman Forum beyond its traditional limits and so created the first nucleus of what was to become the **Imperial Forums**.

Augustus followed the example set by his illustrious predecessor by launching a far-reaching construction program that was destined to continue for much of the imperial age. In particular, following Nero's fire of 64 AD and that of 80 AD, the city was rebuilt to a more rational and functional plan that was also expression of the magniloquent imperial ideology. Rome continued to grow and to acquire grandiose monuments and superb buildings erected by the various ruling dy-

ANCIENT ROME

Primitive Rome, the so-called Roma Quadrata enclosed by the circuit of walls laid out by Romulus, arose and flourished on the **Palatine** hill, where traces of Bronze Age human settlement have been found. From this height, the

Above, the Lupa Capitolina, symbol of the city of Rome. Rome, Capitoline Museums.

Center page: the Colosseum.

Left: detail of the Ara Pacis Augustae, built to celebrate Emperor Augustus' policy of pacification.

nasties: colossal public works, surely, including baths, circuses, theaters, and libraries, but also structures raised for the sole purpose of celebrating imperial grandeur, like honorary columns and triumphal arches.

Ancient Rome achieved its maximum expansion in the second century, when it was divided into 14 districts and counted more than one million inhabitants. Urban growth slowed in the next century, however, and the threat of barbarian invasions spurred the emperor Aurelian (270-275) to ring Rome with a larger and more powerful defensive circle, called the **Aurelian Walls**.

There thus began a long period of decadence during which the city slowly depopulated and construction and building maintenance work was for the most part suspended, with the foreseeable result that Rome's monuments began to fall into ruin. But in the meantime, a new force that was destined to radically change the face of the city had arisen and acquired momentum: the Christian religion. Although initially assailed by imperial policy, it spread first among the lowest classes and later among upper-class citizens, until it permeated even the highest levels of the Roman state.

MEDIEVAL ROME
AND THE FOUNDING
OF THE BASILICAS MAJOR

In parallel with the official acknowledgment of the Christian religion by Emperor **Constantine** (Edict of Milan, 313 AD), the face of the city slowly began to alter. The fist sign of change was the construction of what are known as the **Constantinian basilicas**, which, while still structured along the lines of the Roman buildings of the same name, performed a radically different function: they were no longer civil edifices but places of worship. The first to be built was San Giovanni in Laterano, like the others situated in an outlying district of the ancient city (it is to be noted that the structure of the city center remained substantially the same during the three successive centuries, except for the increasingly-evident signs of a relentless decline). Thus, in 312-315, the basilica of Saint John was raised on the property of the Laterani family, as was the Patriarchate, the first official see of the Bishop of Rome; the Lateran complex remained the center of papal power until the late 14th century, when the papacy chose to move to the **Vatican**. It was in this area, near Nero's Circus where Saint Peter was martyred, that the second of the Constantinian basilicas was built beginning in 320. Together with San Paolo fuori le Mura, founded in 324, and Santa Maria Maggiore, dating to 356, San Pietro in Vaticano (Saint Peter's) and San Giovanni in Laterano marked the extremities of the routes that with their right-angle intersection near the Colosseum sketched the symbolic cruciform plan on which medieval Rome developed. The barbarian invasions of the 5th century and the Gothic War of 535-553 marked the period of Rome's furthest decline; nonetheless, alongside the tituli (the parochial churches that arose near the early Christian places of worship, often in private homes) there began to be built, mainly in the more remote areas of the city, the major **early Christian churches**: San Clemente and Santi Quattro Coronati in the Lateran area; Santa Pudenziana on the Esquiline, Santo Stefano Rotondo and Santi Giovanni e Paolo on the Caelian hill; Santa Sabina, Santa Prisca, and Santa Balbina on the Aventine; San Crisogono, Santa Cecilia, and Santa Maria in Trastevere in the district of that name; Sant'Agnese and Santa Costanza on the Via Nomentana; and Santi Nereo and Achilleo on the Via Appia.

The heart of ancient Rome was for a time disregarded, and was first drawn into the vortex of urban development in the

7th century, when the ban on transforming pagan temples into churches was lifted. There thus began a period of intensive demolition and successive rebuilding during which the ancient construction materials were reused and the existing buildings transformed into sacred edifices (Pantheon, Temple of Fortuna Virilis, Temple of Vesta) that were often entirely decorated with precious mosaics and frescoes. Initially the work of local labor, the decorations were increasingly influenced by Byzantine art (Santi Cosma e Damiano, Sant'Agnese, Santa Maria Antiqua) and this type of early Christian art persisted throughout the early Middle Ages until the Carolingian period, when a rebirth of the city began. Rome by this time was under strict papal control, and on Christmas Day of the year 800, in Saint Peter's, Charlemagne was crowned first emperor of the Holy Roman Empire.

In the first half of the ninth century, the basilicas of Santa Prassede, Santa Maria in Domnica, Santa Cecilia, and San Marco all glistened with splendid mosaics, thanks mainly to Pope Paschal I, but this evanescent blossoming soon ended when the Saracens invaded Rome and sacked even the basilicas of Saint Peter and Saint Paul. In order to better defend the city from these raids, Pope Leo IV had the Vatican enclosed within a circle of stout walls, with its bridgehead in Castel Sant'Angelo, that delimited what was known as the 'Leonine City'. During the next two centuries the city was lacerated by struggles between the imperial powers and the local nobility, and then by the War of Investitures, until in 1084 it was put to fire and the sword by the conquering Normans.

The 12th century was a time of slow but steady civil and political recovery - the Comune was instituted in 1143 and the city senate began meeting on the Campidoglio - as well as of construction. Many of the previously-damaged churches were restored according to the stylistic canons of Romanesque art: San Clemente, Santi Quattro Coronati, Santa Maria in Trastevere, San Crisogono, and Santa Maria in Cosmedin. The Lombard influence is evident in the many Romanesque brick bell towers that rose during the reconstruction of these and other churches (Santa Francesca Romana, Santi Giovanni e Paolo, Santa Maria Maggiore). The masters of Cosmati work were also active during this pe-

THE TALKING STATUES

Among the most interesting and imaginative curiosities in Rome are the so-called 'talking statues'. They of course do not really talk, but they 'speak' through short satirical compositions written on placards anonymously hung around their necks, a tradition that has continued for four centuries. The messages express public discontent with cutting and salacious wit in rhyme and prose.

The most famous of these statues is the **Pasquino,** from which the term *Pasquinade* is derived, usually with the meaning of satirical compositions. A fragment of a Hellenistic marble group representing Menaleus holding the body of Patroclus, the statue was placed at the corner of Palazzo Braschi facing the small square of Parione, a short distance from Piazza Navona, by Cardinal Oliviero Carafa in 1501. The custom of hanging satirical comments began when Roman gymnasium students would, on the Saint Mark's Day (April 25), attach satirical epigrams in Latin to the pedestal of Pasquino.

Other statues soon became used for the same purpose. The first was **Marforio,** the effigy of a river god of the 1st century BC. After that came **Madama Lucrezia,** a huge female bust placed near the church of San Marco, the **Abate Luigi** in Piazza Vidoni, the **Fontana del Facchino** in Via Lata, and the statue of the Silenus, known as **Babuino,** in Via Babuino.

riod: using marbles and other culled material, they created the inlaid floors, portals, ambos, bishops' thrones, and funeral monuments that admirably decorate these and other churches; in the 13th century, in particular, the Vassalletto family decorated the cloisters of San Giovanni in Laterano and San Paolo fuori le Mura with their fanciful columns with mosaic highlights. Mosaic and a fresco decoration also evolved and moved away from the Byzantine models, above all with Jacopo Torriti, the author of the mosaics in the apse of Santa Maria Maggiore and San Giovanni in Laterano, and with Pietro Cavallini, who painted the fine Last Judgment in Santa Cecilia. Both artists were active until the end of the 13th century. During the same period, a recurring theme in civil architecture, the mirror of the emergence and the rivalry of the noble families that unceasingly contended control of the various districts of the city, was the **tower home** (Torre dei Conti, Torre dei Capocci, Torre dei Caetani), some of which were adaptations of ancient Roman buildings, like the Savelli (later Orsini) palace that rose on the ruins of the Theater of Marcellus.

This period of intense artistic fervor was followed by one of the darkest in the city's history: the papacy was transferred to Avignon, France, where it remained from 1309 until 1377. Nor did the return to Rome of Pope Gregory XI in 1378, followed by the Great Western Schism, healed only in 1418, provide any new stimuli to development. This explains why there is little of the Gothic in Rome's churches and city monuments; Roman Gothic flourished only in the late 13th and early 14th centuries (Santa Maria sopra Minerva) and found expression primarily in sculptural works, like the elegant ciboria of San Paolo fuori le Mura and of Santa Cecilia, both by Arnolfo di Cambio.

RENAISSANCE AND BAROQUE ROME

In 1443, Pope Eugenius IV Condulmer returned to Rome after his long exile in Florence, where he had come to know and appreciate the artistic expressions of the Renaissance. A few years later he summoned to Rome the major exponents of that art, among whom Masolino da Panicale and Filarete, respectively the authors of the frescoes in San Clemente and of the bronze portal of Saint Peter's. There thus began an era of true civil and cultural rebirth in the city that followed on the first, timid steps in that direction by Eugenius' predecessor Martin V Colonna. The movement intensified halfway through the century, under Pope Nicholas V Parentucelli; other Tuscan artists continually arrived at the papal court, by that time equal in prestige and splendor to those of many Italian princes. Lorenzo Ghiberti, Donatello, Isaiah da Pisa, Leon Battista Alberti, and Rossellino are only a few of the most celebrated names. In 1452, the pope commissioned Rossellino to redesign the Leonine City and to give Saint Peter's basilica a Renaissance 'face lift' - but actualization of the plans had to await his successors.

In the meantime, the urban development of the city had begun to take the Vatican basilica and the contiguous papal see as its center. Growth proceeded along the three principal routes that from the Vatican branched out toward the other focal points of the city: the Via Peregrinorum (or dei Pellegrini) toward the Ghetto and Saint Paul's basilica, the Via Papalis (or Papale) toward the Campidoglio and San Giovanni in Laterano, and the Via Recta toward the district that had grown up around Santi Apostoli. It was in the latter area, at mid-century, that Pope Paul II Barbo commissioned Palazzo Venezia, a fine example of Renais-

sance civil architecture. But the **Renaissance** secured a truly firm footing in Roman civil and religious architecture (Palazzo della Cancelleria on the one hand and Santa Maria del Popolo, Sant'Agostino, and San Pietro in Montorio on the other), of which Bramante was an inspired exponent, only under Paul II's successor **Sixtus IV** Della Rovere, who was responsible for the building of the Sistine Chapel decorated by Botticelli, Ghirlandaio, Luca Signorelli, and Perugino.

A veritable revolution in art and architecture began in 1503, when **Julius II Della Rovere** ascended the papal throne. Going back to Nicholas V's plans, he commissioned Bramante to restructure Saint Peter's and to build the Via Giulia, which together with Via della Lungara formed new axes for city development parallel to the opposing banks of the Tiber. This new idea of a Renaissance city that bypassed the medieval city embraced by the bend in the river came also to create an alternative circuit linking the Ripa Grande river port in Trastevere to the Vatican, and the Vatican to the major Jubilee basilicas and to the Campidoglio. Under Julius II and

A detail of one of Michelangelo's frescoes in the Sistine Chapel.

his immediate successors, great artists breathed life into the most superb artistic creations of 16th-century Rome: Bramante, the Vatican palaces and courtyards, and later, Raphael the famous Rooms and Loggia and Michelangelo the pictorial decoration of the Sistine Chapel and architectural modifications to Saint Peter's. And many more, of which Peruzzi's Villa Farnesina and Palazzo Farnese, designed by Antonio da Sangallo the Younger, are only two examples. Pope Leo X Medici expanded on the Julian city plan by commissioning Sangallo and Raphael to build the Via Leonina - today's Via di Ripetta. It became the point of departure for urban growth around the 'Tridente' (three streets - Via di Ripetta, Via del Corso, and Via del Babuino - all leading off Piazza del Popolo). Further stimuli to development were supplied, after the interlude of the Sack of Rome in 1527, by Clement VII, another Medici pope.

In 1545, Paul III Farnese called the Council of Trent to define the tenets of Catholic unity (of which Rome came to represent more than ever before the ideal and symbolic center) following the Protestant reform, and thus initiated the Counter-Reformist period, characterized by the emergence of the new ecclesiastical order of the Society of Jesus, founded by Saint Ignatius of Loyola in 1534, for which the Gesù and Sant'Ignazio churches were built. Alongside the Jesuits there sprang up other religious organizations directed by as many orders, like the Theatine monks of Sant'Andrea della Valle and the 'Filippini' of Chiesa Nuova, while the city, above all under Pius IV de' Medici and Gregory XIII Boncompagni, continued to develop, through the works of architects like Giacomo Della Porta, Martino Longhi the Elder, Jacopo del Duca, Pirro Ligorio, Flaminio Ponzio, and Ottaviano Mascherino, along new thoroughfares (Strada Pia, Via Gregoriana, Via Merulana). The new plan was adopted and enlarged upon by Sixtus V Peretti, who with the architect Domenico Fontana laid out more new roads (Strada Felice) to unite the most important sites in the city in a series of theatrical prospects.

In the field of the figurative arts, there arose in the late 1500s the Mannerist school, which counted among its most illustrious exponents the brothers Taddeo and Federico Zuccari, Perin del Vaga, Vasari, and the Cavalier d'Arpino. Quite soon, however, the qualitatively excellent works of this school were challenged by the revolutionary painting of Caravaggio, who decorated the Contarelli Chapel in San Luigi dei Francesi in 1599-1602, during the papacy of Clement VIII Aldobrandini.

Caravaggio's work introduced a new period in art, commonly known as the **Baroque**. The ideas advanced by the painter from Lombardy were later developed by the 'Caravaggeschi' (Orazio Gentileschi, Gherardo Delle Notti, Spadarino, etc.). In parallel, the works of the Carracci family and their pupils, like Domenichino and Guido Reni, but also of artists like Pomarancio, Pietro da Cortona (who was also an architect), and Baciccia showed off another dimension of this innovative pictorial current in counterpoint to the architectural works of Bernini (also the author of admirable sculptures), Borromini, and Maderno. Works of unequaled perfection by the former two architects, in particular, contributed over much of the Seicento,

especially under popes Urban VIII Barberini, Innocent X Pamphili, and Alexander VII Chigi, to giving the city a new, monumental look. San Carlo alle Quattro Fontane, Sant'Ivo alla Sapienza, and the Oratorio dei Filippini are only three of Borromini's best efforts; Bernini, instead, left us Sant'Andrea al Quirinale, the Fontana dei Quattro Fiumi in Piazza Navona, and the Colonnade of Piazza San Pietro.

TOWARD MODERN TIMES: ROME CAPITAL OF ITALY

In the century spanning the year 1700, Rome saw the coronation of the Baroque exploit of 'spectacularizing' the urban fabric with works of imaginative theatrical impact such as the Spanish Steps, by De Sanctis, Filippo Raguzzini's Burrò, and Salvi's Fontana di Trevi. Another outstanding figure of this period was Piranesi, who, among his other merits, with his suggestive engravings threw a new light on the ancient Roman ruins, the use of which for development efforts had during the 1500s and 1600s been one of the cornerstones of Gregorian and Sistine policy.

Love for antiquity and archaeology later became one of the salient features of the neoclassical reweaving of the urban fabric, particularly in the wake of the French occupation in 1809-1814. This interest continued through the Restoration and the return, in 1815, of Pope Pius VII Chiaramonti to Rome. Only in 1864, the brief season of the Mazzini's and Garibaldi's Roman Republic (1849) having ended, and the Italy of the Risorgimento being well on its way toward unification under House of Savoy, did Francesco Saverio Malatesta produce the first city plan to provide for development and restructuring of the city in accordance with modern criteria. This plan was the foundation - once Italian unity had been achieved (1870) and Rome had been proclaimed the **capital city** of the kingdom - for urban renovation that while calling for large-scale demolition, to the principal detriment of the medieval city, also had the merit of improving circulation of traffic and permitting coherent development from the spatial and functional points of view. These same criteria continued to be followed in the late 1800s and early 1900s for the creation of the so-called 'Umbertine Rome'.

The process of modernization of the city (which was not unblemished by speculation) continued into the century and intensified in the 1930s during Fascist rule with work that on the one hand targeted recovery of the monuments of ancient Rome (Via dei Fori Imperiali, the excavations in the Largo Argentina archaeological area, renovation of the Theater of Marcellus and the Ara Pacis) and the Baroque era (Via della Conciliazione) as part of a propaganda effort to focus attention on the ideas of empire and tradition, and on the other embarked on construction of new, modern buildings, which albeit now and then 'rhetorical' were nevertheless eminently functional and architecturally valid (Teatro dei Marmi, Foro Italico, **EUR**).

Luckily only slightly damaged during the second global conflict, post-WWII Rome underwent steadily increasing expansion that was often lacking in architectural consistency but that considerably increased the extension of the city as its population, today about three million, steadily demanded more living space.

EUR, Palazzo della Civiltà del Lavoro. A detail of one of the four sculptural groups of the Dioscuri.

THE JUBILEE YEARS IN CHRISTIAN HISTORY

*T*he Christian Jubilee celebrations originate in Hebrew religious tradition. Biblical law ordered that every half-century there be declared a period of one-year's duration during which debts were remitted, slaves were freed, alienated goods were returned to their former owners, and the arable lands were redistributed. The origin of the word 'jubilee' lies in the Hebrew jobel = ram's horn, and also the name of the instrument that was sounded during the ceremony that proclaimed the Jubilee Year. The first Jubilee in Christian history was declared in 1300 by Pope Boniface VIII, who granted a plenary indulgence; that is, the remission of the temporal penalties for sin for all those faithful who, in respect of the Sacraments, having confessed their sins and received Communion, would also make pilgrimages to Saint Peter's Basilica and to the Basilica of San Paolo fuori le Mura, to the tombs of the two martyrs, at least once a day for a specified time - in the case of the inhabitants for thirty days, in the case of strangers for fifteen.

Over the centuries, the interval between one Jubilee Year and the next changed from fifty years to twenty-five; changes also came about in the modalities of celebration, the rites, and the ceremonials opening and closing the Jubilee Year, also called **Holy Year** or **Holy Year of Jubilee**. If, in fact, the bull published by Boniface VIII prescribed only visits to the tombs of the apostles Peter and Paul and to the two basilicas dedicated to them, Pope Urban VI added Santa Maria Maggiore to the list in 1390 and Martin V, in 1425, added San Giovanni in Laterano. In 1552, Saint Philip Neri lengthened to seven the list of the compulsory church visits for gaining the Roman Jubilee, by adding to the four patriarchal or greater basilicas three lesser basilicas: San Lorenzo fuori le Mura, Santa Croce di Gerusalemme, and San Sebastiano. The obligation to visit all seven of the designated basilicas remained in force until 1950, when their number returned to four. Traditionally, the Holy Year begins on Christmas Eve, when the pope opens the Holy Door, and ends a year later with its closing. Analogous ceremonies then take place in the other three patriarchal basilicas, each of which has its Holy Door. Over the course of the seven hundred years during which this tradition has been observed and which each time has attracted ever larger crowds of pilgrims, there have also been proclaimed extraordinary Jubilees to celebrate especially important occasions, while other, ordinary, Jubilees were suspended for political or historical reasons of various kinds. Certain Jubilees provided the occasion for grandiose **urban renewal** projects that contributed to giving Rome the sublime monumental aspect for which it is known throughout the world. The truly important Jubilee Years declared by the Catholic Church are twenty-seven in number, if we include that of the year 2000.

I (1300) - The first Jubilee Year in Christian history was declared by Boniface VIII Caetani, with the Papal Bull of 22 January. The text of the edict is inscribed on a stone slab in the atrium of Saint Peter's Basilica. Great political and cultural figures, among whom Carlo Martello, Dante, Giotto, and Cimabue, participated in the celebrations.

II (1350) - Proclaimed by Clement VI (Pietro Roger), during the period of the 'exile' when the popes resided in Avignon in France, this Holy Year was superintended in Rome by a papal legate. Many important figures had some part in the celebration of this Jubilee, including Saint Bridget, the patron saint of Sweden.

III (1390) - This was the first extraordinary Jubilee, proclaimed by Urban VI Prignano in an attempt to heal the Great Western Schism. It was continued by his successor Boniface IX Tomacelli, who also declared an unofficial Jubilee in 1400 to celebrate and propitiate the beginning of the new century.

IV (1423) - The second extraordinary Jubilee was proclaimed by Martin V Colonna to celebrate the ending of the Great Western Schism. Partial reconstruction of the city, which had suffered serious damage during the period of neglect that coincided with the exile of the papacy to Avignon, began on occasion of the announcement of this Holy Year. One of the buildings so favored was the Colonna family residence near the church of the Santi Apostoli; it provided a model for other cardinals' homes during the entire Quattrocento.

V (1450) - Nicholas V Parentucelli proclaimed this Jubilee, in which thousands of pilgrims participated, and also changed the interval between Holy Years from fifty to twenty-five years. For the occasion, the pope commissioned the Florentine architect Bernardo Rossellino to draft a plan for restructuring the city and the Vatican area in particular (renovation of Piazza San Pietro, reconstruction of the Basilica itself, and demolition of Borgo Vecchio to make room for a straight line thoroughfare toward Ponte Sant'Angelo) to accommodate the arrival en masse of the Jubilee Year pilgrims; the plan was brought to completion only following the end of the Jubilee.

VI (1475) - The proclamation of this Holy Year by Sixtus IV Della Rovere was preceded by an intensive urban renovation campaign, superintended by the camerlengo Cardinal William

The portraits of Pope Boniface VIII (1295-1303), who promulgated the first Jubilee Year in Christian history (above), and of Pope Sixtus IV (1471-84), during whose pontificate the Sistine Chapel was built and the Holy Year 1475 proclaimed.

Pope John Paul II greeting the crowds of pilgrims to Saint Peter's.

d'Estouteville, that was destined to substantially modify the look of Rome through reorganization of the road network, construction of Ponte Sisto, decoration of the basilicas, and the building or refurbishment of a great number of hospices to care for the pilgrims, among which the Hospital of Santo Spirito in Sassia.

VII (1500) - When he proclaimed this Jubilee, Alexander VI Borgia also introduced the rite of the opening of the Holy Door, which accompanied the display of one of the most precious relics of Christendom: the *Vultur Domini* or Veronica (*vera icona* or 'true icon') preserved in Saint Peter's. The massive urban reorganization efforts that accompanied this Jubilee included the opening of Via Alessandria, which linked Saint Peter's with Ponte Sant'Angelo as had been prescribed in a project styled by Nicholas V. The year 1500 was also the date of the completion Michelangelo's first Roman work: the *Pietà* in Saint Peter's Basilica.

VIII (1525) - Declared by Clement VII de' Medici, this Jubilee was ill-attended due to the wars between Francis I and Charles V that bloodied Europe and caused the Sack of Rome in 1527. The pope brought some of the many substantial urban renewal works promoted by his predecessors Julius II Della Rovere and Leo X de' Medici, to completion. These projects, entrusted to the experienced hands of such great masters as Bramante, Michelangelo, Raphael, and Antonio da Sangallo the Younger, revolutionized the urban fabric of Rome, following the renovation of Saint Peter's Basilica, with the creation of new thoroughfares (Via Giulia, Via Leonina - today's Via di Ripetta - and the Tridente) designed to channel the influx of pilgrims toward the Vatican and the major places of worship linked to the Jubilee ceremonial.

IX (1550) - Proclaimed by Paul III Farnese but officially opened by Julius III, this Jubilee again saw the flocking of numerous pilgrims, who were lodged thanks to Saint Philip Neri, who founded for the purpose the Confraternity of the Holy Trinity. For the occasion - only shortly after Charles V's triumphal entry into the city - a new road link was created between Porta San Sebastiano and Saint Peter's and much urban reorganization work was carried on, including consolidation of the archaeological area lying between the Baths of Caracalla and the Campidoglio. Piazza del Campidoglio was rebuilt to Michelangelo's plans.

X (1555) - Pope Julius III Ciocchi del Monte called this extraordinary Jubilee to celebrate the promise made by Queen Mary Tudor (never fulfilled) to heal the schism between the English and the Roman churches.

XI (1575) - During the Holy Year proclaimed by Gregory XIII Boncompagni, many princes and other important figures from the world of culture and the Church visited Rome. Saint Charles Borromeo and Torquato Tasso are only two of the most illustrious names. Gregory XIII, taking his example from Sixtus IV and heralding the monumental restructuring work ordered by Sixtus V, gave a strong stimulus to the development in terms of reorganization of the urban and monumental fabric of the city.

XII (1600) - The enormous inflow of pilgrims, nearly one and one-half million, prompted Clement VIII Aldobrandini to enlarge the hospice facilities and to create special organs for their coordination. This was also the year in which Giordano Bruno was burned as a heretic in Campo de' Fiori.

XIII (1625) - Proclaimed by Urban VIII Barberini, this Jubilee was marked by a number of important, large-scale urban renewal, architectural, and artistic efforts, most of which were carried out by Borromini and Bernini. The latter was commissioned to rebuild the facade of Saint Peter's Basilica, but he

was above all the author of the celebrated Colonnade in Piazza San Pietro, which he completed under Alexander VII Chigi halfway through the century.

XIV (1650) - The Jubilee Year celebrations of 1650 were presided over by Innocent X Pamphili.

XV (1675) - Although the overall number of pilgrims was low due to the conflicts that raged through Europe, the Holy Year of Jubilee proclaimed by Clement X Altieri was attended by Queen Christina of Sweden, who as a sign of humility washed the feet of the pilgrims lodged in the Hospital of the Santissima Trinità. The arrival of the Swedish sovereign in Rome during the Holy Year provided a stimulus for new works targeting reorganization and beautification of the city. On this occasion the Colosseum was consecrated to the memory of the martyrs during the Roman persecutions.

XVI (1700) - The celebrations were proclaimed by Innocent XII Pignatelli to reinforce the peace achieved among various European nations and were continued by Innocent's successor Clement XI.

XVII (1725) - This Jubilee, declared by Benedict XIII Orsini, was attended by a multitude of pilgrims, among whom four hundred Christian slaves freed by the Mercedarian fathers.

XVIII (1750) - Like that of 1725, this Jubilee proclaimed by Benedict XIV Lambertini saw the flocking into Rome of pilgrims from all parts of the world, including the Americas and Asia.

XIX (1775) - The revolutionary storm clouds that were gathering over Europe and that exploded in France shortly afterwards induced Pio VI Braschi to cut short the duration of this Holy Year.

XX (1825) - The Jubilee of 1800 was not celebrated due to the breaking-off of relations between Napoleon's France and the Holy See; Pope Leo XII Sermattei Della Genga inaugurated the Holy Year that began 25 years later.

XXI (1900) - Political events in Italy - the Risorgimento movements, the wars of independence, the proclamation of the Republic of Rome, the momentary removal of the pope from Rome - forced Pius IX Mastai to suppress the Jubilees of 1850 and 1875. It was only at the beginning of the following century that Leo XIII Pecci was able to finally declare a Holy Year.

XXII (1925) - The Jubilee celebrations proclaimed by Pius XI Ratti were among the best-attended in history.

XXIII (1933) - The proclaimer of this extraordinary Jubilee, celebrating the Lateran Treaty of 1925 that regulated relations between the Holy See and the Italian state, was again Pius XI.

XXIV (1950) - The Holy Year of Jubilee proclaimed by Pius XII Pacelli strengthened international relations and brotherhood among nations following World War II.

XXV (1975) - Paul VI Montini proclaimed this Holy Year.

XXVI (1983) - The last extraordinary Jubilee of the century was declared by John Paul II (Karol Wojtyla) to celebrate the one thousand nine hundred and fiftieth anniversary of the Death of Christ. The duration of this Holy Year (394 days) was also exceptional.

XXVII (2000) - The first Jubilee of the 21st century celebrates the two thousandth anniversary of the Birth of Christ.

THE JUBILEE BASILICAS

The basilicas major:
SAINT PETER'S BASILICA
SANTA MARIA MAGGIORE
SAN GIOVANNI IN LATERANO
SAN PAOLO FUORI LE MURA

The basilicas minor:
SANTA CROCE DI GERUSALEMME
SAN LORENZO FUORI LE MURA
SAN SEBASTIANO

Saint Philip Neri instituted the Jubilee Year tradition of visiting the Seven Churches, adding to the visits to the four major basilicas of San Pietro in Vaticano (Saint Peter's), San Giovanni in Laterano, San Paolo fuori le Mura, and Santa Maria Maggiore those to the three minor basilicas of Santa Croce di Gerusalemme, San Lorenzo Fuori le Mura, and San Sebastiano.

THE VATICAN

*C*enter of Christendom, fulcrum of Western spiritual life, and bastion of the Roman Catholic religion, for ages expression of the glory of the Church Triumphant, the Vatican rises on what was in ancient times called the Ager Vaticanus. In a certain sense the name, derived from vaticinio = vaticination, foreshadowed even in the pagan era the destiny of the site. Here stood Nero's Circus, actually begun under Caligula and only completed by the sadly famous emperor during whose reign Saint Peter, the first shepherd of the Church and a central figure in its history, was martyred. The **tomb of the apostle**, who was buried on the exact spot on which he died, soon became a shrine where many faithful came to pray; so much so that following the Edict of Milan (313) that acknowledged the right to practice the Christian religion, the emperor Constantine ordered construction of a grandiose basilica on the site. Work began a few years later.

The **Basilica di San Pietro in Vaticano (Saint Peter's Basilica)** thus arose in all its magnificence and in a very short time became a key site in Christian geography. Charlemagne was crowned Holy Roman Emperor here on Christmas Day of the year 800; this event marked the Vatican's acquisition of a precise political connotation in addition to its established spiritual power. Enclosed by the **Leonine Walls** built by order of Pope Leo IV, the area, which had theretofore been outside the city pomoerium, became an integral part of the urban fabric of Rome. Nevertheless, for another five centuries the popes continued to prefer the Lateran, which remained the seat of the highest ecclesiastical offices and the center of papal power. Intense construction during the 13th century filled the space around Saint Peter's with buildings designed to house certain administrative bodies of the Roman Curia.

Under Nicholas III, two Dominican monks and architects named Sisto and Ristoro enlarged the original papal palace from which the complex of the **Vatican Palaces**, later adapted to contain the **Vatican Museums** collections, arose. One of their efforts was the Palatine Chapel, on which the **Sistine Chapel** was later built; another a walled garden in which the **Palazzetto del Belvedere** was later erected. With the return of the papacy to Rome in 1377 following its 'exile' to Avignon, the Vatican was chosen as the permanent residence of the popes. There thus began construction work that was to employ hosts of architects and artists for centuries.

Nicholas V advanced the idea of rebuilding the basilica, but work began only in 1506 under Julius II. Bramante's plans were later substituted by designs by Michelangelo, who in the same period also created the **dome of Saint Peter's** and the **Sistine Chapel frescoes**.

With Paul V and Maderno, the basilica took on its final form, while the decoration of the interior continued during the pontificate of Urban VIII with work conducted by Gian Lorenzo Bernini, also author of **Piazza San Pietro (Saint Peter's Square)**. From the Vatican, the popes have uninterruptedly, for centuries, exercised their spiritual and temporal powers. The pope still enjoys jurisdictional power over that which, following the Lateran Treaty of 11 February 1929, is defined as **Vatican City**, the smallest sovereign state in the world. The pope, who is elected by his cardinals during conclaves held in the Sistine Chapel (the word 'conclave' derives from the fact that these secret meetings are held with the doors closed cum clave; that is 'by key'), holds full legislative, executive and judiciary powers in the state, besides being recognized as the supreme power in the world Catholic community. Vatican City mints its own coins and prints its own stamps, supports a radio station, and prints a daily newspaper, L'Osservatore Romano. Order is kept by the famous Swiss Guard, the Vatican police force instituted in 1506, and the security service created in the 1800s.

Aerial view of Saint Peter's Square and Basilica.

Vatican Gardens - An almost perfectly preserved, 16th-century style Italian formal garden.

Fontana dell'Aquilone - Built by Giovanni Vasanzio, the fountain takes its name from the enormous tufa stone eagle atop the rock.

Radio Vaticana - The first station was set up by Guglielmo Marconi in 1931, not far from today's studios, located in a bastion of the ancient Leonine Walls, once home to the astronomical observatory.

Palazzo del Governatorato - Built in the 1930s as the home of the Vatican City administrative offices.

Santo Stefano degli Abissini - Founded by Leo II, the church was granted to the Coptic friars in 1479 by Pope Sixtus IV.

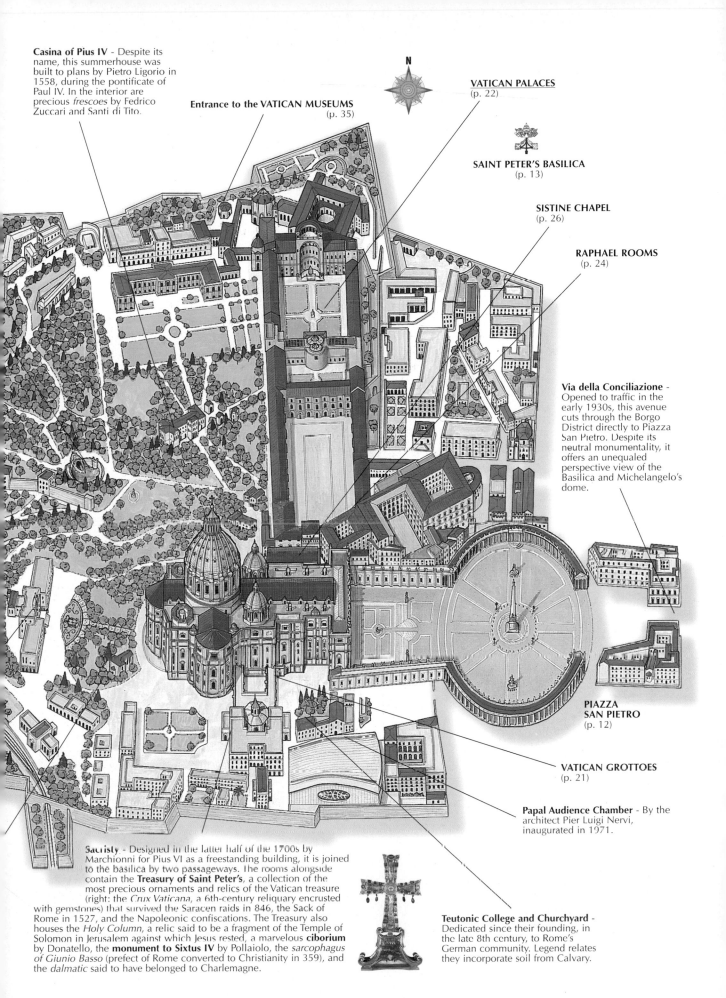

Casina of Pius IV - Despite its name, this summerhouse was built to plans by Pietro Ligorio in 1558, during the pontificate of Paul IV. In the interior are precious *frescoes* by Federico Zuccari and Santi di Tito.

Entrance to the VATICAN MUSEUMS
(p. 35)

N

VATICAN PALACES
(p. 22)

SAINT PETER'S BASILICA
(p. 13)

SISTINE CHAPEL
(p. 26)

RAPHAEL ROOMS
(p. 24)

Via della Conciliazione - Opened to traffic in the early 1930s, this avenue cuts through the Borgo District directly to Piazza San Pietro. Despite its neutral monumentality, it offers an unequaled perspective view of the Basilica and Michelangelo's dome.

PIAZZA SAN PIETRO
(p. 12)

VATICAN GROTTOES
(p. 21)

Papal Audience Chamber - By the architect Pier Luigi Nervi, inaugurated in 1971.

Sacristy - Designed in the latter half of the 1700s by Marchionni for Pius VI as a freestanding building, it is joined to the basilica by two passageways. The rooms alongside contain the **Treasury of Saint Peter's**, a collection of the most precious ornaments and relics of the Vatican treasure (right: the *Crux Vaticana*, a 6th-century reliquary encrusted with gemstones) that survived the Saracen raids in 846, the Sack of Rome in 1527, and the Napoleonic confiscations. The Treasury also houses the *Holy Column*, a relic said to be a fragment of the Temple of Solomon in Jerusalem against which Jesus rested, a marvelous **ciborium** by Donatello, the **monument to Sixtus IV** by Pollaiolo, the *sarcophagus of Giunio Basso* (prefect of Rome converted to Christianity in 359), and the *dalmatic* said to have belonged to Charlemagne.

Teutonic College and Churchyard - Dedicated since their founding, in the late 8th century, to Rome's German community. Legend relates they incorporate soil from Calvary.

11

PIAZZA SAN PIETRO (SAINT PETER'S SQUARE)

A sacred, uniquely evocative setting, imbued with profound religious and symbolic connotations: Piazza San Pietro is perhaps the most famous square in the world. Since the Middle Ages it has welcomed and been a gathering place for countless multitudes of pilgrims come to visit Saint Peter's Basilica, the center of Christianity, and has offered a vital space for the functions of the religious life of the city. The square was built over a part of the ancient Vatican Circus (or Nero's Circus, though in reality built almost entirely during Caligula's reign), of which there remains the so-called **Vatican Obelisk**, transported here in 37 BC from Alexandria, where it decorated Caesar's Forum. Called in medieval times the *aguglia*, it stood at length beside the basilica, until in 1596 Sixtus V ordered Domenico Fontana to move it to its present site. In 1613, Paul V bid Carlo Maderno build a **fountain** to its right; half a century later, a 'twin' fountain by Carlo Fontana, placed symmetrically with respect to the first, was added. Again under Sixtus V, the original bronze globe that topped the obelisk (today in the Capitoline Museums), and that was believed to contain the ashes of Caesar, was replaced with that pope's family emblem, the mountains and the star, topped by a crucifix containing a fragment of the Holy Cross of Christ's Crucifixion.

In the mid-17th century, when the monumental work of rebuilding Saint Peter's Basilica was well-delineated, attention naturally shifted to the square before it, which was built by Gian Lorenzo Bernini between 1656 and 1667. The feeling of triumphal spectacularism lent by the genius of the Baroque architect and sculptor to this immense masterpiece was not entirely dictated by artistic considerations; he also imbued his design with profound symbolic significance, to the point that the entire opus may be interpreted as a monumental allegory.

The great **portico** that opens out from the facade of the basilica to form two hemicycles delineated by a quadruple row of Tuscan columns supporting an entablature animated by a procession of *statues of saints* and the immense *coats-of-arms* of Pope Alexander VII, during whose reign the work was realized, is a symbolic embrace by the Church that would welcome and protect all the faithful of the world in this life and in that to come. The vast elliptical space (240 meters in width), so theatrically defined by the two hemicycles, is also possessed of many symbolic references. Arisen as the last forum of Rome and dedicated to Christianity, it owes its form to that of the circuses of the ancient *Urbe*, and in particular to the Colosseum: the square may thus be said to play the role of historical *trait-d'union* between the early Church, persecuted as were its martyrs who in the amphitheaters were put to death, and the glory of the Church Triumphant, in which Christ and the saints portrayed in the statues are participants. But the elliptical form is also evocative of the Firmament, in which, according to the theory of Copernicus, coeval with construction of the square, the planets describe such orbits, and of the Universe, understood as the space-time dimension in which the obelisk, which stands at the geometrical center of the ellipse and is the gnomon of an immense sundial, symbolizes the sun and alludes to the all-importance of the pope, the Vicar of Christ on Earth.

Saint Peter's Square, Via della Conciliazione, and the Borgo district seen from above Saint Peter's Basilica.

SAINT PETER'S BASILICA

The original Saint Peter's basilica was ordered built by Constantine on the site on which the saint was martyred in Nero's time and his body then buried, and from the very first the sanctuary drew crowds of faithful pilgrims. Begun in 324, the enormous five-aisled structure was completed only in 349, although it had already been consecrated and opened to worship in 326.

A great number of sacred buildings, oratories, cloisters, and baptisteries, were later built all around the monumental basilica, and all were decorated with precious mosaics, statues, and various, refined ornaments of different provenance. The complex reached the Renaissance intact; in 1452, Pope Nicholas V commissioned Rossellino to enlarge the apsidal portion of the basilica. But another half century was to pass before the original structure was completely revolutionized, when Pope Julius II commis-

Saint Peter's Basilica. Michelangelo's dome and the facade.

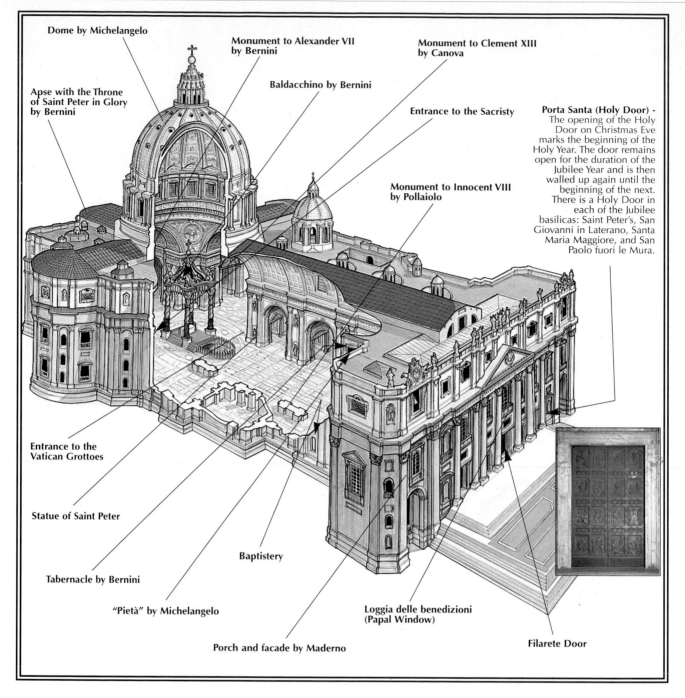

Dome by Michelangelo

Monument to Alexander VII
by Bernini

Monument to Clement XIII
by Canova

Apse with the Throne
of Saint Peter in Glory
by Bernini

Baldacchino by Bernini

Entrance to the Sacristy

Porta Santa (Holy Door) -
The opening of the Holy
Door on Christmas Eve
marks the beginning of the
Holy Year. The door remains
open for the duration of the
Jubilee Year and is then
walled up again until the
beginning of the next.
There is a Holy Door in
each of the Jubilee
basilicas: Saint Peter's, San
Giovanni in Laterano, Santa
Maria Maggiore, and San
Paolo fuori le Mura.

Monument to Innocent VIII
by Pollaiolo

Entrance to the
Vatican Grottoes

Statue of Saint Peter

Baptistery

Tabernacle by Bernini

"Pietà" by Michelangelo

Loggia delle benedizioni
(Papal Window)

Filarete Door

Porch and facade by Maderno

sioned Bramante to renovate the basilica. The architect from the Marches region of Italy demolished the earlier edifice almost in its entirety, also making a clean sweep of the structures that has risen around it in order to make room for a grandiose building that according to his plans would have been on a Greek cross plan with a central dome. At Bramante's death Raphael took over and suggested transforming the structure into a Latin cross by lengthening the entrance bay, while retaining the idea of the dome.

The two designs alternated for years as supervision of works passed from one architect to another; finally, in 1546, Michelangelo again opted for Bramante's original design, while making slight modifications to the dimensions and the structure to make it smaller and slimmer, and to the design of the **dome**, which although based on Brunelleschi's cover for Florence's cathedral appeared absolutely innovative and revolutionary. Thus the dome, completed by Giacomo Della Porta and Domenico Fontana in 1588-89, consisted of a tambour supported by 16 buttresses hidden by binate columns; between the columns of each pair open the large windows with tympana. The double-shell dome reaches upward above the tambour in sections with 16 ribs, on which three orders of oculi open.

To the sides are two **small domes**, by Vignola, with purely decorative functions and not in correspondence to the Clementine and Gregorian Chapels underneath.

At the death of the master from Tuscany, supervision of works again passed from hand to hand among many architects, until under Pope Paul V the Latin cross plan returned to favor. Maderno added three chapels per side and lengthened the nave as far as the present **facade**, which he completed in 1614. On 18 November 1626, in the one thousand three hundredth anniversary year of the original consecration, Urban VIII finally consecrated the new basilica. Maderno's work to a certain extent penalized Michelangelo's project by obstructing the full view of the dome, which is visible only in part behind the monumental facade with gracious *clock faces* by Valadier at either end. On either side of the facade stand two huge neoclassical statues of *Saint Peter* and *Saint Paul*.

The announcement of the election of a new pope is made from the central balconied window on the facade, known as the **Loggia delle benedizioni**, from which papal blessings are normally given. The **porch**, proportionally as vast as the interior, is imaginatively and elegantly decorated with statues, friezes, and stuccowork; it shelters the *Navicella mosaic*, designed by Giotto for the original basilica but restored and moved many times, showing *Christ inviting Peter to walk on the water*. Five entrances open at the back of the porch: the stupendous central **portal**, which leads in to the basilica, is a 15th-century work by Filarete; the last on the right is the **Holy Door**, which is solemnly opened by the pope to inaugurate Jubilee Years, and closed during another just as solemn ceremonial at the end of each.

The **interior**, in all its seeming boundlessness, is the symbol of the Church Triumphant, and the profuse and opulent decoration only accentuates the sublime atmosphere of the glorification of Christianity.

This feeling of monumentality emerges from a simple glance at the **nave**, with its *ceiling* that was richly decorated under Pius VI in 1780, the *stars* set into the floor to indicate the size of the world's largest churches, the *holy water*

Porch of Saint Peter's Basilica. The 'Navicella' mosaic designed by Giotto.

Saint Peter's Basilica. A view of the interior.

stoups supported by massive marble putti, and the venerated **statue of the seated Saint Peter** imparting the blessing, probably by Arnolfo di Cambio, near the last pillar on the right.

But as soon as he crosses the threshold, the visitor's eye is drawn by the great bronze **Baldacchino** with its tortile columns. It is the fruit of felicitous collaboration by Bernini, Borromini, and Duquesnoy that absorbed the artists' energies from 1624 through 1633.

Under the host of angels that crowns the daring structure, almost 30 meters in height and for the construction of which Pope Urban VIII Barberini sacrificed the Pantheon bronzes, is the *papal altar* at which only the pope may celebrate Mass; it stands over the *confessio*, decorated by Maderno and illuminated by 95 eternal flames, built over the tomb of Saint Peter. Above the Baldacchino, the inner shell of Michelangelo's dome is decorated with *mosaics* designed by the Cavalier d'Arpino.

In the space behind the altar, in the colossal **apse** or tribune, is the splendid **Throne of Saint Peter in Glory**, a late work by Bernini (1656-1665), who pressed into service all his astounding art as a sculptor and decorator in a complex play of stucco, gilt work, sculptures, and reliefs. The *bronze throne* supported by the statues of the *Doctors of the Church* contains the wooden throne that (historically unfounded) tradition relates was used by Saint Peter. To the left of the monumental tribune is the *monument to Pope Paul III* by Guglielmo Della Porta; to the right, Bernini's *monument to Pope Urban VIII*.

The first chapel in the **right aisle**, decorated by Bernini in such a manner as to mask the narrowing at the third arch, where Maderno's extension is grafted to Michelangelo's original structure, contains the celebrated **Pietà** by Michelangelo, sculpted by the Tuscan master in 1498-1499 for the Charles VIII's legate to the Holy See. The third is the *Chapel of the Holy Sacrament*, which contains Bernini's resplendent **Tabernacle**, a ciborium inspired by Bramante's Tempietto di San Pietro in Montorio and flanked by two kneeling angels.

Beyond the *monument to Gregory XIII*, the

Interior of Saint Peter's. Michelangelo's Pietà, sculpted halfway through the millennium.

Facing page: Bernini's celebrated Baldacchino above the papal altar in Saint Peter's Basilica.

Interior of Saint Peter's.
The statue of Saint Peter attributed to
Arnolfo di Cambio, and Bernini's 'Gloria',
centering on the Throne of Saint Peter.

Left, a view of the interior of
Michelangelo's dome.

Facing page: Bernini's monument to
Pope Alexander VII, created using a
rich array of marbles.

Interior of Saint Peter's.
Left, the bronze monument to Pope Innocent VIII by Pollaiolo;
above, Canova's monument to Clement XIII.

author of the reform of the calendar that now bears his name, is the *Gregorian Chapel* completed by Giacomo Della Porta in 1583.

Further on, the **right transept** gives access to the *Chapel of Saint Michael* with before it the **monument to Clement XIII**, a masterpiece by Canova dating to about 1790.

Across the apse on the left side of the basilica is the corresponding *Colonna Chapel* containing the relics of Saint Leo I the Great, to whom the beautiful marble altarpiece by Algardi showing *Leo the Great Halting Attila* alludes.

In the adjacent passageway a somber skeleton holding an hourglass calls attention to Bernini's **monument to Pope Alexander VII** that introduces the **left transept**. Past the *Clementine Chapel*, built like the corresponding chapel in the right aisle by Della Porta, is the **left aisle** with the lavish *Choir Chapel*.

In the following passageway is the bronze **monument to Innocent VIII** cast by Pollaiolo in 1498. At the level of the first chapel is another masterpiece by Canova, the *Stuart Monument*, tomb of the last members of the family; the grace of the two genies with their upside-down torches is striking. Last to open on the nave is the **baptistery**, with its *baptismal font* adapted from an ancient Roman sarcophagus.

the **Chapel of Nicho**
Scenes from the Lives (
more ground-floor roo
nucleus of the Vatican
In 1473, Sixtus IV con
chapel for the papal ce
Sistine Chapel. The d
artists of the Tuscan an
Iuricchio and Perugino
with the Life of Moses
under Nicholas V wa:
who in the late 1400s
Apartments, compose
dence itself and three
section was carried o
ous rooms take their
Room, the Umbrian a
the sibyls and the pr
Messiah; the decorati
on the figures of prop
faith. In the Liberal *
Arts of the Trivium (G
Quadrivium (Geome
panels adorned with
The Saints' Room, a
orated with Scenes fr
Church; in the Room
assisted by many of
1500 and was comp
cos and frescoes by
Before the work orde
Pope Innocent VIII h
build what is now ca
est part of the Bel
Palace, as a place o
the slopes of the Vat
And this was the w
papal throne in 150.
one from the other,
to be united to forr
charged Bramante, a
work for the rebuild
this operation. The
designed two extre
(later reserved for th
There was thus crea
tile del Belvedere. 1
ified through consti
mid-1500s by Pirro
erroneously believe
hand, instead, was
ment of Palazzo V
posed orders of arc
1514, by Raphael,
Romano, Perin de
coed the loggias. 1
up this harmonious
were decorated w
thirteenth shows
Raphael also deco
Palazzo Vaticano,
which Julius II ha
artists of great v
Sodoma.
In the same perio
Sistine Chapel by
frescoed the ceilii
former, the great I
Testament, and ir
ing on the central
lunettes he paint
Hebrew families
The work begun
his successor, Le
rentine Renaissa
Between 1536 ar

Interior of Saint Peter's, Chapel of the Holy Sacrament.
Bernini's Tabernacle, inspired by Bramante's Tempietto di
San Pietro in Montorio.

VATICAN GROTTOES

This important sacred site underneath the Vatican basilica
contains the mortal remains of the popes and the *tomb of
Saint Peter*, over which the first church was raised. The
intricately configured series of rooms in the Vatican Grottoes may be divided into three principal areas. The first are
the **Old Grottoes** that extend through a vast cavity
between the floor of the present basilica and that of the
original building, under the nave and aisles of the upper
construction. They contain the **tombs** of many popes,
including that of *Boniface VIII* (who proclaimed the first
Jubilee Year) by Arnolfo di Cambio, and those of the most
recent popes like *John XXIII, Paul IV*, and *John Paul I*, but
also the sepulchers of important temporal rulers such as
Emperor Otho II and *Queen Christina of Sweden*. Many of
the altars, sculptures, frescoes, and mosaics that decorated
the original basilica are also installed here. The **New Grottoes**, called thus because their restoration postdates that of
the Old Grottoes, are arranged in a semicircle with many
radial chapels alternating with niches with statues of the
Apostles by Mino da Fiesole and other masters of the same
period. The whole is built around the **Chapel of Saint
Peter**, built on the site of the tomb of the first pope and
richly decorated under Clement VIII.
The Bocciata Chapel contains the interesting 14th-century

The tomb of Saint Peter.

fresco by Pietro Cavallini of the *Madonna and Child* that
once adorned the atrium of the old basilica.
A third level underlying the Vatican Grottoes as such is
host to a large **pre-Constantinian necropolis**, dating to
the first through the fourth centuries. Among the many
pagan tombs there are also those of Christians, including
the original burial place of Saint Peter.

SAINTS PETER AND PAUL IN ROME

The dawn of the Roman Church is tied to the figures of Saints Peter
and Paul, emblems of Christian doctrine. Their presence in Rome, during their lifetimes and after, had a profound influence on the religious
as well as historical destiny of the city.
Linked to the memory of the two saints are important religious sites,
first among them **St. Peter's Basilica**, built where the Apostle was
martyred and buried. Born with the name Simon in Bethesda in the
1st century BC, Peter was a fisherman who, upon meeting Jesus,
became a disciple. It was Christ who changed his name to Cephas,
which in Aramaic means 'stone' ('stone' resembles 'Peter' in many lan-
guages). Jesus also conferred to Peter primacy over the other apostles (Matthew, 16, 13-20), just as the popes, as the successors of
Peter, have primacy over the bishops. After the death of Christ and
the Pentecost, Peter preached for a long period in Jerusalem, where
he was arrested in about 41 AD. He managed to escape from prison
with the help of an angel, who broke his chains. These chains would
later miraculously link themselves to the chains that held the Saint in
Rome and they are still venerated in the church of **San Pietro in Vincoli** in Rome.
From Palestine, Peter took refuge in Rome, where for almost 20 years
he found hospitality in many homes. One such house was that of the
patrician Pudens, where the church of **St. Pudentiana** stands today.
According to tradition, Peter was again captured and imprisoned in
the **Mamertine Prison**, where he baptized his jailers and then escaped
disguised in a slave's cape, his feet bandaged because of the sores
from his chains. In flight along the Appian Way, after losing his bandages where the church of **Santi Nereo ed Achilleo** now stands, he
encountered Christ at the site of today's church of **'Domine quo vadis?'**
and decided to return to Rome to face his martyrdom. He was martyred in 64 or 66 at Nero's Circus in the Vatican, crucified head down.
St. Paul was martyred in the same period on the Via Laurentina. The
Apostle of the Gentiles was beheaded and, according to tradition, his
head rebounded three times, giving birth to three founts, later to be
marked by the **Abbazia delle Tre Fontane** (Abbey of the Three Fountains). Paul's body was moved to a cemetery on the Via Ostienses,
where the **Basilica di San Paolo** was built. Born in Tarsus into a Jewish family, Paul was a soldier of the Roman army. He miraculously converted after being struck blind near Damascus and preached throughout Greece and Asia Minor. He arrived in Rome in 61, bound in chains
and awaiting Imperial judgment. Found innocent, he departed for
Spain, returning to Rome three years later and living, according to tradition, in a house near the present church of **San Paolino alla Regola**
where he was arrested.

RAPHAEL ROOMS

The master began frescoing what are now known as the Stanze di Raffaello (Raphael Rooms) in 1509. The work, which continued into the following years under Leo X, revolves around themes that celebrate the power of Faith and the Church.

The first room to be frescoed was the **Room of the Segnatura**, called thus because it was here that the pope signed official documents; Raphael's sure touch gleams from all the frescoes, from the *Dispute of the Blessed Sacraments*, depicting the glorification of the Eucharist, to the *School of Athens*, which brings together in a grandiose architectural frame the wise men and the philosophers of ancient times and the seigneurs and the artists of the Renaissance cultural scene, all gathered around the figures of Plato and Aristotle, and to the *Parnassus*, an allegorical celebration of the arts impersonated by the mythological figures of the Muses and the pagan gods. In the alternating medallions and panels of the ceiling, almost as a symbolic compendium of the frescoes on the walls below, Raphael painted allegorical representations of the Sciences and the Arts (*Theology, Justice, Philosophy, Poetry, Astronomy*) together with emblematic episodes referred to them (*Adam and Eve*, the *Judgment of Solomon*, *Apollo and Marsyas*).

From 1512 to 1514, Raphael worked on the decoration of the **Room of Heliodorus**, where he frescoed historical episodes that at once illustrate divine intervention in favor of the Church and glorify the salient episodes of Julius II's reign, according to an iconographic program dictated by the same pope. *Leo I Halting Attila* alludes to the Battle of Ravenna in 1512 at which the future Leo X defeated the French; the *Miracle at Bolsena* illustrates the institution of the Corpus Domini by Urban IV and also calls to mind the vow made by Julius II before the siege of Bologna; the biblical episode of the *Expulsion of Heliodorus from the Temple* refers to the pope's struggle against the enemies of the Church; the *Liberation of Saint Peter* alludes to the liberation of Leo X from his imprisonment after the Battle of Ravenna. The next two years, until 1517, were dedicated to the **Room of the Fire in the Borgo**, which takes its name from the principal fresco, *The Borgo Fire of 847 AD*, inspired by the figure of Leo IV who extinguished the fire by making the sign of the cross. This and the other frescoes in the room (the *Battle of Ostia*, the *Oath of Leo III*, the *Coronation of Charlemagne*), executed almost entirely by Raphael's pupils under the strict guidance of the master, make specific reference to Leo III and Leo IV, illustrious predecessors of Leo X, during whose pontificate the room was decorated. The **Sala dei Palafrenieri** also contained wall paintings by Raphael, which were destroyed and later replaced by other frescoes ordered by Gregory XIII in the late 1500s.

The decoration of the **Hall of Constantine** is instead certainly the work of one of Raphael's most important followers, Giulio Romano. Following the death of the master he led a team of artists who illustrated in fresco episodes from the life of Constantine: the *Baptism of Constantine*, the *Battle of the Milvian Bridge*, the *Apparition of the Cross*, and *Constantine's Donation*.

Room of Heliodorus. Raphael, Expulsion of Heliodorus from the Temple.

Facing page:
Room of the Segnatura. Raphael,
School of Athens *(top)* and
Dispute of the Blessed Sacraments
(bottom).

Museo Missionario Etn
Missionary Ethnologica
a rich collection of obje
most remote parts of th
collected by Catholic r
was founded in 1926,
in Palazzo del Lateran
here by Giovanni XXIII

Museo Pio-Cristiano
- Arranged in 1854
by order of
Pius IX to
house a
sizeable
collection of
material
found in the
catacombs
and the oldest
of Rome's
basilicas.

PINACOTECA VATIC
(p. 38)

Gallery of th
gallery, cont
finds, owes it
marble cande

Tapestry Gallery
tapestries it contains
of Europe's finest w
that of Brussels th
Chapel tapestries to

Biblioteca Apost
Apostolic Librar
Sixtus V in the late
rich collec
engravi
incunabula, and p
ground-floo

Map Gallery
maps of
territories, drawn b
in

THE VATIC

*T*he original n
Vatican Pala
ings that arose
was the simple
the early sixth
remains today,
- who at the tim
no - during the
was adjacent.
grew in import
turies it hosted
to Rome for the
The site had in
IV ordered bui
which both the
theless, the cou
ing centuries th
don: the exten:
the twelfth cen
further enlarge

THE SISTINE CHAPEL

Between 1475 and 1481, Pope Sixtus IV charged Baccio Pontelli with design of a new pontifical chapel; the vast rectangular hall with a barrel-vaulted ceiling was built by Giovannino de' Dolci. Mino da Fiesole, Giovanni Dalmata, and Andrea Bregno subdivided the space into two parts with a marble *choir screen* and also created the *Cantoria* or choristers' gallery, while a veritable host of great artists participated in the pictorial decoration, including figures of such caliber and renown as Botticelli, Ghirlandaio, Perugino, Luca Signorelli, and Cosimo Rosselli.

In 1506, Julius II decided to have the **ceiling**, which at the time was blue and strewn with stars, frescoed as well, and entrusted the immense project to the genius of Michelangelo, already employed in reconstruction of Saint Peter's Basilica. The Tuscan master began painting the vast surface (almost 800 square meters) in May of 1508, and completed the work four years later. Michelangelo's composition consists of a series of Old Testament scenes; continuity is assured by plastic and pictorial architectural elements in which emblematic and symbolic figures provide narrative 'hinges' and iconographic links among the different episodes. Michelangelo's innovative colors have been revealed in all their original splendor by recent restoration.

The twelve figures in question are **Prophets and Sibyls**, the heralds of the coming of the Messiah: *Jeremiah*, the *Persian Sibyl*, *Ezekiel*, the *Erythraean Sibyl*, *Joel*, *Zachariah*, the *Delphic Sibyl*, *Isaiah*, the *Cumaean Sibyl*, *Daniel*, the *Libyan Sibyl*, and lastly *Jonah*, in ecstasy at the moment of his exit from the whale's belly. Together with the vigorous pairs of *Ignudi* supporting garlands and medallions,

Sistine Chapel. One of the lunettes with a figure from the 'Ancestors of Christ' series by Michelangelo, following restoration.

In the foldout, an overall view of the ceiling of the Sistine Chapel frescoed by Michelangelo, following restoration.

the twelve figures frame the nine panels of the **Stories of the Genesis**: *God Dividing Light from Darkness*; *God Creating the Sun and the Moon and Plants*; *God Dividing the Waters from the Land and Creating the Fishes and the Birds*; the incredibly famous **Creation of Adam** and the *Creation of Eve* at the center; *Original Sin*; the *Sacrifice of Noah*; the *Flood*; and the *Drunkenness of Noah*. In the triangles at the four corners of the vault are other biblical episodes: *Judith and Holophernes*, *David and Goliath*, the *Punishment of Haman*, and the *Brazen Serpent*. The lunettes and the spandrels over the windows contain equally splendid frescoes of the **Ancestors of Christ**. Twenty-five years after completing the ceiling, Michelangelo returned, at Pope Paul III's bidding, to crown his opus with a great fresco on the back wall of the chapel. Thus in 1536-1541 the artist created what many feel is his absolute masterpiece - the **Last Judgment**, centering on the figure of Christ Judge surrounded by a superbly innovative composition of the hosts of the elect and the damned - for the realization of which the earlier frescoes by Perugino had to be destroyed.

Sistine Chapel. Michelangelo's frescoes of the Creation of Adam *(above) and* Original Sin *(below) on the ceiling, following restoration.*

On the following pages:

Sistine Chapel. Overall view of the Last Judgment *by Michelangelo, following restoration.*

Sistine Chapel, 15th century frescoes on the side walls. Above, Scenes from the Life of Moses *by Sandro Botticelli; below,* Moses' Journey into Egypt *by Perugino.*

On the facing page, a side wall of the Sistine Chapel. In the upper portion, frescoes by Michelangelo: figures of the 'Ancestors of Christ' in the lunettes, and below, four figures from the series of 'Popes'. In the lower band, 15th-century frescoes: Perugino, Handing Over the Keys to Saint Peter, *and Cosimo Rosselli,* Last Supper.

Above, a bird's-eye view of the Vatican Museums.

VATICAN MUSEUMS

From the very first, the complex that is today called the Palazzi Vaticani and that is the result of a long process of construction and transformation has hosted splendid collections of art assembled by the various popes. The supreme pontiffs also enriched their collections by patronizing the arts and employed entire generations of Italian and foreign artists in the creation of masterpieces on commission.

*The many collections, from those of Greek, Roman, Etruscan, and Egyptian antiquities to those of books and paintings (the latter now in the celebrated **Pinacoteca Vaticana**) slowly filled the available rooms, halls and galleries as they were built - and in many cases provided the impetus for their construction. The arrangement of the collections has changed over the centuries in relation both to the increase in available space and to changes in the criteria in vogue for the organization and cataloging of works in museums, and the buildings gradually became museums to all effects. The first step in this direction was taken in the late 1700s by Clement XIV, who transformed the Palazzetto del Belvedere into the museum that, following the reorganization ordered by Clement's successor Pius VI, took the name of **Museo Pio-Clementino**.*

*In the first half of the following century, that passion for archaeology and antiquity that was a hallmark of Neoclassical taste induced two popes, Pius VII and Gregory XVI, to create certain of the cardinal institutions of the Vatican museum complex: the former founded the **Museo Chiaramonti**, to the decoration of which even Canova contributed and for which the Braccio Nuovo was expressly built; the latter pope organized the **Museo Gregoriano Etrusco** and the **Museo Gregoriano Egizio** in seventeen rooms.*

*Later on in the 19th century, Pope Leo XIII, to whom we owe restoration of myriad parts of the Vatican complex, opened to the public many rooms which theretofore had been reserved for the pope and the highest members of the ecclesiastical hierarchy. The first such revelation was the Borgia Apartments, which later became the seat of the **Collection of Modern Religious Art** inaugurated by Pope Paul VI in 1973.*

*The creation of new museums went on all through the twentieth century: John XXIII had both the **Museo Missionario Etnologico**, instituted in 1926 to house the material exhibited at the Missionary Exhibit of the 1925 Jubilee, and the **Museo Pio-Cristiano**, founded in 1854 by Pius IX to organize the paintings, inscriptions, reliefs and sculptures from the catacombs and the ancient Roman basilicas, moved to the Vatican from their original homes in the San Giovanni in Laterano complex.*

MUSEO PIO-CLEMENTINO

In 1771, Clement XIV organized the first of the Vatican museums, when in the rooms of the Palazzetto del Belvedere he installed the primitive Renaissance nucleus of the collection of antique statuary theretofore in the **Cortile Ottagonale**, designed by Bramante and enlarged by Michelangelo Simonetti in 1773. Clement XIV's successor Pius VI further enlarged the collection and extended the museum space into other parts of the Vatican complex. Close by the Cortile Ottagonale, in what is called the **Gabinetto di Apollo**, was placed one of the sculptures that most aroused the interest of scholars of antiquities, such as Winckelmann and Goethe: the celebrated *Apollo del Belvedere*, a fascinating work attributed to Leocares and discovered in the 1400s near the church of San Pietro in Vincoli. The **Gabinetto dell'Apoxyomenos** owes its name to another masterpiece of ancient sculpture, a Roman copy of a work by Lysippos of an athlete scraping sweat from his body, unearthed in the mid-1800s in Trastevere. The **Gabinetto del Laocoonte** contains the homonymous sculptural group found in the 1500s in Nero's *Domus Aurea* and inspired by the famous Trojan War episode of the priest Laocoön and his sons being strangled by two serpents sent by Athena after the failure of the Trojan horse hoax, revealed by the priest of Troy. The work enormously influenced the art of the late Renaissance, above all that of Michelangelo. The **Gabinetto dell'Hermes** owes its name to a copy, dating to Hadrian's reign, of a statue by Praxiteles portraying the god in the guise of psychopompos; that is, the conductor of the souls of the dead to the afterworld. The statue that lends its name to the **Gabinetto del Perseo** is, instead, of Neoclassical matrix. It was sculpted in 1800 by Antonio Canova and was inspired by the *Apollo del Belvedere*. In 1776, Pius VI commissioned, of Michelangelo Simonetti, the **Sala degli Animali** to contain exhibits of sculptures and fragments of Roman mosaics having animals as their subjects. The most famous piece in this highly singular collection is the Roman copy of Skopas' statue portraying *Meleager* with a dog and the head of a wild boar. Under Innocent VIII, the Palazzetto was enlarged with the aim of creating new exhibit spaces, among which the **Galleria delle Statue**, which contains many fine sculptural works such as the *Apollo Sauroktonos*, the *Sleeping Ariadne*, the *Resting Satyr*, and the *Barberini Candelabra*. Simonetti also built other rooms in which he used perspective effects to exalt the works of art they contain. This is the case of the **Sala delle Muse**, home to the celebrated *Belvedere Torso* that inspired Michelangelo's nudes in the Sistine Chapel, of the **Sala Rotonda**, where we find the *Otricoli Jupiter* and the colossal gilded bronze statue of *Hercules*, of the **Sala a Croce Greca**, custodian of the *sarcophagus of Constantia*, Constantine's daughter, and that of *Saint Helena*, the emperor's mother, and of the **Gabinetto delle Maschere**, home to the famous *Venus of Cnidos*. Clement XIV had previously readapted certain rooms in the building to host the collections; this is the case of the **Galleria dei Busti**, which exhibits examples of imperial Roman lapidary portraiture among the world's most famous; for example, the busts of *Caracalla*, of *Caesar*, and of *Augustus*.

MUSEO CHIARAMONTI

The Museo Chiaramonti, founded by order of Pius VII (Barnaba Chiaramonti) in the early 1800s and laid out by Antonio Canova, was arranged in the first portion of the eastern gallery designed by Bramante to link the Palazzetto del Belvedere with the Palazzo Vaticano, and was then extended into the Galleria Lapidaria, created to provide a home for the Vatican's profuse collection of inscriptions on stone, and into the Braccio Nuovo, built expressly to house the works which were excluded from the spaces offered by the other galleries. In a space decorated in strict accordance with the canons of Neoclassical art, the first section of the museum presents various exhibits of Roman statuary of Greek inspiration: gods of Olympus, like the statue of *Athena*, a copy of a Greek original by the school of Myron, alternate with mythical heroes, like the *Hercules with his Son Telephos*, and figures of

MUSEO GREGORIANO ETRUSCO

Roman times, such as the portrait of a *priest of Isis*, also known as *Scipio Africanus*, or the anonymous *male head* veiled in the typical garb of the ritual sacrifices. The **Galleria Lapidaria**, accessible only for reasons of study, instead offers a sweeping panorama of pagan and Christian

inscriptions, most of which come from necropoli and catacombs. The collection was begun by Clement XIV for the famous epigraphist Gaetano Marini and augmented by Pius VI and Pius VII.

The **Braccio Nuovo**, built by Stern in 1817 across the Cortile Belvedere parallel to the gallery of the Biblioteca Apostolica, is another wide and luminous gallery, interrupted at its center by a vast apsed hall that contains masterpieces of Roman statuary. Of special note are the so-called *Augustus of Prima Porta*, showing the emperor, wearing a finely-engraved suit of armor, in the act of haranguing his subjects, with at his feet a cherub, the symbol of Venus, protectress of the *gens Julia*; the statue of the *Nile*, discovered in the early 1500s near Santa Maria sopra Minerva, which together with the *Tiber* (now in the Louvre) adorned the Temple of Isis and Serapis; and the celebrated *Doryphoros*, with its perfectly balanced proportions, a copy of the bronze original by Polycleitus.

In the first half of the 19th century, interest in Etruscan studies and investigation of the Italic populations of the pre-Roman era sparked organization of systematic campaigns of excavations at many sites in the Papal State of the time in areas such as Cerveteri, Tarquinia, Vulci, and Veii. The finds were cataloged and arranged in a museum instituted especially for that purpose in 1837 by Gregory XVI; the collection later grew by donations and other acquisitions. The museum itinerary begins with series of interesting *funerary urns* documenting the early Iron Age civilizations in Etruria and Latium. A complete tomb exhibit, showing the objects that normally accompanied the dead, has been reassembled from the material found in the *Regolini-Galassi Tomb*: bronze objects, ceramic and bucchero vases (bucchero was a typically Etruscan black clay mixture), and finely-worked gold pieces.

Among the exquisite examples of the urns in which the Etruscans preserved the ashes of their dead is the outstanding *Calabresi Urn*, from the 7th century BC. The *Mars of Todi* is instead a precious illustration of the heights reached by this culture in the art of bronze casting.

But the major attraction of the museum is its collection of ceramics, with vases of various types, either decorated with figures or simply crafted in one-tone clay, and in particular the superb **Benedetto Guglielmi Collection** that brings together interesting ancient black- and red-figured vases.

Facing page: Museo Pio-Clementino. Apollo del Belvedere and the sculptural group of Laocoön and his sons.

Museo Gregoriano Etrusco. Above, the interior of a Laconian cup showing the torture of Prometheus; below, an Attic bowl depicting Oedipus and the Sphinx.

PINACOTECA VATICANA

This exceptional collection of paintings, founded by Pope Pius VI, is one of the world's most prestigious and boasts masterpieces of undeniable beauty that span an arc of time from the 12th through the 18th centuries. Although deprived of the many works removed to France in the late 1700s following the Treaty of Tolentino (and recovered only in part about twenty years later thanks to the efforts of Canova), over the years the gallery incorporated other works, in part from the sacristy of Saint Peter's and in part from the summer residence of the popes in Castel Gandolfo. The paintings are arranged in chronological order, beginning with the 'primitives'. This part of the collection contains panels of enormous value such as *Mary Magdalen* by Veneziano, the *Madonna with Child* by Vitale da Bologna, *Saint Francis* by Giunta Pisano, and the *Last Judgment* by Friars Giovanni and Niccolò, a precious panel of the Roman Benedictine milieu painted in the late 11th or early 12th century. The *Scenes from the Life of Saint Stephen* by

Pinacoteca Vaticana. Giotto and disciples, the Stefaneschi Polyptych. *Above, the rear; below, the front.*

Bernardo Daddi leads into the following section, dedicated to Gothic painting and centering mainly on Giotto and his followers. Among the works by the great Tuscan master is the *Stefaneschi Polyptych*, commissioned during Giotto's Roman sojourn by Cardinal Stefaneschi for one of the altars in the old Saint Peter's Basilica. It is accompanied by such beautiful paintings as Simone Martini's *Redeemer*, the *Madonna del Magnificat* by Daddi, and the *Nativity* by Giovanni di Paolo.

Beato Angelico's stay in Rome is evinced by such intensely evocative works as the *Scenes from the Life of Saint Niccolò di Bari* and the *Stigmata of Saint Francis*, to which works by Filippo Lippi and Benozzo Gozzoli play delicate counterpoint. Two singular examples of the work of Melozzo da Forlì as a fresco painter are the fragments of the fresco that once decorated the apse of Santi Apostoli with the *Ascension*, destroyed in the 1700s, and the immense mural that embellished the first seat of the Biblioteca Apostolica; it is a work dating from the second half of the 15th century illustrating *Sixtus IV Appointing Bartolomeo Sacchi Prefect of the Library*.

Melozzo ushers in a more mature phase of 15th-century painting: alongside works by foreign masters such as Lucas Cranach, the author of a dramatic *Pietà* in typically Nordic tones, are the *polyptychs* by Carlo and Vittorio Crivelli. But it is the Umbrian school which triumphs, with its evocative Renaissance works like the *Coronation of Maria* by Pin-

Pinacoteca Vaticana. Raphael, Coronation of the Virgin.

Pinacoteca Vaticana. Raphael, Transfiguration.

turicchio and Perugino's *Virgin with Child and Four Saints*. These paintings introduce one of the most famous and interesting sections of the gallery, which contains some of Raphael's finest paintings: the *Transfiguration*, his last master-piece, commissioned in 1517 by Giulio de' Medici, then cardinal and future Pope Clement VII, the *Madonna di Foligno*, painted for Sigismondo Conti, Julius II's personal secretary, and the ten *Tapestries*, created in 1515-1516 by Flemish weavers after Raphael's cartoons, that once hung in the Sistine Chapel on occasion of the conclaves and the most solemn ceremonies.

Another great master, Leonardo, is represented with the sketch for a painting of *Saint Jerome*. This particularly significant work reveals interesting facets of the chiaroscuro technique and the compositional methods used by Leonardo. The 16th-century section also contains a great number of paintings of the Venetian school, including the acute *Portrait of the Doge Nicolò Marcello* by Titian and works by Veronese. The consequence of the evolution of painting in the 1500s was inevitably the interesting works of the Tuscan and Roman Mannerist schools, represented here by Vasari (*The Martyrdom of Saint Stephen*), Carracci (*The Sacrifice of Isaac*), and the Cavalier d'Arpino (*Annunciation). The works of some of the greatest exponents of the Baroque revolution are also on exhibit: first and foremost the *Deposition* by Caravaggio, painted in the very early 1600s, but also paintings by Guido Reni (*The Crucifixion of Saint Peter*) and Domenichino (*The Communion of Saint Jerome*).

Other fascinating rooms dedicated to 17th- and 18th-century painting hang canvases by Italian artists active in Rome, such as Pietro da Cortona, Orazio Gentileschi, and Baciccia, and also by foreign masters like Poussin, Van Dyck, and Rubens.

The portion of the museum specifically concerned with 18th-century painting also comprises a number of surprising works by Giuseppe Maria Crespi, Giaquinto, and Donato Creti.

Pinacoteca Vaticana, Raphael, Madonna di Foligno.

MUSEO GREGORIANO PROFANO

The original nucleus of the museum, which was initially located in the Palazzo del Laterano, dates from the first half of the nineteenth century, when Pope Gregory XVI began systematic arrangement of the many Greek and Roman finds unearthed during the course of the archaeological excavations conducted in the territory of the former Papal State. In 1970, the extensive collection was transferred to the Vatican, in spaces built especially for the occasion by order of Pope John XXIII by the architects Fausto and Lucio Passarelli.

The museum is divided into five sections containing Greek sculpture and works exemplary of the various phases in the development of Roman sculptural art, from that of copying and adapting the Greek models to independent production in the imperial age and late antiquity. Among the most important works of Greek origin are the *fragments of sculptures from the Parthenon* and the *head of Athena*, a celebrated expression of the art of Magna Graecia. The influence of Greek and Hellenistic art was for a long time a fundamental influence in the evolution of Roman art; this was especially true in the field of sculpture, which took its first steps by copying ancient models, and is the case of the statues of *Marsyas* and of *Athena*, reproductions of the renowned bronze group cast by Myron in 460 BC that stood at the entrance to the Athens acropolis, or of the *Chiaramonti Niobe*, inspired by a famous sculptural group attributed to Skopas.

In the late republican era and the first years of the empire, Roman sculpture began to strike out on its own, above all in the sector of portraiture, with both full-figure *statues* and *busts* of famous personages and of the emperors and their family members. Many reliefs, like that of the *Vicomagistri Altar*, representing a sacrificial procession, also stand precious witness to the unfolding of religious and civil life in Roman society. Funerary art, which revealed itself especially prodigious in the production of *sarcophagi* (to which the museum dedicates an entire section) sheds much light on the myths of ancient times (*Adonis, Oedipus, Phaedra*, etc.) through the reliefs that decorate the coffins. The myths and beliefs of oriental origin that pervaded the Rome of the first and second centuries AD are clearly evident in the works grouped in the last section, including the lovely *Mithras Slaying the Bull*, a typical expression of late Roman art.

Facing page: Pinacoteca Vaticana, Leonardo da Vinci, Saint Jerome.

Pilgrims in Saint Peter's Square; Pope
John Paul II at the window of the
Papal Apartments; aerial view of Saint
Peter's Basilica and Square.

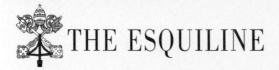

THE ESQUILINE

The present precinct of the Esquiline, created in 1870 when Rome was proclaimed the capital of Italy, occupies the eastern slopes of the Esquiline Hill. The name is derived from the Latin escolere, or 'living beyond', in reference to its suburban status outside of the Servian walls. The hill was typically the site of cemeteries in its early history. This use continued at least until Augustus, when the area was annexed to the city and transformed into a residential quarter for wealthy supporters of the Imperial court. Here lived the famed Maecenas, the personal counsel of Augustus and above all the animator of the most important cultural circle of antiquity. He was a friend of the poets Horace and Virgil (who also lived here) and owned immense gardens, known as the Horti Mecenatiani, which abounded in marvelous and precious works of art. With the decay of Rome, the green slopes became overgrown, the patrician villas fell into decay, and the area slid into a long and silent oblivion. The hill nevertheless became a popular site for the founding of churches and monasteries, which rose on some of the most antique Roman tituli. Among these are **Santa Prassede**, *built at the well where St. Praxedes had piously gathered the remains of some 2,000 Christian martyrs, and* **Santa Pudenziana,** *built on the house owned by her father Pudens, who had provided hospitality to St. Peter there. These two daughters of Pudens, Praxedes and Pudentiana, were martyred and gave their names to the two churches, both built between the 4th and 5th centuries.*

Also on the Esquiline is one of the four Jubilee basilicas of Rome, **Santa Maria Maggiore**, *built on the summit of the hill after it was whitened by a miraculous blizzard in August of 356, an event that had been foretold in a dream about the Virgin by Pope Liberius. The area maintained its rustic appearance through the Middle Ages, settled mostly by churches, convents and religious welfare institutions that had sprung up in connection with the latter. In the second half of the 16th century, the Esquiline witnessed somewhat of an urban rebirth with the creation, under Sixtus V, of a network of streets. Santa Maria Maggiore provided one of the hubs, with the strada Felice emanating from one side of it and connecting it with the church of Trinità dei Monti, and the Via Merulana (begun by Pope Gregory XIII for the Jubilee of 1575) on the other side, connecting it with the basilica of St. John Lateran. After Sixtus V had his villa built near the hill, other villas with large gardens were built in the area, forming until the 1800s an unbroken strip of such mansions adjacent to the Aurelian walls. However, they were all demolished when Rome became the capital of unified Italy, replaced by a regular street plan and new buildings, designed in the eclectic and classicist styles typical of the era. The reshaping of the urban fabric continued in the 1900s, extending to the Viminale, the hill facing the Esquiline, and home of the monumental* **Palazzo del Viminale**, *now the Ministry of the Interior.*

Santa Pudenziana - The church was built over the house of the Roman senator Pudens, whose daughters were the Saints Praxedes and Pudentiana; Pudens was known to have provided hospitality to St. Peter during his apostolate in Rome. The ancient *titulus*, perhaps dating from the 2nd century, was replaced in the late 4th century by a church, which, although extensively rebuilt during the Middle Ages and the Renaissance, is still partially visible in the present building. Works carried out during medieval times are evident on the exterior with the Romanesque **campanile**, from the early 13th century, and the facade, with its lovely **portico**

featuring two antique fluted columns and an 11th-century frieze representing the *Lamb of God* among *St. Peter, Pudens, Pudentiana and Praxedes*. Inside, the apse contains splendid *mosaics* from the 4th century with *Christ Triumphant* enthroned and surrounded by the *Apostles* and the *Saints Pudentiana and Praxedes*, who are offering crowns. In the background are the *Cross, Heavenly Jerusalem*, and the *symbols of the Evangelists*. Also of note is the **Caetani Chapel**, on the left side of the nave, begun by Francesco da Volterra in 1598 and completed by Maderno in 1614.

San Lorenzo in Panisperna - The church, which rises above a double stairway next to a shaded courtyard with several **medieval houses**, was built under Constantine on the site of the saint's martyrdom. It was restored in the early 1300s and again in the 1500s, when the **campanile** was added. The interior contains frescoes, attributed to Pasquale Cati and influenced by the work of Michelangelo, that depicted the *Martyrdom of St. Laurence.*

Aerial view with the basilica of Santa Maria Maggiore in the foreground.

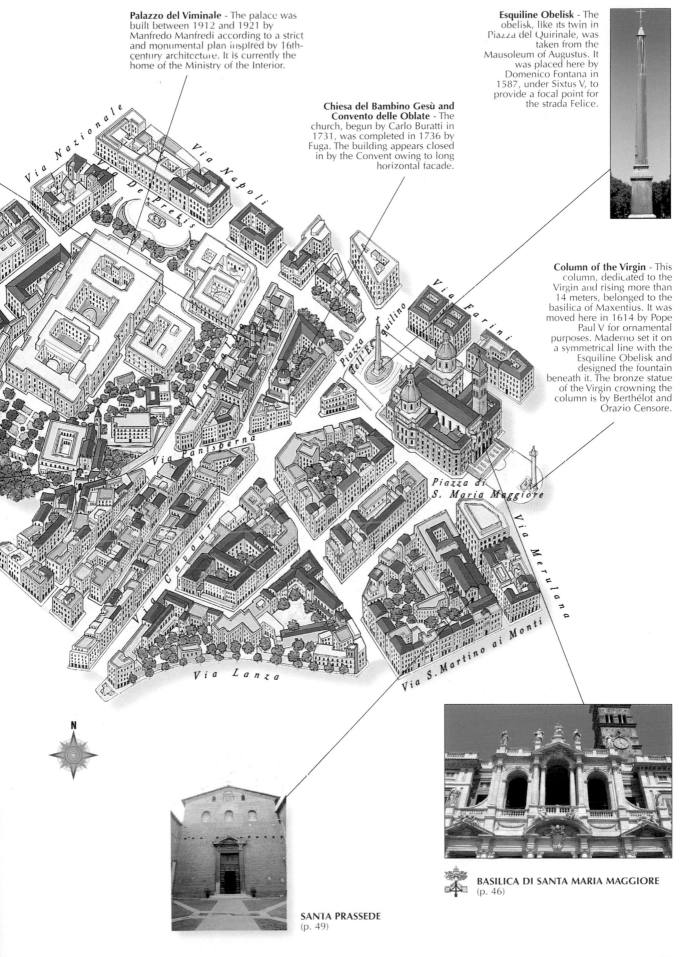

Palazzo del Viminale - The palace was built between 1912 and 1921 by Manfredo Manfredi according to a strict and monumental plan inspired by 16th-century architecture. It is currently the home of the Ministry of the Interior.

Chiesa del Bambino Gesù and Convento delle Oblate - The church, begun by Carlo Buratti in 1731, was completed in 1736 by Fuga. The building appears closed in by the Convent owing to long horizontal facade.

Esquiline Obelisk - The obelisk, like its twin in Piazza del Quirinale, was taken from the Mausoleum of Augustus. It was placed here by Domenico Fontana in 1587, under Sixtus V, to provide a focal point for the strada Felice.

Column of the Virgin - This column, dedicated to the Virgin and rising more than 14 meters, belonged to the basilica of Maxentius. It was moved here in 1614 by Pope Paul V for ornamental purposes. Maderno set it on a symmetrical line with the Esquiline Obelisk and designed the fountain beneath it. The bronze statue of the Virgin crowning the column is by Berthélot and Orazio Censore.

Via Nazionale

Via Napoli

Via De Pretis

Via Farini

Via dell'Esquilino

Via Panisperna

Piazza dell'Esquilino

Piazza di S. Maria Maggiore

Via Cavour

Via Merulana

Via S.Martino ai Monti

Via Lanza

N

SANTA PRASSEDE
(p. 49)

BASILICA DI SANTA MARIA MAGGIORE
(p. 46)

Santa Maria Maggiore, with its 18th-century facade, the richly decorated interior of the Paolina Chapel, and the frescoed cupola by Cigoli.

BASILICA DI SANTA MARIA MAGGIORE

Tradition has it that on the night of August 5, 356, under the pontificate of St. Liberius, the Madonna appeared in a dream to both the saint and a noble Roman, asking them to build a sanctuary dedicated to her on the summit of the Esquiline Hill, the ancient mons Cispius, which appeared covered with snow. When snow was found on the hill the following morning, the pope ordered that there be built around the whitened perimeter a basilica, which he called Liberiana after himself, and Santa Maria ad Nives, after the miraculous event. In reality, the date does not correspond historically to that of the basilica of Santa Maria Maggiore, which was instead consecrated by Pope Sixtus III as the Mother of God following the Council of Ephesus in 431. Despite the many restorations carried out over the centuries, the building has closely maintained its typical early-Christian basilican plan, even as it remarkably summarizes the long period of artistic and architectural styles going from the Romanesque to the late Baroque.

In the **facade** alone this intermingling of vastly different elements can be appreciated in all its magnificence: the 18th-century **portico** by Ferdinando Fuga gives way to the me-

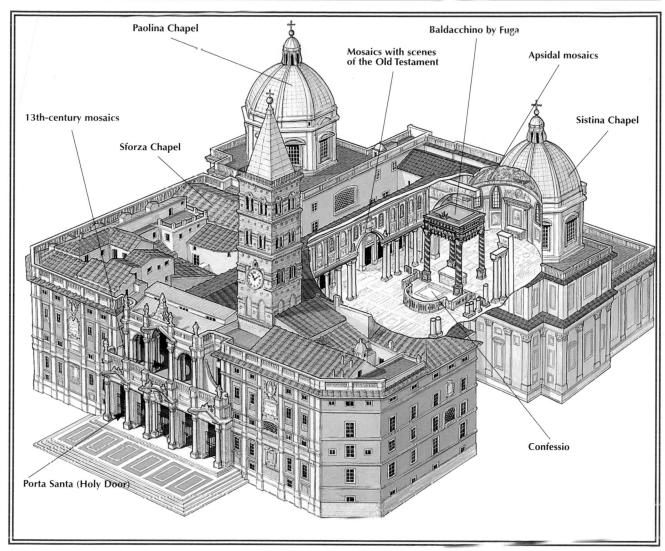

Paolina Chapel

Baldacchino by Fuga

Mosaics with scenes
of the Old Testament

Apsidal mosaics

13th-century mosaics

Sistina Chapel

Sforza Chapel

Confessio

Porta Santa (Holy Door)

Santa Maria Maggiore, the cupola of the Sistina Chapel.

dieval facade, featuring splendid 13th-century polychrome **mosaics** representing the *Miracle of St. Mary of the Snow*. The contrast is also repeated in the juxtaposition of the two 17th-century structures that clasp the facade to the tall **campanile**, still Romanesque although dating from the 14th century. The **apsidal facade**, also from the 1600s, is a work of great harmony by Carlo Rainaldi, who managed to connect with an elegant yet simple structure the two symmetrical 16th-century **cupolas** that cover the Sistina and Paolina chapels.

The interior plan of the basilica is striking for its original appearance, even with the later coffered **ceiling** by Giuliano da Sangallo, who used the first gold brought from the Americas to decorate it. The interior still shows in its essential lines the original structure of the 5th century, from which date, although with some significant later

alterations, the 36 mosaic panels depicting *Scenes of the Old Testament* and adorning the walls of the **nave**. The mosaics in the **apse** provide a superb corollary to those of the nave: the mosaic of the triumphal arch represents *Events in the Life of Jesus* and dates to the founding of the church, while those of the apsidal vault depict the *Incoronation of the Virgin* and were produced in 1295 by Jacopo Torriti, who made the mosaics that originally adorned the apse of St. John Lateran. Also interesting are the *baldacchino* by Fuga and the **confessio**, restored in the 1800s by Vespignani to hold the relics of the crib of the Infant Jesus. A great profusion of art works produced in different periods decorate the aisles and their chapels, perhaps too overwhelming to be seen in just one visit. At the beginning of the **right aisle** is the *Baptistery*, built by Flaminio Ponzio in 1605 and adorned with frescoes by Passignano and beautiful sculptures.

Opening at the end of the aisle is the **Sistina Chapel**, commissioned to Domenico Fontana by Sixtus V in 1585 for his *funerary monument*, which is placed next to the tomb of St. Pius V. The chapel, built in the full spirit of the Counter Reformation and decorated with marble from the *Septizodium* on the Palatine, is topped by a cupola and has two smaller side chapels. From here is the entrance to the **Oratory of the Holy Nativity**, which originally held the relic of the crib of the Infant Jesus. This still holds the fine crèche with the statues of *St. Joseph*, the *Magi*, the *oxen* and the *donkey*, all by Arnolfo di Cambio, while the statues of the *Virgin* and the *Infant Jesus* are by Valsoldo. A curiosity: here, in his family tomb, marked by a simple stone, is buried Gian Lorenzo Bernini.

In perfect symmetry with the Sistina Chapel is, at the end of the **left aisle**, the **Paolina Chapel**. Commissioned by Pope Paul V to hold his *sepulchral monument*, the chapel was completed by Flaminio Ponzio in 1611 following the same plan of its twin chapel on the right side. However, this chapel contains works of even greater artistic value: the painted decorations are by some of the most important artists of the Baroque age. The frescoes on the cupola are by Cigoli, while those on the spandrel are by Il Cavalier d'Arpino. The paintings on the lower sections of the chapel are instead by Guido Reni and Passignano. The genius Rainaldi designed the **altar**, which contains beautiful decorations in semiprecious stone, while the bas-relief by Maderno depicts *Pope Liberius tracing the perimeter of the basilica*, inspired by the mosaic on the medieval facade. The altar contains a fine Byzantine *Madonna*, which according to tradition was painted by St. Luke. The last among the numerous masterpieces of this church is the **Sforza Chapel**, designed by Michelangelo in 1564, the year of his death, and executed by his pupil Giacomo Della Porta.

Santa Maria Maggiore,
the mosaics on the facade, a view of the wooden ceiling by Giuliano da Sangallo and, below, left, a detail of the apsidal mosaic by Jacopo Torriti with the incoronation of the Virgin (late 13th century).

Below, right, the splendid apsidal mosaics of Santa Pudenziana with Triumphant Christ *surrounded by the figures of the Apostles and of* Saints Pudentiana *and* Praxedes *offering crowns (4th century).*

SANTA PRASSEDE

This early Christian basilica, still almost intact in its essential design and containing some of the most beautiful masterpieces of high medieval mosaics, was built in the 5th century on the site where St. Praxedes and her sister Pudentiana, daughter of the Roman senator Pudens, gathered the remains of some 2,000 martyrs of the Christian church in a well, before they themselves were martyred for their gesture of piety and religious faith. Around the well stood the ancient *titulus*, upon which Pope Paschal I had the basilica built in the 9th century. The church has undergone only partially alterations, including the addition of several pilasters that support the 13th-century wooden ceiling. The brick **facade** also dates from the 9th century, and the 15th-century doorway is preceded by a court and a double atrium with an external Romanesque **portico**.

In the **interior**, medieval pilasters and 16 columns, which support an architrave partially composed of antique fragments, separate the aisles from the central nave, while a porphyry disk on the pavement near the entrance marks the spot where the well of St. Praxedes was located. But the most interesting feature are undoubtedly the fine **mosaics** dating from the time of Paschal I that adorn the apse and the Chapel of St. Zeno. The **triumphal arch** in front of the presbyterian enclosure is decorated with a mosaic of *Celestial Jerusalem*, approached by the crowds of the Elect: at the top is the image of *Christ among the Angels and Saints*, including St. Praxedes and her sister St. Pudentiana. The area of the **presbytery**, with a ciborium in the center, is decorated with the *Twenty-four Elders of the Apocalypse*, who extend their arms offering crowns to the *Lamb of God*, the *Archangels*, the *Evangelists* and the *Apostles*, here symbolically represented. The **apsidal bowl** instead presents the *Redeemer* among the *Saints Peter, Paul, Praxedes, Pudentiana, Zeno* and *Paschal I*, who is presenting a model of the church and has a square halo because he was still living when the mosaics were produced. Below is a strip bearing the *Lamb of God* with 12 other *sheep*, symbolizing the Apostles, the two *holy rivers* and the two *holy cities*, Jerusalem and Bethlehem.

The **Chapel of St. Zeno**, once call the 'Garden of Paradise', opens towards the aisle with a front composed of a Classical doorway flanked by two columns, an inset window with an antique urn placed in front of it and a mosaic with *Christ*, the *Virgin* and *Saints*. But the masterpiece of this chapel created by Paschal I in honor of his mother Theodora, who is buried here and portrayed with a square halo in the niche on the left side, is without doubt the **vault**, in which four *Angels* hold a medallion with an image of *Christ*. Around this, other figures form part of the retinue of the *Madonna*, perhaps a later work, depicted in the niche of the altar. Next to that, a small chapel holds the so-called *Column of the Flagellation*, a venerated relic brought here from Jerusalem in the Middle Ages and said to be the one in which Jesus was beaten. The church also contains other works of great value and beauty: the *funerary monument of Bishop Santoni* is the first work, dated 1614, executed by Bernini in Rome, while also interesting is the **confessio**, with two *sarcophagi* containing the bodies of the two sister Saints and numerous other *relics* of martyrs.

Santa Prassede, the interior and a detail of the triumphal arch and apse.

The Chapel of St. Zeno, in Santa Prassede, the mosaic on the vault and the upper part of the entrance.

Porta San Giovanni - Built by Jacopo Del Duca during the pontificate of Gregory XIII, in 1574, to replace the older Porta Asinara.

Porta Asinara - Originally, this was a minor gateway from which issued the Via Asinara; it was enlarged by order of Honorius, who also had added the enclosure around the entrance and the two semi-cylindrical towers.

BASILICA DI SAN GIOVANNI IN LATERANO
(p. 52)

Triclinium of Leo III - Repaired in the 18th century and enclosed in a sort of exedra by Ferdinando Fuga, the mosaic portraying *Christ and the Apostles, Saint Peter Crowning Leo III, and Christ Investing Pope Sylvester and Constantine* is all that remains of the dining room (*triclinium*) of the ancient Patriarchate, the papal palace commissioned by Leo III in the late 8th century.

Scala Sancta - The 16th-century building was commissioned by Sixtus V. As we read in an inscription in the interior, it unites in a single building the **Scala Sancta** itself and the **Chapel of Saint Lawrence** or *Sancta Sanctorum* (Holy of Holies). According to a 15th-century tradition, the staircase is that of Pilate's praetorian palace, up which Jesus walked to submit to Roman judgment. Tradition again dictates that it be climbed by the faithful on their knees, reciting specific prayers on each of the 28 steps. The *Sancta Sanctorum* is instead a surviving portion of the original papal palace built in the late 1200s during the pontificate of Nicholas III. It is decorated with fine Cosmati work and contains extremely precious relics, including the celebrated image of the *Savior* called the *Acheiropoeton*; that is, not painted by human hand but the product of prodigious divine intervention.

Lateran Obelisk - This most ancient and tallest of Rome's obelisks was transported here in 1587 by Domenico Fontana from the Circus Maximus, where it had been raised by order of Constantius II in 357. It was originally part of the Egyptian Temple of Ammon in Thebes.

Santi Marcellino e Pietro - The ancient church dedicated to the two martyrs and saints was founded in the 4th century; it was totally rebuilt in 1751 by Girolamo Theodoli in forms that show the influence of Borromini both in the interior and in the stepped dome.

Ospedale del Salvatore - Also known as the **Ospedale di San Giovanni**, this hospital was founded in 1348 by the Compagnia del Santissimo Salvatore *ad Sancta Sanctorum*, and remodeled during the 15th century. The facade on the square is the 17th-century work of Carlo Rainaldi and Giacomo Mola.

Piazza di Porta S. Giovanni

Piazza di S. Giovanni in Laterano

Via Merulana

Via di S. Giovanni in Laterano

Via Labicana

Lateran Palace - Domenico Fontana built today's palace for Sixtus V in 1586-1589 on the earlier Patriarchate, for centuries the papal residence, of which it retained the original layout. The massive, squared-off building, with its distinctive three almost identical facades, takes its inspiration from the models typical of the sober Counter-Reformist style in architecture, of which Palazzo Farnese is the outstanding example. Beginning in the mid-19th century, the Lateran Palace became the home of the Museo Gregoriano Profano, the Museo Pio-Cristiano, and finally, in the 1920s, the Museo Missionario Etnologico; all three collections are now in the Vatican. Today, the Lateran is home to only the **Museo Storico Vaticano**: it occupies the rooms of the papal apartments, which include the Sala della Conciliazione built on the ancient Hall of the Popes of the Patriarchate.

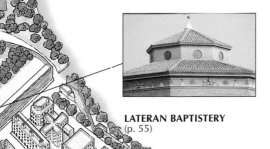

LATERAN BAPTISTERY
(p. 55)

THE COSMATI MASTERS

Between the 12th and 13th centuries, a succession of several generations of marble workers, decorators, and architects in Rome created some of the most interesting works of the late Romanesque period. These works were characterized by precious polychrome marble inlays and by mosaic highlights achieved by applying glass paste or gold tesserae to structures (cloisters, campanile, pavements) or to religious objects (ambones, thrones, altars, ciboria).
The use of the common name of 'Cosmati' comes from *Cosma*, a particularly widespread name among members of various family groups that for two centuries perpetuated this artistic tradition. Among them the oldest was the family head, Paolo, who in or around 1148 produced with his sons the ciborium for **San Lorenzo fuori le Mura**. The most important family unit was the one headed by Lorenzo, with his son Jacopo and grandson Cosma worked on the restoration of several churches during the 12th century (**Santa Maria in Trastevere, San Clemente, Santa Maria in Cosmedin**). The Cosmati of the Vassalletto family continued the tradition in the 13th century, and among their many works executed the cloisters of **San Giovanni in Laterano** and **San Paolo fuori le Mura**.

SANTI QUATTRO CORONATI
(p. 56)

THE LATERAN

*I*n early imperial times, the territory that extended east of the Caelian hill within the circle of the **Aurelian Walls**, in which both **Porta Maggiore** and **Porta Asinara** opened, was chosen by some of the richest and most important Roman patrician families as their place of residence. One of these was the Plauzi Laterani, the owners of a villa surrounded by a great estate which after being incorporated into the state lands under Nero was donated by Fausta, wife of Constantine, to Pope Melchiades, who made it his residence and that of his successors; the district takes its name from the Laterani family. A number of important monuments of antiquity, such as the well-known equestrian statue of Marcus Aurelius, which was moved to the Campidoglio in the 1500s, the **Castrense Amphitheater**, built under Septimius Severus and Elagabalus, and some public works, such as the **Claudian** and **Neronian aqueducts** that supplied much of the city water system, were located here. Alongside the papal residence, the so-called Patriarchate, which extended with its crenellated towers and its many wings well beyond the perimeter of today's **Lateran Palace**, Constantine commissioned the construction of **San Giovanni in Laterano** in 311-314. It was the first basilica of the Christian world and the cathedral of the city of Rome. A short distance from the center of papal power arose the Sessorian Palace, the last imperial residence of ancient Rome. It was here that Constantine's mother Saint Helena had transported a great quantity of relics from the Holy Land; to house them, the basilica of **Santa Croce di Gerusalemme** was later built not far away.
Outside the Aurelian Walls, along the Via Tiburtina, Constantine commissioned construction of another basilica, **San Lorenzo fuori le Mura**. Although originally intended to perform strictly cemeterial functions as a place of burial for the earthly remains of saints and martyrs, it was quite soon flanked by a true place of worship, the so-called Basilica Minor or Pelagian Basilica, from the name of the pope who ordered its construction. In the Middle Ages, another church fused with the earlier one to give rise to today's basilica dedicated to Saint Lawrence, which much later underwent massive restoration to repair the damage suffered during World War II. Not far away, near the Lateran basilica in the direction of the slopes of the Caelian hill, is another important place of worship: the 4th-century church of the **Santi Quattro Coronati**, which was given its unique aspect, still in perfect repair today, in the Middle Ages.
Following the 'exile' in Avignon and return of the papacy to Rome in 1377, the Patriarchate slowly declined. The Vatican in fact came to be preferred as the seat of papal power, and from that time onward tarnished the fame enjoyed theretofore by the Lateran complex. The Lateran also ceased to be the theater of that resplendent ceremonial linked to the installation of the newly-elected pope, who came with a long and opulently-appointed procession from Saint Peter's to his see and took possession of the cathedral basilica as Bishop of Rome. The Patriarchate was almost totally demolished during the radical urban renewal work promoted by Sixtus V, which in 1585-1589 involved the opening of the routes linking Santa Maria Maggiore, the Colosseum, and the Via Appia Antica, the placement of the **Lateran Obelisk** at their crossing, and the construction of the new papal palace, of the **Loggia delle Benedizioni**, and of the **Sancta Scala** building.
During the following two centuries the scenic Sistine renovation was integrated by construction of the **Ospedale di San Giovanni** or 'of the Holy Savoir', the creation of a new facade for the basilica, and the recovery of the **Triclinium of Leo III**. Finally, during the 19th and the early 20th century, the many villas immersed in luxuriant gardens, in which the area abounded, disappeared to make way for the new urban fabric of Umberto I's weaving, with its monumental buildings in eclectic and classicist styles more suitable to Rome as capital of Italy.

The Lateran Obelisk, of ancient Egyptian origin.

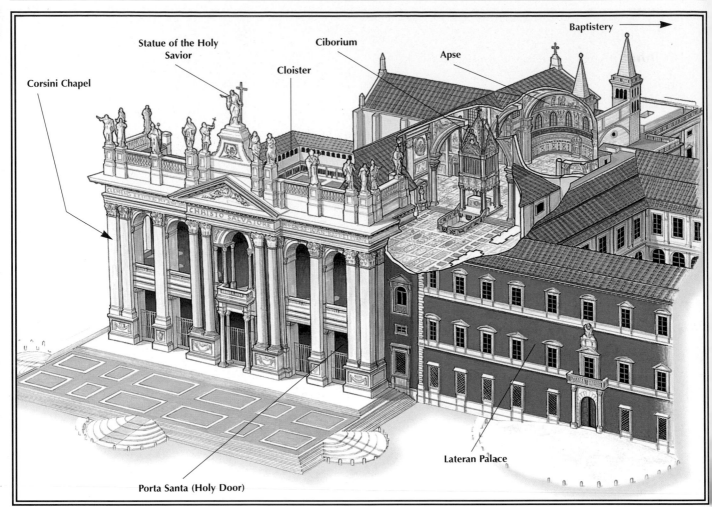

Corsini Chapel

Statue of the Holy Savior

Cloister

Ciborium

Apse

Baptistery

Porta Santa (Holy Door)

Lateran Palace

San Giovanni in Laterano.
The 13th-century cloister, a masterpiece
of Cosmati marblework.

BASILICA DI
SAN GIOVANNI IN LATERANO

The cathedral of Rome and the ancient center of papal power during the entire Middle Ages, the Basilica of San Giovanni in Laterano was founded by Pope Melchiades in 311-314 on land belonging to the Plauzi-Laterani family granted to him by the wife of the emperor Constantine. It is therefore also the oldest Christian basilica in the world, since its foundation predates that of Saint Peter's by about fourteen years. San Giovanni also differs from Saint Peter's in the very different way in which it was constructed, having been restructured and rebuilt a little at a time with no single project and above all proceeding with the idea of preserving the primitive structure. And indeed, although it underwent sometimes quite radical renovation, the layout of the basilica is still quite similar to the original.

Thus, if on the one hand the **foundations** incorporate the remains of the very oldest structures, the exterior walls are those of the early Middle Ages, although reinforced, while the cloister and the two **bell towers** date to the 13th century.

The work conducted in the 1500s by Domenico Fontana and by Giacomo Della Porta included the **transept** and the **side facade** erected near the papal window commissioned by Sixtus V. The first of these creations was frescoed by a group of Mannerist painters, under the direction of the Cavalier d'Arpino, with *stories from the Bible, scenes from the life of Constantine,* and salient phases of the *construction of the basilica.*

San Giovanni in Laterano.
The main facade, and a view of the interior showing
the Cosmatesque-style floor.

We might say that until the 16th century the internal structure of the building, with a nave and four aisles divided by tall stands of columns and enhanced by a fine Cosmatesque **floor**, remained almost intact. But its condition was so critical that on occasion of the Jubilee of 1650 Innocent X had the **interior** completely remodeled by Borromini and although the artist was constrained in his work by considerations of conservation, he nevertheless succeeded admirably in expressing his genius as an architect. In the **nave**, he left intact the beautiful wooden **ceiling**, designed by Piero Ligorio and decorated by Daniele da Volterra in 1562-1567, and limited his intervention to creating in the twelve pillars the same number of recesses to receive *statues of the Apostles*.

In the four **aisles**, he preferred simple decoration with heads of angels and cherubs, and instead highlighted the architectural purity of the pillars, arches, and vaults. Here, Borromini excogitated a genial decorative solution that reused the many sculptures of the *medieval and Renaissance tombs*, in Baroque aediculae of his own design. One of these, at the first pillar of the intermediate right aisle, instead houses a fragment of a fresco, attributed to Giotto, of *Pope Boniface VIII announcing the first Holy Year in 1300.*

Interior of San Giovanni in Laterano. A view of the presbytery and the 16th-century wooden ceiling.

Facing page: one of the 12 statues of the apostles that line the nave of San Giovanni in Laterano.

Below: in the interior of San Giovanni in Laterano, the frescoed panels of the ciborium.

Not far from this aedicula are others with the funeral monuments of prelates, nobles, and famous popes: *Sylvester II*, who in the Middle Ages was known as a worker of miracles, *Alexander III*, and *Sergius IV*.

Another interesting monument is that in the intermediate left aisle to *Elena Savelli*, decorated by Jacopo Del Duca, a qualified pupil of Michelangelo's, with an expressive bust and refined reliefs, all in bronze.

The **confessio**, instead, contains the funeral monument to *Pope Martin V*; the tombstone is a masterpiece of the Renaissance by the Florentine artist Simone Ghini.

Above, almost as though it were watching over the **papal altar**, at which only the pope is permitted to celebrate Mass, is the Gothic-style **ciborium** made for Urban V in 1367 by Sienese masters and ornamented with twelve panels frescoed by Barna da Siena; it contains, in silver *reli-*

quaries, the heads of the apostles Peter and Paul.

The **apse**, beyond the presbytery, was completely remodeled under Leo XIII, who commissioned reinstatement of the original mosaic by Jacopo Torriti (also the author of that in Santa Maria Maggiore) and Fra' Jacopo da Camerino, whose self-portraits are the two figures kneeling alongside the *Apostles* between the windows.

Off the far left aisle open two of the basilica's masterpieces, the Corsini Chapel and the **cloister**, in which in the third decade of the 13th century the Cosmati of the Vassalletto family demonstrated their skillful hand with marble. The cloister is a vast arched portico with small columns of differing forms, some of which are highlighted with mosaic.

Above the archways runs a richly-adorned entablature, also decorated with mosaics and sculpted marble lions' heads; under the portico are some remains of the architecture and decoration of the ancient basilica, among which fine sculptures taken from the *funeral monument to Cardinal Annibaldi* by Arnolfo di Cambio, and the original bronze door of the Scala Sancta. The **Corsini Chapel** is instead the work of the Tuscan architect Alessandro Galilei, who built it in 1732-1735 to contain the funeral monument to Pope Clement XII Corsini with the *statue* of the pope by Giovan Battista Maini.

Galilei was also the author of the solemn, monumental main **facade**, on which stands the *statue of the Holy Savior* surrounded by those of the titular saints of the basilica, *John the Baptist* and *John the Evangelist*, and those of the *Doctors of the Church*.

Lateran Baptistery. The interior, with the circle of two superposed orders of columns; below, the mosaics of the narthex and those of the apse and the arch of the Chapel of Saint Venantius.

LATERAN BAPTISTERY

This small and very ancient building, also known as San Giovanni in Fonte, is essentially that commissioned by Constantine. It was nevertheless amply remodeled many times, most importantly in the 5th century under Sixtus III and in 1657 under Urban VIII.

The octagonal plan, the model for many a later baptistery, reveals an interior organized around a central space delimited by two orders of overlapping porphyry and white marble columns, at the center of which stands a green basalt *urn* with a bronze cover, once used for baptism by immersion.

All around are chapels: the **Chapel of Saint John the Baptist** preserves the massive 5th-century bronze *doors*; the **Chapel of Saint Venantius** and the **Chapel of Saint Rufina** are still decorated with fine *mosaics* from the 5th and 7th centuries, respectively; the **Chapel of Saint John the Evangelist** also boasts a bronze *portal* dating to 1196 and *mosaics* from the second half of the 5th century.

Santi Quattro Coronati.
A view of the cloister and three of the frescoes in the Oratorio di San Silvestro depicting Scenes from the History of Saint Sylvester and Constantine; on the top left, Emperor Constantine kneeling as he donates the symbolic tiara to Saint Sylvester (the 'Donation of Constantine').

SANTI QUATTRO CORONATI

This church, erected in the 4th century, was dedicated to the four soldiers Severus, Severianus, Carpophorus, and Victorinus, who according to an ancient tradition were martyred because they refused to kill four Dalmatian sculptors who had in turn refused to sculpt the likeness of a pagan divinity. Other sources name the sculptors as the martyrs, but whatever turn events actually took, the church has always been the chosen place of worship of Rome's stonecutters and marble-workers.

The original building was renovated in the 9th century and later, after having been destroyed by the Normans, was rebuilt under Pope Paschal II. The convent, the cloister, and the Oratorio di San Silvestro were added in the 12th and 13th centuries.

The entrance, under an arch surmounted by a distinctive Romanesque **bell tower**, opens on a series of **courtyards** and **porticoes** that lead to the church proper. The three-aisled **interior**, with its *women's gallery*, is one of the most extraordinary surviving examples of medieval architecture, and is all but perfectly intact. The columns supporting the asymmetrical archways, the Cosmatesque *floor* in part composed of ancient Roman paving stones, and the remains of many frescoes all suggest to the church's evocative past.

The enormous **apse**, which embraces all three aisles, was decorated in the 17th century by Giovanni da San Giovanni with frescoes of the *Martyrdom of the Four Crowned Saints* and the *Glory of All Saints*, which includes some angels with curious female traits that earned for the work the nickname of 'Coro delle Angiolesse'. Under the presbytery is the **crypt**, where the relics of the four titular martyrs are preserved. The left aisle instead gives access to the **cloister** of the convent, with its distinctive archways supported by small columns adorned with water lily leaves; at the center is a singular *fount* for ablutions, from the time of Paschal II.

The second exterior courtyard of the church leads into the **Oratorio di San Silvestro**, with its perfectly-preserved original decoration painted in 1246 by Venetian masters of Byzantine training, showing the *Last Judgment* and *Scenes from the History of Saint Sylvester and Constantine*. An ancient legend recounts how the emperor's leprosy was healed by the saint, who Constantine had called in after Saint Peter and Saint Paul had appeared to him in a dream; Sylvester cured the emperor by baptism and in gratitude the emperor granted him lands by a document known in history as the Donation of Constantine. But the historical inaccuracy of the story was proven in the 15th century by Lorenzo Valla.

Nero's Aqueduct - This aqueduct was built by Nero as a branch of the *Aqua Claudia* to supply the *Domus Aurea* on the Oppian hill and the nymphaeum of the Temple of the Divus Claudius on the Caelian hill. Domitian extended it to the Palatine to supply water to the imperial residence.

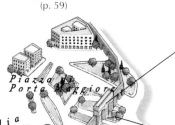

BASILICA DI SAN LORENZO FUORI LE MURA
(p. 59)

Porta Maggiore - Originally built by the emperor Claudius in 38 AD to allow the *Aqua Claudia* and *Anio Novus* aqueducts to bridge the *Via Praenestina* and the *Via Labicana*, this structure was later incorporated into the Aurelian Walls. The architectural composition, with two openings with aediculae and columns formed of blocks of travertine, is striking.

Tomb of Eurysaces - This sepulcher of the late republican era, apparently that of the rich baker Marcus Vergilius Eurysaces, came to light in 1838 following the demolition of the bastions erected by Honorius. The structure, which much influenced the architecture of the Fascist era, includes a relief showing Eurysace overseeing bread-making.

Castrense Amphitheater - This construction, begun by Septimius Severus and completed by Elagabalus, was originally part of the Sessorian Palace, the private home of the last emperors of Rome. It was later incorporated in the Aurelian Walls, from which its first-story arches and columns emerge.

BASILICA DI SANTA CROCE DI GERUSALEMME
(p. 57)

Santa Croce di Gerusalemme. Cross by Valadier (1803).

BASILICA DI SANTA CROCE DI GERUSALEMME

Perhaps the most important of the three minor Jubilee basilicas, Santa Croce di Gerusalemme has been known since the Middle Ages as the 'basilica of the relics' due to the great number of mementos of saints and martyrs it contains. Its official name derives from the soil of the Holy Sepulcher in Jerusalem brought here by Constantine's mother Saint Helena and placed, together with the precious relics of the Cross and the Passion of Christ, in a hall of her private home, the Sessorian Palace. The atrium was converted some decades later into a church, called the Sessorian Basilica after the palace; it was completely rebuilt in the 12th century by Pope Lucius II.

The **bell tower**, with its Cosmatesque aediculae, and the **cloisters** are the only external elements to have survived the 18th-century restoration promoted by Pope Benedict XIV and performed by Domenico Gregorini and Pietro Passalacqua, authors of the creative convex **facade** inspired by Borromini's style. The two architects also transformed the medieval narthex into a luminous and lively elliptical **atrium** that nevertheless preserves traces of the original decoration in the fine 14th-century crucifix frescoed in the adjoining left chapel.

The **interior** is divided into a nave and two aisles by twelve columns, four of which are enclosed in the 18th-century pillars. Although architecturally less successful, it is by no means less significant, with its beautiful wooden *ceiling*, the false vault of which is decorated with the *Apotheosis of Saint Helena* by Gia-

The atrium and a detail of the facade of Santa Croce di Gerusalemme; below, the interior with the 18th-century baldachin and the fresco in the apse.

quinto, who was also the author of the paintings decorating the **apse** and the **presbytery** - to the exception of the *Legend of the Holy Cross*, a masterful 15th-century fresco by Antoniazzo Romano. The 16th-century *tomb of Cardinal Quiñones*, by Sansovino, stands in the back of the apse; over it is the marble and gilded bronze *tabernacle* designed by Maderno. To the right of the apse, steps lead to the **Chapel of Saint Helena**, founded by Constantine, that contains the soil of the Holy Sepulcher under its floor; the titular saint is portrayed in a modified Roman statue on the altar. The **mosaic** that adorns the upper portion of the walls and the vault is a Renaissance work variously attributed to Melozzo da Forlì and Baldassare Peruzzi.

The adjacent Gregorian Chapel was commissioned by Cardinal Carvajal, whose tomb is in the apse. Of less artistic and architectural importance, but of inestimable religious value, is the **Chapel of the Relics**, containing the fragments of the True Cross, the Holy Thorns of Christ's Crown, a portion of the cross of Saint Dismas the Good Thief, and other significant sacred relics. The **Sessorian Library**, in the adjoining convent, is also of interest with its frescoes by Pannini.

BASILICA DI SAN LORENZO FUORI LE MURA

Although severely damaged by the World War II bombings, San Lorenzo still preserves much evidence of its remote and illustrious past. In truth, it arose from the fusion of the Pelagian Basilica, dedicated to Saint Lawrence, and Honorius' church dedicated to the Virgin, commissioned by the popes Pelagius II (6th century) and Honorius III (13th century), respectively. The Pelagian Basilica stood alongside the primitive Constantinian building that was destined for purely cemeterial functions and contained the relics of the titular saint, which were later moved to the adjacent Pelagian building. The lovely **portico** created by the Vassalletto family Cosmati workers, incorporating ancient columns with Ionic capitals, dates to the 13th century; under the portico are a number of *ancient tombs* and remains of medieval *frescoes*. Alongside are the monastery, with its beautiful **cloister**, and the late 12th-century Romanesque **bell tower**.

The **interior** shows evident signs of the origin of the building as the fusion of two churches that while contiguous were laid out on different axes: the front portion has a nave and two aisles divided by twenty-two ancient columns; the rear church, which forms the presbytery and the apse of the present-day basilica, has three aisles divided by columns that probably came from the earlier Constantinian building and upper **women's galleries**, marked out by small columns with a Byzantine cast. Examples of the alacritous activity of the Cosmati can also be found in the interior of the basilica: the beautiful mosaic *floor*, unfortunately damaged by the WWII bombings, the two *pulpits*, the *ciborium*, the *paschal candelabrum* and the *bishop's throne* at the back of the choir.

The **mosaic** that decorates the triumphal arch with *Jesus with Saints Paul, Stephen, Hippolytus, Peter, Laurence and Pope Pelagius* instead dates to the 6th century.

San Lorenzo fuori le Mura. The Romanesque bell tower and the 13th-century portico; below, the bishop's throne with the Cosmati work frontals, and a view of the cloister.

Rocca dei Savelli and Giardino degli Aranci - Only the ramparts remain of the heavy fortress built under Alberic II in the 10th century and then taken by the Savelli around the year 1000. In the 1930s, it was incorporated into a public park with cluster pines and orange trees. Before that, the area was owned by the Dominicans of the adjacent Santa Sabina.

Monument to Mazzini - The statue of the hero of the Risorgimento, or Italian unification, was made by Ettore Ferrari in 1929 and placed here for the centenary of the Roman Republic.

Santi Bonifacio e Alessio - The original early Romanesque building, probably dating from the 8th century, was redesigned several times during the 16th and 18th centuries, mostly distorting the primitive plan of the church. The *crypt*, however, is still intact. The 18th-century interior, which one enters through a doorway erected by Honorius III, still has part of the Cosmatesque *pavement* and two *small columns*, also Cosmatesque, in the apse. In the left aisle is a well, said to belong to the house of St. Alexis, and the staircase, set off by a precious Baroque framework, under which the saint slept for the many years he lived there. In the crypt are the relics of St. Thomas of Canterbury. The campanile is from the 13th century.

SANTA SABINA
(p. 64)

Priorato dei Cavalieri di Malta - Between 1764 and 1766 Cardinal Rezzonico gave Giovanni Battista Piranesi the opportunity to put into practice his great talent for architecture, which until then had only been evident in his designs and projects. The design of the complex–for the Order of the Knights of Malta, who had occupied the site since the 1300s–demonstrated the creative inspiration of this master. This can be seen in the decorations: stele, obelisks, heraldic emblems, panoplies and aedicules are integrated with the essential architectural lines, reflecting a neo-classic spirit. The taste for the scenographic arrangement of the whole is demonstrated by the *view of the cupola of St. Peter's*, which can be seen through a keyhole in the main doorway.

Santa Prisca - The church, dating from antiquity, was built on the home of the matron Priscilla and her husband Aquila, parents of the martyr Prisca, to whom the church is dedicated. The house was cited in the *Epistle* of St. Paul and known for having given hospitality to St. Peter. The remains of a *Roman house* are still visible, along with those of a 3rd-century **Mithraeum** containing sections of frescoes related to that Eastern religion. Next to that is the *crypt*, where the relics of the saint are kept. The church was restored several times, shortened and almost rebuilt in 1456 as a consequence of a partial collapse. The facade was redesigned by Carlo Lambardi in the 17th century. Inside, above the high altar, is the *Baptism of St. Prisca*, a 17th-century masterpiece by Passignano.

Santa Maria del Priorato - In designing this small church, Piranesi combined the most important styles in the religious architecture of Rome: on the one hand, the severity of the **facade**, inspired by the Counter-Reformation, is mixed with ornate decorations, while the interior, with the finely ornamented symbols of the Order of Malta, is a fanciful 17th-century transposition of the stylistic canons of Borromini.

Sant'Anselmo - The church, linked to the monastery of the same name, was built in the late 1800s in the Romanesque style with a trussed ceiling and mosaic decorations in the apse.

Bastione della Colonella - Commissioned by Paul III as a reinforcement to the Aurelian walls, the bastion was designed by Antonio da Sangallo the Younger.

The Pyramid of Gaius Cestius - This peculiar funerary monument of Gaius Cestius, designed in the likeness of an Egyptian pyramid, was built in 12 BC and ended up within the perimeter of the Aurelian walls 200 years later. The structure, about 36 meters high, is made of mortar covered by blocks of volcanic tufa stone, with a sepulchral chamber inside.

N

Via di S. Maria in Cosmedin

Clivo Pubblicio

Via delle Terme Deciane

Via di S. Sabina

Via S. Domenico

Via S. Alessio

Via Marmorata

THE AVENTINE

*Initially placed outside of the Servian walls, the Aventine Hill, with its two summits known as the Grande and Piccolo Aventino, fell inside of the city walls, thus gaining the right of intra moenia, only with the construction of the Aurelian walls. The only remaining traces of this latter wall is the **Porta San Paolo**, located in the lower section of the hill. The area had already changed its original appearance by the time the Aurelian walls were built, passing from a populous quarter, prevalently inhabited by plebs, to one of the most exclusive residential areas of the city with many villas, including one belonging to Trajan. The oldest Roman law, the Lex Acilia (456 BC), in fact allowed the plebeians, originally composed of the Latin populations brought here by Ancus Martius, to settle on the Aventine.*

Numerous hypothesis exist about the origin of the name of the hill: one is that it derived from the oats (avena) cultivated on the hills and sold in the valley below; another links it to the temple of Jupiter Inventor, built according to legend by Hercules to thank the god for allowing him to find his herds stolen by the giant Cacus, whose grotto was here; the third hypothesis, the most plausible, is that it derived from the Latin word aves, that is, from the birds at the Saxum Sacrum that had given augurs to Remus, who had chosen the heights as his point of surveillance and where he was buried. From that came the name of Remurio, which the hill was also called.

Another name attributed to the Aventine was that of collis Dinae, the hill of Diana, in reference to the great temple dedicated to the goddess erected here by Servius Tullius as a place of common worship for the Latin cities and enlarged by Augustus with the construction of the sumptuous porticoes. Near the Temple of Diana rose the Temple of Minerva, which housed from the 3rd century BC the College of Writers and Actors, who were responsible for organizing the Ludi Scaenici, public performances with sacred themes in which the

hymns of the gods were sung. Another important temple on the Aventine was that of Juno Regina, built under Furius Camillus in 392 BC to hold the effigies of the goddess brought to Rome from the conquered Etruscan city of Veio.

*On its southern side, the hill dominated the Emporium, the important Tiber port with porticoes and storehouses, the so-called Horrea, where merchandise, especially oil conserved in special amphorae, was kept. The earthenware fragments of the amphorae, heaped in a precise spot near the port, eventually created the so-called **Monte Testaccio**, around which a populous residential district developed in the 1900s. This area marked the extreme perimeter of the ancient city and was the site of one of the city's most peculiar tombs, the **Pyramid of Gaius Cestius**, enclosed two centuries later by the Aurelian walls. The hill suffered terrible devastation during the barbarian invasions and was nearly reduced to open country and almost depopulated, with the exception of those living in the monastic communities that had settled on the hills. The Grande and Piccolo Aventino were in fact the site of some of the most prestigious medieval tituli: **Santa Sabina**, **Santa Prisca**, **Santi Bonifacio e Alessio**, **San Saba**. Given its eminent position above the Tiber, it was also the site of many forts. One of these was the **Rocca dei Savelli**, whose ramparts were transformed into public gardens and today offer an outstanding view of the city. The area, sparsely populated until the 1900s, remained nearly unaltered for centuries, with the exception of the 18th-century buildings designed by Piranesi. On the site of a former Benedictine monastery, which subsequently belonged to the Templars and then the Hospitalers, the architect built the **Priorato dei Cavalieri di Malta** for the Order of the Knights of Malta, and the church of **Santa Maria del Priorato**. Branching out of Porta San Paolo is Via Ostiense, with one of the four major pilgrimage basilicas, **San Paolo fuori le Mura**. Nearby is the **Abbazia delle Tre Fontane**, the site of the martyrdom of the St. Paul.*

Porta San Paolo - The gate is situated at the beginning of the ancient Via Laurentina and Via Ostiensis, which corresponded to the two original arches still visible from the inside. These were changed into a single arch on the exterior by Honorius. The gate was called Porta Ostiensis in antiquity and owes its present name to the vicinity of the Basilica of San Paolo fuori le Mura. The two heavy semi-circular towers house the **Museo della Via Ostiense**, which contains archaeological findings and models of the ancient road connecting Rome with the port of Ostia.

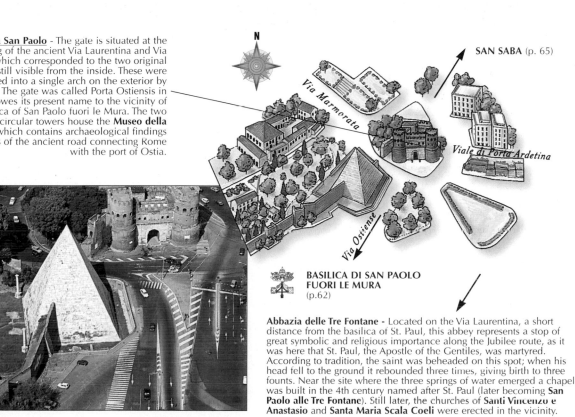

SAN SABA (p. 65)

BASILICA DI SAN PAOLO
FUORI LE MURA
(p.62)

Abbazia delle Tre Fontane - Located on the Via Laurentina, a short distance from the basilica of St. Paul, this abbey represents a stop of great symbolic and religious importance along the Jubilee route, as it was here that St. Paul, the Apostle of the Gentiles, was martyred. According to tradition, the saint was beheaded on this spot; when his head fell to the ground it rebounded three times, giving birth to three founts. Near the site where the three springs of water emerged a chapel was built in the 4th century named after St. Paul (later becoming **San Paolo alle Tre Fontane**). Still later, the churches of **Santi Vincenzo e Anastasio** and **Santa Maria Scala Coeli** were erected in the vicinity.

San Paolo fuori le Mura:
*a general view of the facade and the
quadriporticus, a detail of the facade
mosaic of a* benediction by Christ.

*Middle, the large nave with the
frescoed triumphal arch.*

Below, the Cosmatesque cloister.

BASILICA DI SAN PAOLO FUORI LE MURA

St. Paul's is the second largest of the four major Jubilee basilicas after St. Peter's and, for that matter, one of the largest churches in the world. Founded under Constantine, the basilica has unfortunately come to us in its modern version following the fire of 1823 that destroyed the original structure and, with it, its Byzantine, Renaissance and Baroque restorations that had characterized the history of the building. The church is preceded by a vast **quadriporticus**, with a statue of St. Paul by the artist Obici at its center. This structure leads into the actual basilica, with its monumental dimensions (132 meters long, 65 meters wide and 30 meters high).

The **nave** is set off by 80 colossal granite columns and is topped by the 19th-century coffered ceiling. A unique mosaic frieze extends to the aisles, with *portraits of the popes*, from St. Peter until modern times, recounting the long history of the Catholic Church. To the right of the main doorway is the 11th-century *Porta Santa*, in bronze and decorated with *scenes from the Old and New Testament*, which is opened at the beginning of the Jubilee year.

The 19th-century reconstruction nevertheless contains numerous pieces of the original structure that escaped the flames and were restored. The *triumphal arch* is decorated with splendid mosaics dating from the time of Pope Leo the Great (5th century). They portray *Christ between two angels, the symbols of the Evangelists*

and the 24 *Elders of the Apocalypse*. There are also 13th-century *mosaics* by Pietro Cavallini created for the facade of the basilica.

The **apse** is also decorated by a large *mosaic* depicting in the center *Christ giving blessing*, the work of Venetian artists who executed it in the Byzantine style under Pope Honorius III. A short distance ahead, at the edge of the transept and preceded by the confessio, is the *high altar*. Its stupendous *ciborium* is an elegant work in the Gothic style executed in 1285 by Arnolfo da Cambio and a certain Pietro, erroneously confused with Cavallini. To the right of the altar is the *Easter candle*, more than 5 meters high and illustrated by Pietro Vassalletto and Niccolò d'Angelo in the late 12th century with reliefs portraying human, vegetable and animal motifs mixed with religious scenes.

The **transept**, totally rebuilt in the 19th century, nevertheless contains numerous relics of the Baroque restoration of the basilica, especially in the *Chapels of St. Stephen, of the Crucifix* and of *St. Laurence*, all designed by Maderno. Among interesting works of art found here are a 14th-century *Crucifix* in the second chapel, attributed to Cavallini, whose tomb is also there. Vassalletto, with the other Cosmati, was also responsible for the **cloister** connected to the basilica. Like the cloister of St. John Lateran, that of St. Paul's displays refined columns in a great variety of forms, with mosaic highlighting. The columns support small arches, above which are set beams decorated with fanciful inlays of polychrome marble and with a mosaic inscription in gold letters on a blue background.

Located in the cloister are the **Sala del Martirologio**, or the Oratory of St. Julian, the **Baptistery**, the **Sala Gregoriana**, the **Chapel of Reliquaries** and the **Pinacoteca**, with several interesting works of art, including a *Flagellation* by Bramante and a *Crucifix with St. Brigid* by Cigoli.

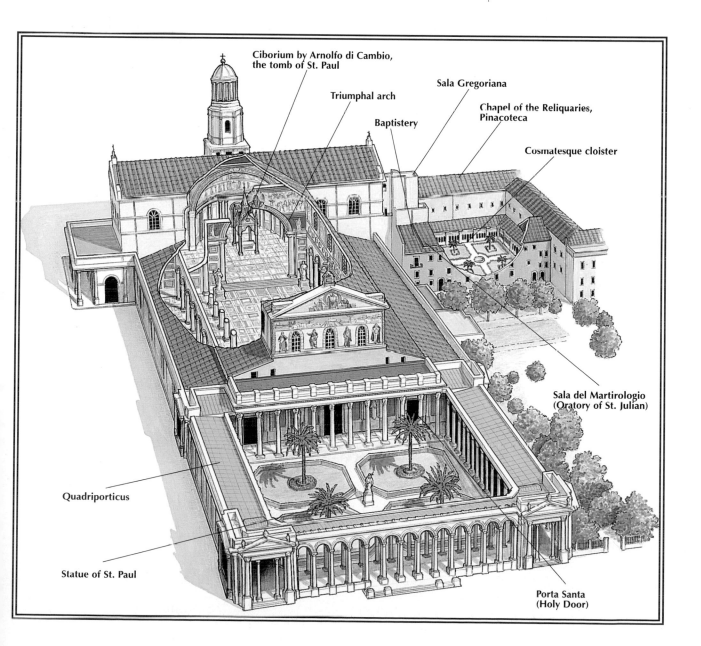

Ciborium by Arnolfo di Cambio, the tomb of St. Paul

Triumphal arch

Sala Gregoriana

Baptistery

Chapel of the Reliquaries, Pinacoteca

Cosmatesque cloister

Sala del Martirologio (Oratory of St. Julian)

Quadriporticus

Statue of St. Paul

Porta Santa (Holy Door)

Santa Sabina, view of the church, with a section of the right exterior, the interior and, below, the side portico and the exterior of the apse.

SANTA SABINA

The church of Santa Sabina is without a doubt one of the most complete examples of early Christian architecture in Rome. The church was brought back to its primitive splendor in the 1900s with restorations that eliminated several structures added by Domenico Fontana and Francesco Borromini between the late 1500s and the first half of the 1600s. The church was founded in 422 by Peter of Illyria and covered an older building that belonged to a Roman matron named Sabina, then confounded with the Umbrian saint of the same name, for whom the primitive *titulus Sabinae* was built. The adjoining **convent** is linked to the figure of St. Dominic; in the 13th century, he oversaw the building of the harmonious **cloister**, which looked out at the *chapter house* and the saint's *cell*.

The brick **exterior** of the church has a series of windows with their original *transenna* in selenite, a very fragile building material, while a 15th-century **portico** leads to the atrium, containing architectural fragments from the church brought to light during the 20th-century restoration. The main doorway here, perhaps originating from a building of the Imperial age, holds two very precious 5th-century cypress *doors*. These are decorated with rich frames bearing animal and flora motifs that still hold 10 of the 28 original panels depicting *scenes from the Old and New Testaments*.

The **interior** of the church has a basilican plan with columns setting off the nave from the two aisles. Its form recalls the basilicas of Ravenna, and like them it was decorated with mosaics. Of the original mosaics, however, there remains only a fragment above the door with an inscription commemorating the founding of the church by Peter of Illyria under the pontificate of Caelestunus I, while the two female figures symbolize, respectively, the Church as born from the conversion of Gentiles (*Ecclesia es gentibus*) and as born from the conversion of the Jews (*Ecclesia es circumcisione*). The apsidal mosaics were in-

San Saba,
the interior, a detail of the antique schola cantorum *and, below, the Cosmatesque bishop's throne.*

stead removed and in their place Taddeo Zuccari executed frescoes reproducing the same theme of *Christ seated among the Apostles.* A decorative inlay of porphyry and serpentine with motifs symbolizing chalices and crosses runs between the arcades of the **nave**, in the center of which stands the *burial stone of Muñoz de Zamora* (14th century) with the mosaic effigy of the Provincial General of the Dominicans in mosaic. Farther ahead is the *enclosure of the schola cantorum,* dating to the pontificate of Eugenius II (9th century), decorated with Byzantine style elements depicting plants and animals. In the **right aisle** is a curious relic placed atop a small column: a black stone that according to tradition Satan threw at St. Dominic to break him away from his prayers. A short distance away is a 16th-century *chapel* with frescoes by Zuccari and the Renaissance *funerary monument of Cardinal Auxia*, with its unique Latin inscription, from the school of Andrea Bregno.

SAN SABA

Descending the summit of the so-called Grande Aventino, and climbing back up the hill known as the Piccolo Aventino, one arrives at the church of St. Saba, preceded by a 13th-century Romanesque porch and a large forecourt. The church, dedicated to the monk saint Sabas who founded the first monastic communities in Asia Minor, was built in the 7th century and largely restructured in the 13th and 15th centuries. The site is also bound to the figure of St. Sylvia, mother of St. Gregory the Great, who in the 5th century founded the primitive oratory upon which the present church was built. The last restoration, by Cardinal Francesco Piccolomini, produced the **portico** and **gallery with loggia** as well as the fresco on the triumphal arch. Under this were found some interesting objects from the

Roman and medieval periods, including a fine *sarcophagus* and a relief depicting a *Horseman with a falcon* from the 8th century. The fine doorway, decorated with refined Cosmatesque mosaic highlights, leads into the rather simple and bare **interior**, curiously divided into a nave and three aisles as a result of incorporating an ancient portico that abutted on the left aisle. The original nave and aisles, each of which terminates in apses, contain numerous works that testify to the building's medieval past, such as the *bishop's throne*, the *high altar*, and the remains of the *ambones* (pulpits) and of the *schola cantorum*, standing side by side in the right aisle. The primitive mosaic decorations have mostly disappeared and been replaced by *frescoes*, some of which, dating from the 13th century, are from the Subiaco school. Some *fragments of wall paintings* (7th-9th centuries) from the church and the fortified convent that rose next to it are exhibited in the corridor of the *sacristy*, where the entrance to the *subterranean oratory* founded by St. Sylvia is located.

ANCIENT ROME

THE CAMPIDOGLIO AND THE FORUM BOARIUM, THE ROMAN FORUM, THE IMPERIAL FORUMS AND THE MONTI DISTRICT, THE OPPIAN HILL, THE PALATINE, THE BATHS OF CARACALLA, THE GHETTO AND THE SANT'ANGELO DISTRICT, ISOLA TIBERINA, PIAZZA ESEDRA AND THE UMBERTINE QUARTERS, PIAZZA DEL POPOLO AND THE CAMPO MARZIO DISTRICT

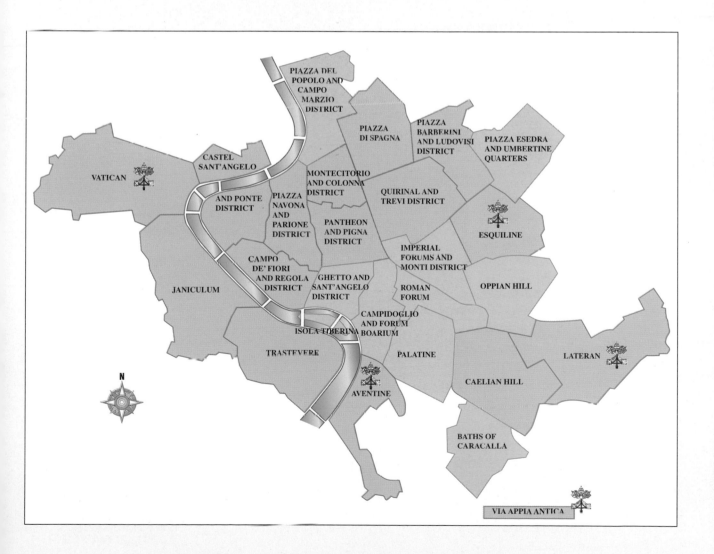

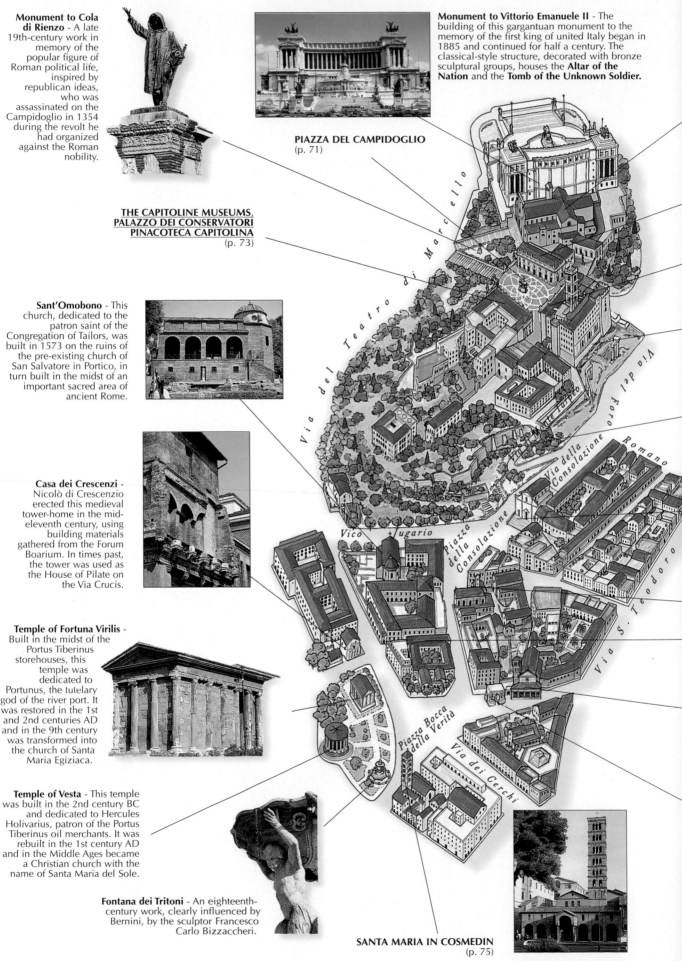

Monument to Cola di Rienzo - A late 19th-century work in memory of the popular figure of Roman political life, inspired by republican ideas, who was assassinated on the Campidoglio in 1354 during the revolt he had organized against the Roman nobility.

Monument to Vittorio Emanuele II - The building of this gargantuan monument to the memory of the first king of united Italy began in 1885 and continued for half a century. The classical-style structure, decorated with bronze sculptural groups, houses the **Altar of the Nation** and the **Tomb of the Unknown Soldier**.

PIAZZA DEL CAMPIDOGLIO
(p. 71)

THE CAPITOLINE MUSEUMS, PALAZZO DEI CONSERVATORI PINACOTECA CAPITOLINA
(p. 73)

Sant'Omobono - This church, dedicated to the patron saint of the Congregation of Tailors, was built in 1573 on the ruins of the pre-existing church of San Salvatore in Portico, in turn built in the midst of an important sacred area of ancient Rome.

Casa dei Crescenzi - Nicolò di Crescenzio erected this medieval tower-home in the mid-eleventh century, using building materials gathered from the Forum Boarium. In times past, the tower was used as the House of Pilate on the Via Crucis.

Temple of Fortuna Virilis - Built in the midst of the Portus Tiberinus storehouses, this temple was dedicated to Portunus, the tutelary god of the river port. It was restored in the 1st and 2nd centuries AD and in the 9th century was transformed into the church of Santa Maria Egiziaca.

Temple of Vesta - This temple was built in the 2nd century BC and dedicated to Hercules Holivarius, patron of the Portus Tiberinus oil merchants. It was rebuilt in the 1st century AD and in the Middle Ages became a Christian church with the name of Santa Maria del Sole.

Fontana dei Tritoni - An eighteenth-century work, clearly influenced by Bernini, by the sculptor Francesco Carlo Bizzaccheri.

SANTA MARIA IN COSMEDIN
(p. 75)

SANTA MARIA IN ARACOELI
(p. 70)

**MUSEI CAPITOLINI,
PALAZZO NUOVO**
(p. 72)

PALAZZO SENATORIO
(p. 70)

Tabularium - Built in 78 BC to preserve the documents (*tabulae*) of the Roman state. The massive tufa foundations underneath Palazzo Senatorio and remains of the upper arches are still visible on the Forum side of the hill.

Tarpeian Rock - The site recalls Tarpeia, the girl who betrayed Rome by opening the gates of the Arx to the invading Sabines.

Santa Maria della Consolazione - Part of the **facade** and the **interior** decoration of this three-aisled church in severe late Renaissance style is attributable to the genius of Martino Longhi the Elder, who worked on its construction from 1583 to 1600. The side chapels are decorated with exemplary works of the Roman Mannerist school.

Sant'Eligio dei Ferrari - This building, on the site of the former small church of Santi Giacomo e Martino, was granted in 1453 to the corporation of blacksmiths (*fabbri ferrai*), of whom the titular saint is patron. It was completely restored in the Baroque era; in its richly-decorated interior are interesting 16th- and 17th-century paintings.

SAN GIOVANNI DECOLLATO
(p. 74)

SAN GIORGIO IN VELABRO
(p. 74)

N

Arch of Janus - Built by Constantine in the 4th century BC as a covered passageway. The outside decoration includes many niches that once housed statues and the effigies of divinities on the keystones of the arches. In the Middle Ages, the Frangipane family used the arch as the base of a tower, which was later demolished together with the original roof of the arch.

THE CAMPIDOGLIO AND THE FORUM BOARIUM

*T*he soaring heart of religious and civil life of ancient Rome, with its temples dedicated to the greatest of the guardian deities of the city, the Campidoglio still conserves a symbolic valence as the center of municipal power, seated since the Middle Ages in the halls of **Palazzo Senatorio**. To the north, on the highest and steepest spur of the hill, where the church of **Santa Maria in Aracoeli** stands, are the arx, the fortified citadel that represented Rome's last bulwark, and the Temple of Juno Moneta (or Admonisher), built by Furius Camillus after his victory over the Gauls as a warning to all the enemies of Rome. It was also the site of the first Roman mint. The so-called Asylum Romuli - *the site where the first king of Rome had offered hospitality to the neighboring peoples - was linked to the arx by a clivus; the southern knoll of the Capitoline was instead home to the gigantic* **Temple of Jupiter Optimus Maximus**, *founded by Tarquinius Priscus in the 6th century BC and often rebuilt, and of other significant places of worship like the temples of the Fides Publica and of Jupiter Feretrius. The latter was Rome's first temple, said to have been founded by Romulus. With the passing of the centuries, the monumental Roman buildings fell into ruin and the land gradually returned to pasture, earning for itself the name of 'Monte Caprino' (hill of the goats). In the Middle Ages a small complex of public buildings rose in place of the ruins, but it was not until the 16th century that Michelangelo gave the summit its present-day look.*
At the foot of the southern spur, the so-called **Tarpeian Rock** from which traitors were thrown, there opened out in ancient times the Forum Boarium, the cattle market, and its continuation, a sacred area that ran down to the Portus Tiberinus, an extremely important trading port on the Tiber. The Forum Boarium is today an area rich in evocative vestiges of the past and emblematic places of worship. In the part nearest the Campidoglio, on the site now occupied by the church of **Sant'Omobono**, are the remains of two very ancient temples founded by Servius Tullus and dedicated one to Fortune and the other to the Mater Matuta.
The **Temple of Fortuna Virilis** and the **Temple of Vesta**, built in the portion of the Forum Boarium nearer the port on the Tiber, have instead come down to us almost intact, as has the four-faced **Arch of Janus** under which the merchants of the ancient forum took shelter in bad weather.

Perin del Vaga. Tarquinius Priscus Founding the Temple of Jupiter on the Capitoline Hill.

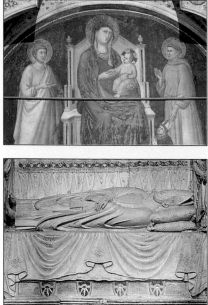

SANTA MARIA IN ARACOELI

The date of construction of this church, a true jewel of medieval architecture, is uncertain: it is variously dated to the time of Constantine and to that of Gregory the Great. The most probable hypothesis, however, is that by which it was built in the 8th century for the Greek monks. The good friars were supplanted first by the Benedictines and later by the Franciscans, who in the 13th century enlarged and restructured the building to plans probably by Arnolfo di Cambio. This phase of work was concluded with the construction of the steep **staircase** inaugurated in 1348, but in the centuries that followed further remodeling partially altered the pre-existing medieval building.

The suggestive **interior** is divided into a nave and two aisles by columns from various monuments of ancient Rome, and is home to works of great artistic importance. The Bufalini Chapel preserves late 15th-century frescoes by Pinturicchio of *Stories from the Life of Saint Bernardino*, considered one of the artist's masterpieces, but the remaining chapels, the transepts and the aisles are certainly no less noteworthy. For example, in the Savelli Chapel in the right transept is the beautiful *tomb of Luca Savelli*, attributed to Arnolfo di Cambio, which integrates a finely-decorated Roman sarcophagus with a lovely 14th-century marble structure with mosaic inlays. Another interesting funerary monument is the Cosmatesque *tomb of Cardinal Matteo d'Acquasparta*, in the left transept, set in a Gothic aedicula decorated with a fresco attributed to Cavallini.

PALAZZO SENATORIO

This building stands on a site on which functions linked to the political life of the city have always been carried on. It was originally that of the **Tabularium**, an impressive building housing the state archives, ordered built by Quintus Lutatius Catulus in 78 BC. In the eighth century, the senate of Rome met in the Curia, but when this old building was damaged and isolated by the marshes that were invading the forum, it was decided to reorganize administrative activity in another location. The first site chosen was the cloister, today no longer in existence, of Santa Maria in Aracoeli, but later, as city independence grew and with it the prestige of the senators, a more fitting meeting-place was sought.

Thus, in 1143, work began for construction of a new building on the ruins of the *Tabularium*, then used as a storehouse for salt. In 1160 the college of senators was already meeting in the halls of the new building. It was remodeled in 1299, when

Interior of Santa Maria in Aracoeli. Above, the tomb of Cardinal Matteo d'Acquasparta and the fresco of the Virgin Enthroned with Two Saints *above it; right, the tomb of Luca Savelli.*

Palazzo Senatorio, seat of Rome city government, at the top of the cordonata, *with on the left Palazzo Nuovo and on the right Palazzo dei Conservatori.*

a loggia and two corner towers were also added. The building was severely damaged by the assault of the troops of Holy Roman emperor Henry VII but was restored in the early 15th century under Pope Boniface IX, who donated it to the city of Rome. Halfway through the same century, Pope Nicholas V had the central tower added, but the building took on its modern-day look only a century later, under Pope Paul III, who charged Michelangelo with redesigning it. Michelangelo in person directed the work of building the **staircase**; it was later decorated by order of Sixtus V with the statue of the goddess *Roma Capitolina*, originally Minerva, in the center niche, and those of the *Nile* and the *Tiber* (originally the *Tigris*), brought to the Capitoline from the Baths of Constantine on the Quirinal hill, in those on each side. The work planned by Michelangelo was completed, with some liberties taken, between 1582 and 1605 by Giacomo Della Porta, Girolamo Rainaldi, and Martino Longhi the Elder. The latter architect is the author of the brick **bell tower** that replaced the medieval turret.

The two statues of the Dioscuri on the balustrade of Piazza del Campidoglio and the porphyry and marble Roma Capitolina in one of the niches on the staircase of Palazzo Senatorio.

PIAZZA DEL CAMPIDOGLIO

The plans drawn up by Michelangelo in 1547 for the Campidoglio extended to include remodeling of the space separating **Palazzo Nuovo**, **Palazzo Senatorio**, and **Palazzo dei Conservatori** that was the site of the ancient *Asylum Romuli*, and the creation of the so-called **cordonata**, the elegant access ramp leading to the square. In Michelangelo's plans the balustrade was conceived as an integral part of the square itself. It was decorated in 1585 with the statue of the **Dioscuri** brought here from their temple in the city ghetto to replace the statues selected by the artist, which were instead placed in Piazza del Quirinale. The decoration was completed in the following decades with the sculptures called *Marius' Trophies* and the statues of *Constantine* and his son *Costantius II*. The *paving* of the square, with its dynamic pattern of arches, was designed to appear convex - a probable allusion to a representation of a world of which Rome was the symbolic capital. The *equestrian statue of Marcus Aurelius* (today replaced by a copy; the original is in the Capitoline Museums) was brought here by Pope Paul II from the Lateran in 1538 and installed at the center, on a pedestal designed by Michelangelo.

Piazza del Campidoglio. A view toward the city; at the center of the square, the copy of the equestrian statue of Marcus Aurelius that has replaced the restored original, now in the Capitoline Museums.

THE CAPITOLINE MUSEUMS

The Capitoline Museums house one of the world's oldest and most prestigious public art collections, containing mostly statues from the Classical age, some of which are of considerable historic-artistic importance and undisputed fame. The collections are portioned out between Palazzo Nuovo and the facing Palazzo dei Conservatori, which is also home to the Pinacoteca Capitolina.

The history of the Capitoline Museums collections greatly predates the construction of the palaces in which the works are housed today and in which they were arranged beginning in 1734 by order of Pope Clement XII. The original nucleus was the Lateran collection of Roman bronzes donated to the City of Rome by Sixtus IV in 1471. Other donations followed rapidly: popes Leo X and Pius V contributed, in the 1500s, with some of the world's most important examples of classical statuary, and two centuries later the collection of Cardinal Albani was added. Later, under Benedict XIV, the museums acquired many works from Hadrian's Villa in Tivoli.

The last massive donation was the Castellani collection, to which were later added many works unearthed during the excavation work carried on when Rome was made capital of Italy.

Capitoline Museums. The Sala degli Imperatori in Palazzo Nuovo and on the right, two busts: above, Marcus Aurelius *and below,* Hadrian.

Palazzo Nuovo. The equestrian statue of Marcus Aurelius.

PALAZZO NUOVO

In 1734, Palazzo Nuovo became the first of the various exhibition centers making up the Capitoline Museums. This building houses many of the most interesting examples of Roman statuary, including one of the most complete collections of imperial Roman portraiture anywhere. The Sala degli Imperatori in fact contains *65 busts of Roman emperors*, exhibited in chronological order around an evocative statue of the *Seated Helena* in which the head of Constantine's mother is set on the body of a 5th-century BC Greek original. The masterful **Marcus Aurelius** may be considered as being a latecomer to this museum. His gilded bronze equestrian statue, for centuries at the center of the Campidoglio square, found a permanent home here following a decade of restoration concluded in 1990. Thought in the Middle Ages to be the effigy of Constantine (and for this reason not destroyed), the statue served as a model for the equestrian statues of the Renaissance. Other works on display in the halls of Palazzo Nuovo include the famous *Capitoline Venus*, a Roman copy of a Hellenistic original, the *Wounded Amazon*, and the *Dying Galatian*, unearthed in the Horti Sallustiani together with the *Galatian Killing his Wife*, which is today on exhibit in the Palazzo Altemps Museum.

PALAZZO DEI CONSERVATORI AND PINACOTECA CAPITOLINA

Since the Middle Ages the seat of one of the most important city magistratures, Palazzo dei Conservatori was completely restructured to Michelangelo's plans beginning in 1563. Guidetto Guidetti and Giacomo Della Porta, pupils of the great Tuscan artist, collaborated on realization of the harmonious **facade** with its massive pilaster strips and crowning balustrade adorned with statues. The original destination of the palace is evident in the splendid Sale dei Conservatori, which are now used as exhibit space for some of the most celebrated of the works in the Capitoline collections: for example, the *Spinario* and the *She-Wolf* (**Lupa Capitolina**), a marvelous bronze from the 5th century BC. The twins, quite probably the work of Antonio del Pollaiolo, were added in the Quattrocento when the statue was raised to the status of symbol of the city.

A few Gothic arches of the original 15th-century building still remain in the courtyard, which also contains evocative fragments, among which the head and one hand, of the *colossal Constantine*, the magniloquent statue that once stood in the apse of the Basilica of Maxentius. The museum as such is housed in the rooms and galleries of one of the wings of the palace, and contains such masterpieces as the *bust of the emperor Commodus*, the *Esquiline Venus*, the *Warrior Hercules* and the *Punishment of Marsyas*, found together with other statues in the Horti Lamiani and the gardens of Maecenas' villa on the Esquiline.

The Castellani collection, which includes many black-and red-figured *Greek vases*, is a very interesting section of this museum, which continues on into the Braccio Nuovo and the Museo Nuovo. During reorganization of the latter exhibit space, much attention was paid to the reconstruction of those sculptural groups that once adorned public and sacred buildings in ancient Rome.

The museum itinerary is brought to a close with the **Pinacoteca Capitolina**, established in 1748 in the other wing of the palace by Benedict XIV. His primary intention was to provide a home for the numerous paintings belonging to the Sacchetti and Pio di Savoia collections. Among the many important works on exhibit here are paintings by Titian, Tintoretto, and Guido Reni, as well as Caravaggio's celebrated *Saint John the Baptist.*

Pinacoteca Capitolina. Saint John the Baptist by Caravaggio.

Palazzo dei Conservatori. The head of what was once the colossal statue of Constantine.

Palazzo dei Conservatori. The celebrated Lupa Capitolina, *a work dated to about the 5th century BC to which the twins were added in the Renaissance. Symbol of the city of Rome, the statue recalls the legend of Romulus and Remus, descendants of Aeneas and sons of Mars and Rhea Silvia. The twins, thrown into the Tiber by Amulius, the usurper of the throne of Alba Longa, were saved and nursed by a she-wolf and lived to become the founders of Rome. Romulus became the first king of the city on the Palatine hill.*

Palazzo Nuovo. The Dying Galatian.

The interior of San Giorgio in Velabro, with the splendid Cosmatesque ciborium; below, two details of the fresco in the apse of the Virgin with Saints George, Peter, and Sebastian.

SAN GIORGIO IN VELABRO

This church, built probably in the 6th century near the *Velabrum*, the marsh where according to legend Romulus and Remus were found, was initially dedicated to Saints George and Sebastian, the patrons of the cavalry and of weapons. The name of the former titulary took root in common usage when Pope Zachary brought the head of the saint here as a relic. In the ninth century, under Pope Gregory IV, the church was partially reconstructed in Romanesque style: the side naves were added and the apse and the presbytery, in which a stupendous Cosmatesque **ciborium** was installed, were remodeled.

New modifications to the original structure came about in the 12th century with the addition of the Ionic **portico** and the **bell tower**.

The vault of the apse was decorated near the end of the following century with frescoes of *Christ, the Virgin, and Saints George, Peter, and Sebastian* that are attributed to Pietro Cavallini but are more probably the work of his pupils.

SAN GIOVANNI DECOLLATO

The Confraternita di San Giovanni Decollato (Confraternity of Saint John the Beheaded) was founded in 1488 with the support of the Florentine city-state; the task of the brothers was to provide spiritual and material assistance to those condemned to death. The area of the ancient church of Santa Maria de Fovea was chosen to provide the sodality with an appropriate place of worship, and in the early 1500s, construction of a new complex dedicated to Saint John, the patron saint of Florence, was begun.

The church, with its *oratory* and the adjacent *cloister* and *cemetery* where the bodies of the executed were buried, was completed halfway through the century. The buildings are fully Counter-Reformist in spirit and represent an excellent expression of full-blown Roman Mannerism, especially in the interior decoration. The ornamentation of the church is the result of a harmonious mix of *stuccowork*, *inlays*, and *marbles* that provide a fitting frame for the many frescoes by artists of the caliber of Zucchi, Vasari, and Pomarancio.

The oratory, which includes the *Camera Storica della Confraternita* with its collection of the instruments used in meting out capital punishment, is richly decorated with frescoes of the Tuscan Mannerist school.

San Giovanni Decollato. The monumental facade.

SANTA MARIA IN COSMEDIN

When, in the late 19th century, Sardi's beautiful Baroque facade was demolished, the church of Santa Maria in Cosmedin rediscovered its early medieval aspect. This is in fact the period (6th-7th century) in which the original building was raised on the ruins of the Roman *Annona* - the offices superintending the Forum Boarium and other trade forums - and of the 5th-century BC temple of Ceres with the conjoined *Ara Maxima*, from the structure of which the crypt of the church is said to have been created. About two centuries after its construction, Pope Hadrian I commissioned some decorative work (hence the appellative 'Cosmedin') and donated the building to the Greek friars who had escaped the iconoclastic persecutions that ravaged the Byzantine east. Further work was carried out under Pope Calixtus II during the first quarter of the 12th century, when the graceful Romanesque **bell tower**, with its several orders of windows, and the portico were built. The portico shelters the celebrated **Bocca della Verità**, a Roman drain cover in the form of the mask of a river god that according to medieval tradition would 'bite' anyone who dared tell a lie with his hand inserted between the jaws.

In the highly evocative **interior**, besides the iconostasis and the frescoes in the apse, which were substantially retouched in the nineteenth century, are one of the most beautiful cosmatesque *floors* in Rome and an elegant *Gothic ciborium*, a late 14th-century work by Deodatus of Cosma.

The neoclassical **sacristy** is instead the setting for a precious and brilliantly-colored gold-ground mosaic depiction of the *Epiphany*. It is actually a fragment of an 8th-century work of much greater size from the Chapel of John VII in the ancient Vatican Basilica.

Santa Maria in Cosmedin.
Left, the Bocca della Verità under the portico;
above, an aisle;
below, a detail of the mosaic of the Epiphany in the sacristy
and a detail of the Cosmati work floor.

Phocas' Column - This last monument to have been erected in the Forum, in 608 by Smaragdo, exarch of Italy, in honor of the Phocas, was originally topped by the gilded bronze effigy of the emperor of Byzantium.

Arch of Septimius Severus - On the attic of this majestic construction with three passageways delineated by composite columns is an inscription dedicating the arch to Septimius Severus and Caracalla in the name of the Senate and the People of Rome (S.P.Q.R.: *Senatus Populus Que Romanus*). It was erected in 203 AD in memory of the glorious victories of the Mesopotamian campaigns, illustrated in the reliefs.

Curia - The meeting-place of the Roman senate beginning in Tullus Hostilius' time (*Curia Hostilia*) was rebuilt by Sulla in 80 BC (*Curia Cornelia*) and again as the *Curia Julia* by Caesar, who moved the building to its present location.

CAESAR'S FORUM (p. 79)

SANTI LUCA E MARTINA (p. 91)

SAN GIUSEPPE DEI FALEGNAMI, MAMERTINE PRISON (p. 89)

Temple of Concord - Very little is left of this ancient building erected by Marcus Furius Camillus in 367 BC to celebrate the agreement between the patricians and the plebeians and rebuilt in 121 BC by the consul Lucius Opimius in memory of the victory over Gaius Gracchus. The temple was rebuilt for the third time under Tiberius.

Temple of Vespasian - Built by Domitian in 81 AC in honor of his father Vespasian and his brother Titus. There remain three beautiful Corinthian columns supporting an architrave decorated with friezes showing sacrificial objects.

Temple of Saturn - Erected in 497 BC by Titus Tatius, the first dictator of Rome, on the site of the ancient altar dedicated to Saturn, the temple was restored many times before it was rebuilt in 42 BC by Lucius Munatius Plancus, one of Caesar's generals, with the booty from the Syrian campaign. The eight surviving columns date to the reconstruction of 283 AD.

THE ROMAN FORUM

*The valley between the Capitoline, Palatine, Quirinal, Esquiline, and Caelian hills was until the ninth century BC only marginally occupied by human settlements; most of the area was a **necropolis** begun by the inhabitants of those Iron Age villages that rose on the surrounding heights, which, two or so centuries later, formed what is known as the Septimontium, the area on which the city of Rome later developed. In that period the area was mostly submerged by a series of bogs which extended from the Velabrum swamp, near the Forum Boarium, to the Lacus Curtius, the pool formed by the waters of the streams descending the hills. Among these were the Amnis Petronia that originated in a spring on the Quirinal, the Nodinus and the Spino; their waters were augmented by those of a number of springs like the Tullianum that arose near the prison of the same name built by Ancus Marcius (better known as the **Mamertine Prison**) and the Fount of Juturna, the nymph who in Virgil's account was the devoted sister of Turnus, king of the Rutulii. One of the oldest Roman altars stood on this site. The swampy condition of the area persisted until the 7th century BC, when Tarquinius Priscus built the **Cloaca Maxima**, an ingenious sewer system capable of draining off the surface water to the Tiber. The inlet of the Cloaca in the Forum was marked by the **Sacellum of Venus Cloacina**, rebuilt during the imperial age.*
Even before that time, the Forum Magnum or Romanum, as it was called at the time (the word 'forum' probably derives from fores = enclosure and door), already boasted a number of important buildings that had begun to rise under the diarchy of Romulus and Titus Tatius, king of the Sabines stationed on the Quirinal hill, who had

Porticus of the Dei Consentes - Although the original construction is believed to date to the fourth century BC, it was Domitian who consolidated the structure by building a raised base on which he set a portico. After falling into ruin, it was rebuilt in 367 AD and decorated with statues of gods arranged in pairs: Jupiter and Juno, Neptune and Minerva, Vulcan and Vesta, Apollo and Diana, Mars and Venus, and Mercury and Ceres.

Basilica Julia - Construction of this immense structure divided into five naves by columns was begun in 54 BC by Caesar. It was completed by Augustus and restored during Diocletian's time.

Temple of Caesar - Dedicated to the Divus Julius in 29 BC by Augustus but almost entirely destroyed in the 15th century.

Temple of Augustus - Although traditionally called thus, the building was actually one of the entrance atriums of the imperial palaces on the Palatine. Two important religious buildings were erected over it in the Middle Ages: the church of **SANTA MARIA ANTIQUA** (p. 89) and the Oratorio dei Quaranta Martiri.

Temple of Castor and Pollux - This temple, inaugurated in 484 BC, was restored in 117 BC by Lucius Metellus Dalmaticus with the spoils from the Dalmatian campaign. It was totally rebuilt by Tiberius in the early Ist century AD; the ruins we see today date to that period.

Temple of Antoninus and Faustina - Built in 141 AD and transformed in the Christian era into the church of **SAN LORENZO IN MIRANDA** (p. 90), built over the remains of the cella of the ancient temple, of which there remain the facade with the colossal columns in Euboeian marble.

Regia - According to tradition, the Regia was originally the residence of Numa Pompilio, who took his architectural inspiration from the Etruscan models. Later it was the seat of the *pontifex maximus*; it was rebuilt in 148 BC and again in 36 AD by Domitius Calvinus.

Temple of the Divus Romulus - This temple, begun by Maxentius and completed by Constantine, has remained practically intact thanks to its having been transformed, in the Middle Ages, into the atrium of the church of **SANTI COSMA E DAMIANO** (p. 90); the bronze door is the late Imperial Age original.

Basilica Aemilia - The only remaining basilica of the four built during the republican era following Rome's victory over Carthage. It dates to 179 BC and was restored many times over the centuries until its destruction by the Vandals in the Sack of Rome of 410 AD.

Temple of Vesta - All that remains of this ancient circular temple are the ruins of its last reconstruction by Septimius Severus. A small niche cut in the podium contained the *sacra*, the objects that according to legend were brought to Italy by Aeneas and with which the destiny of the city was intertwined.

Basilica of Constantine and Maxentius - Begun by Maxentius, this stately structure had three naves divided by pilasters and columns, the last of which was moved to the square of the Basilica of Santa Maria Maggiore in 1613. Following the Battle of the Milvian Bridge in 312 AD, in which Maxentius lost his life, the victorious Constantine modified the original orientation of the building and completed it; he also added precious decorations in the form of statues and fine marbles.

ARCHAIC NECROPOLIS
(p. 76)

Antiquarium Forense - This museum conserves the most important archaeological finds brought to light by the excavations in the Forum and Necropolis areas.

SANTA FRANCESCA ROMANA
(p. 91)

Temple of Venus and Rome - Hadrian built this enormous temple in 121 AD at the very edge of the Forum in the direction of the valley in which the Colosseum was built. To do so he demolished the remains of Nero's *Domus Aurea* and the gigantic statue of the same emperor that had given the name to the amphitheater. The temple had two apsed cellae, dedicated one to Venus the progenitrix of the *gens Julia*, and the other to the goddess Rome, the personification of the Empire.

House of the Vestals - This building, traditionally attributed to Numa Pompilio, was the home of the priestesses of Vesta. It was rebuilt by Nero following the fire of 64 AD and was later restructured many times. The adjacent buildings along the *Via Sacra* were in imperial times used as shops.

Arch of Augustus - The remains of this triumphal arch, erected in 19 BC in honor of the emperor's victory over the Parthians, are unfortunately sketchy. The monument had three barrel-vaulted archways decorated with aediculae displaying the *fasti consolares* and the *fasti trionfales*: lists of the names of consuls and records of triumphs from the foundation of the Republic through Augustus' time. Statues of defeated warriors and a bronze quadriga with the emperor in triumph were also part of the decoration.

Arch of Titus - Built by Domitian to celebrate the exploits of Titus, victor over the Jews and despoiler of Jerusalem, who is shown in the panels that decorate the interior side walls of the single archway. Titus is portrayed in triumph, crowned by Victory and riding on a quadriga led by the goddess Rome and preceded by the most important Roman officials, in a procession carrying the spoils from Solomon's Temple to Rome.

Piazza del Colosseo

COLOSSEUM
(p. 81)

ARCH OF CONSTANTINE
(p. 88)

Via dei Fori Imperiali

N

A panoramic view of the Roman Forum with the Arch of Titus in the background and the ruins of the Temple of Vesta on the right.

Below, a detail of one of the Corinthian columns of the Temple of Vespasian.

here stipulated with the first king of Rome a pact of alliance at the end of the war sparked by the notorious rape of the Sabine women. The pact was sealed by construction of the Volcanal or Altar of Vulcan, a red-painted polished rock erected near the Comitium against the Capitoline arx. The route taken by the two kings following stipulation of the pact instead became that of the **Via Sacra**, along which for centuries the most important religious processions and the many triumphs of victorious generals and emperors proceeded and continued on to the Campidoglio. To Romulus, who was entombed in the Forum, tradition ascribes the construction of a temple dedicated to Jupiter Stator near the site of the Arch of Titus, of which there today remains only the foundation and on which in the Middle Ages the Frangipane family installed a tower. Romulus' successor Numa Pompilio instead chose the forum as his place of residence and founded on it the so-called **Regia**, which later became the seat of the pontifex maximus and the home of the archives of the Annales Maximi, books reporting the principal events of each year. The structure also embraced the Sacrarium of Mars, where the ancilia, the lances and shields sacred to the god were kept. Legend recounts how these objects fell prodigiously from the sky and were possessed of the power to announce impending war through the noise generated by their spontaneous oscillation. It is to the same Numa Pompilio that ancient sources also attribute the foundation of the **Temple of Vesta** and the adjoining **House of the Vestals**. The priestesses, originally six in number and later ten, were selected from among the daughters of the most illustrious of Rome's patrician families. They served for thirty years, during which time they presided over the rites of the cult of Vesta, an ancient divinity of the hearth and the fertility of the land. Among the duties of the Vestals was that of assuring that the goddess' symbolic flame never went out, and that of preserving the sacra, the objects traditionally brought to Italy by Aeneas. These included the famous Palladium, an extremely ancient effigy of Minerva taken from a Trojan temple. The prestige and the veneration enjoyed by these priestesses was such that if a man condemned to death were lucky enough to encounter one of them before his execution his sentence was suspended. The Vestals also presided over the solemn feasts in honor of the goddess, the Vestalia, that were celebrated on 9 June of every year. They lived in the building dedicated to their order, a sort of ante litteram convent in which the statues of the Virgines Vestales Maximae (the senior members of the order) are still visible. On the ground floor of the building were rooms used for the production of flour and for cooking food, while above were the rooms of the priestesses, each with heated bath.

But the Forum was not only an important religious center constellated with ancient places of worship. Just as many commercial activities were conducted here, the Forum was also home to all those activities pertinent to politics and the administration of the state. The senate met in the **Curia** founded by Tullus Hostilius and for that reason called the Curia Hostilia; the popular assemblies were held in the space in front of the Curia, called the **Comitium**, under which tradition placed the tomb of Romulus marked by a slab of black marble called the **Lapis Niger**. A cippus with the oldest known Latin inscription, dating to the 6th century BC and relating to a sacred law, still bears mute witness to the importance of the site.

The forum was enlarged under Numa Pompilio's successors, and after the Tarquin dynasty was ousted it acquired new and sumptuous buildings. One of the most important of these was the **Temple of Saturn**, a god much venerated in antiquity. The temple also protected the public treasure, or Aerarium Saturni, called thus because of the god's link to the mythical Golden Age, an era of peace and harmony, in remembrance of which the Saturnalia were celebrated every year from 17 through 23 December. In the same period, the **Temple of the Dioscuri** was built by the son of the dictator Aulus Postumius in fulfilment of a vow made to the divine twins before the battle against the Latins near Lake Regillus, led by Tarquinius Superbus. Castor and Pollux are said to have fought at the side of the Romans in that battle and also to have announced the Roman victory to the people as they watered their horses at the Fount of Juturna. It was to commem-

The remains of the House of the Vestals (left) and the Basilica Julia (right).

Below right: the distinctively circular form of the Temple of Vesta in an aerial view.

Below left: the architrave of the Temple of Saturn resting on columns with Ionic capitals. The inscription recalls a fire that damaged the temple.

orate this episode that the temple was built near the spring. On more than one occasion the temple was chosen as the meeting-place of the senate, while the temple podium, decorated with the rostra of enemy warships, took on the function of an orators' tribune and was used even by Caesar for the promulgation of the Agrarian Law.

The advent of republican government gave a new significance to the Forum, which had increasingly become the vibrant nucleus of the public activities of the Roman populace and of their political representatives. The emblematic site of this function was the Tribunal, a high podium from which the orators harangued the crowd assembled in the square. It was decorated with the **rostra**, the bronze beaks mounted on the prows of warships for ramming enemy ships; the rostra of the Tribunal were those taken from the warships of Antium in 338 BC following the decisive battle in the Latin War and exhibited in celebration of the might of Rome. A honorary column erected alongside the rostra feted Gnaeus Maenius, the victor of this important battle; a century later the Colonna Rostrata was raised nearby to celebrate the victory of Gaius Duilius over the Carthaginian fleet at Mylae (Milazzo).

During the course of the 2nd century BC, the center of public affairs in Rome acquired further spaces for their performance. First and foremost there were the basilicas, large rectangular halls the roofs of which were supported by columns, designed to host the organs for settling legal controversies (tribunalia) and as a place for conducting business transactions. The first of the basilicas built in the Forum was the Basilica Porcia, erected in 184 BC to the west of the Comitium by the censors Marcus Porcius Cato and Lucius Valerius Flaccus as the site for the gatherings of the tribunes of the plebs. It was destroyed during the uprisings of 52 BC. The **Basilica Aemilia**, originally called the Basilica Fulvia, was built in 179 BC by Marcus Fulvius Nobiliores and Marcus Aemilius Lepidus with the booty from the war against the Aetolians. Another important building of this type was the Basilica Sempronia, built against the Palatine facing the Lacus Curtius; it was linked to the memory of the patrician Marcus Curtius, who, weapons in hand, hurled himself on horseback into the chasm in which the lake is said to have formed, to fulfil the expectations of the auguries, which stated that the earth would close up if the Romans threw into it that which they valued most highly; that is, their weapons and their courage.

The **Basilica Julia**, the seat of the court of the Centumvirs, was built on the site of the Basilica Aemilia as part of the works promoted for reorganization of the forum by Gaius Julius Caesar, between 54 and 44 BC. The great leader soon saw how inadequate the Roman Forum was to meet the needs of a population which had by that time grown to many hundreds of thousands in the city of Rome alone; after 48 BC and to commemorate the victory over Pompey at Pharsalus, he decided to enlarge the forum beyond the Curia, which he had moved and rebuilt as the Curia Julia, with the construction of a new complex of sacred and civil buildings. The new **Caesar's Forum** developed as a vast porticoed square opening in front of the facade of the **Temple of Venus Genetrix**, the patroness of the gens Julia from which Caesar descended, portrayed in the cella of the building in a famous sculpture by the Greek master Archesilaos. Celebrated paintings of Medea, Ajax, and Cleopatra, by Timomachus of Byzantium, also decorated the temple.

The portico, which was later embellished with works of art taken from the territories conquered by the Roman troops, delimited a rectangular open area with at its center the gilded bronze equestrian statue of Caesar. On the side toward the Forum, near the Curia where the church of Santi Luca e Martina stands today, there were instead a series of tabernae housing shops and schools.

In 29 BC, on the site on which Caesar's body had been cremated and where Mark Anthony had publicly read

The great arches of the Basilica of Maxentius.

A stretch of the Via Sacra, for centuries the route of devotional and triumphal processions.

quered entire populations, and had annexed the most disparate territories. To celebrate these exploits, there arose near the Temple of Caesar two triumphal arches dedicated by the senate to the emperor. The first, the so-called **Arch of Augustus** or Parthian Arch, commemorated the recovery of the Roman insignia taken from Crassus by the Parthians in 55 BC; the second recalled the victory at Actium.

As is easy to understand from the type of works carried out by Augustus, for the forum the beginning of the imperial era meant a clear change of purpose away from the commercial-administrative and political functions and toward representation of Rome's historical memory and its traditions. Development now continued principally beyond the original site and took the form of erection of the so-called Imperial Forums in the wake of the example provided by Caesar and followed by Augustus. Besides restoration and reconstruction of the previously-existing buildings, many new monuments were erected by order of the senate and the emperors, all celebrating the power of Rome.

To the first emperor of the Flavian dynasty was dedicated the **Temple of Vespasian**, built by Vespasian's son Domitian near the **Temple of Concord**. Domitian was also responsible for the construction, in front of the Basilica Julia, of the seven **Honorary Columns** that framed the larger-than-life equestrian monument to the emperor, which was, however, demolished by senate order following the issuance of the damnatio memoriae that posthumously condemned him to cancellation of all his effigies.

In celebration of his brother Titus' victories over the Jews, which culminated in the destruction of Jerusalem in 70 AD, Domitian erected the **Arch of Titus**, with reliefs depicting the salient phases of the campaign and the destruction of the Solomon's Temple, the spoils from which were solemnly carried into Rome on the Via Sacra below the site of the arch. The **Arch of Septimius Severus** was built in the heart of the forum area on the tenth anniversary of this emperor's ascent to the throne to celebrate his victories over the Parthians, the Arabs, and the Adiabenians. The precedent Antonine dynasty was instead responsible for construction of the **Temple of Antoninus and Faustina**, in honor of Antoninus Pius and his wife Faustina, and the completion of the **Temple of Venus and Rome** begun under Hadrian.

In the fourth century it was Maxentius, co-ruler, with Constantine, of the empire, who enriched the Forum with new monuments. In honor of his son, who died as a child in 307, Maxentius raised the **Temple of the Divus Romulus** to replace the Temple of the Penates that had been demolished to make room for the so-called **Basilica of Maxentius**, in turn completed by Constantine who placed a colossal statue of himself in the apse; fragments of this work are on exhibit in the courtyard of Palazzo dei Conservatori. The last monument dedicated to the pagan cult to be erected in the Forum was the **Porticus of the Dei Consentes**, built in 367 by the prefect

his testament, Augustus built the **Temple of Caesar** to commemorate the great Roman leader. The building had a semicircular podium decorated with the rostra taken from Mark Anthony's ships following the battle of Actium. Some years later, in 20 BC, the emperor set the **milarium** at the center of the forum square. This bronze-covered marble column marked the point of departure of the roads of the Empire and bore engravings of the distances separating Rome from the various cities. The eternal city had by this time expanded its dominion to far-off lands, had con-

of Rome Vettius Agorius Prenaestatus, friend of Julian the Apostate, on the earlier podium with seven atria built under Domitian. The structure was decorated with gilded statues of the twelve principal gods of Olympus. Finally, in 608, with the raising of **Phocas' Column**, the glorious season of the Roman Forum could be said to have been concluded.

With the decline of the Empire and the progressive depopulation of Rome into the Middle Ages, the area richest in historical memories of the Eternal City waned in importance: the ancient bogs returned; the monuments, toppled during the barbarian invasions, sank into the ground until all that was visible was here and there a stone emerging from the overgrown fields used as pastures. The glorious Forum Magnum of ancient times had become the much more prosaic Campo Vaccino, or cows' field.

A view of the Forum showing the remains of the Temple of Saturn, Phocas' Column, and the Arch of Septimius Severus; in the background, the remains of the Tabularium below the Campidoglio.

The Roman Forum, with a portion of the Via Sacra, the Temple of Antoninus and Faustina on the left, and the Temple of Vesta on the right; in the background, Santa Francesca Romana and the Colosseum.

The Arch of Titus, built in his honor by his successor Domitian in memory of the Jewish campaign of 70 AD.
A relief frieze on the architrave shows the triumph of Vespasian and Titus over the Jews; in the panel at the center of the coffered vault of the single passageway is the relief of the Apotheosis of Titus.

Facing page: the exterior of the Colosseum and a view of the immense arena with the cavea.

In the foldout: details of the scale model of ancient Rome in the Musei della Civiltà Romana, with the forums, the Colosseum, the Palatine area, and the Circus Maximus.

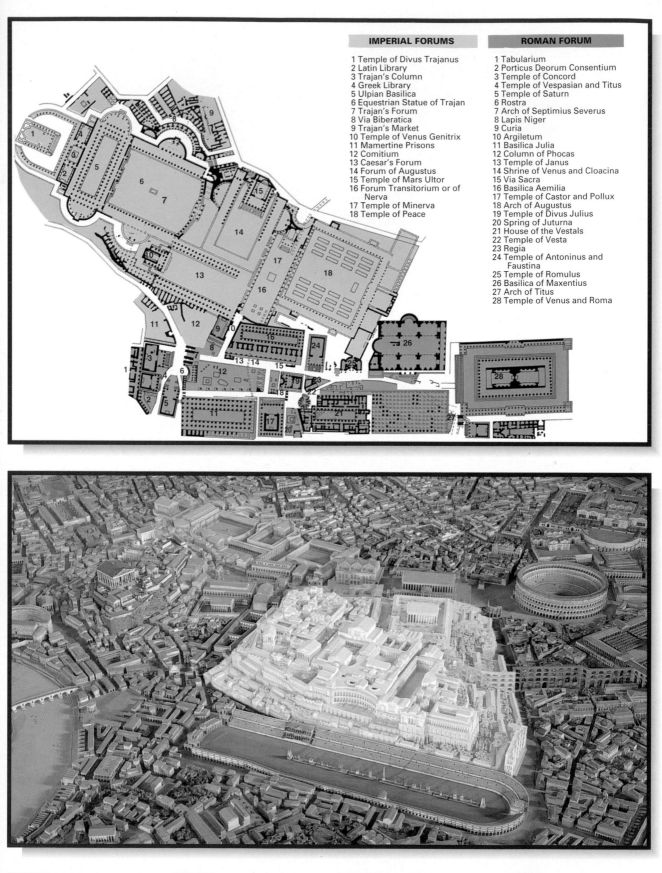

IMPERIAL FORUMS	ROMAN FORUM
1 Temple of Divus Trajanus	1 Tabularium
2 Latin Library	2 Porticus Deorum Consentium
3 Trajan's Column	3 Temple of Concord
4 Greek Library	4 Temple of Vespasian and Titus
5 Ulpian Basilica	5 Temple of Saturn
6 Equestrian Statue of Trajan	6 Rostra
7 Trajan's Forum	7 Arch of Septimius Severus
8 Via Biberatica	8 Lapis Niger
9 Trajan's Market	9 Curia
10 Temple of Venus Genitrix	10 Argiletum
11 Mamertine Prisons	11 Basilica Julia
12 Comitium	12 Column of Phocas
13 Caesar's Forum	13 Temple of Janus
14 Forum of Augustus	14 Shrine of Venus and Cloacina
15 Temple of Mars Ultor	15 Via Sacra
16 Forum Transitorium or of	16 Basilica Aemilia
Nerva	17 Temple of Castor and Pollux
17 Temple of Minerva	18 Arch of Augustus
18 Temple of Peace	19 Temple of Divus Julius
	20 Spring of Juturna
	21 House of the Vestals
	22 Temple of Vesta
	23 Regia
	24 Temple of Antoninus and
	Faustina
	25 Temple of Romulus
	26 Basilica of Maxentius
	27 Arch of Titus
	28 Temple of Venus and Roma

IMPERIAL FORUMS   ROMAN FORUM   PALATINE   CAMPIDOGLIO

THE COLOSSEUM

Following the fire of 64 AD that destroyed a goodly part of the city, Nero decided to build his grandiose *Domus Aurea* on the Oppian hill. It was linked to the facing Palatine hill by a cryptoporticus, part of which is still standing. The depression between the two heights was the site of gardens and a man-made lake, not far from which, to mark the entrance to the palace, there stood a colossal gilded bronze statue of the emperor as Sun God. In 72 AD, Vespasian ordered that the lake be drained in order to build an amphitheater, construction of which continued under Titus until the year 79. These two emperors, both of the Flavian dynasty, were responsible for the first name given the building, which was known in antiquity as the **Amphiteatrum Flavium**.

The name Colosseum dates instead to the Middle Ages and refers to the colossal statue of Nero that Hadrian had moved near the celebrated monument. The amphitheater was inaugurated in 80 AD with spectacles and games that lasted, according to sources of the time, one hundred days, during which thousands of wild animals and many gladiators were killed in combat. When, under Domitian, the top tier was completed with the construction of an attic and the supports to which the *velarium* (an immense tent that shielded the spectators from the sun), the structure had a capacity of 50,000 spectators, who sat in the *cavea*, an area separated from the enormous elliptical arena, 86 meters by 54, by a podium protected by a balustrade. It was here that important personages were seated, while a special box was reserved for the emperor and the Vestals. The cavea, built entirely of marble, was subdivided into orders and sectors; the seats were occupied from lower to higher in accordance with social standing, the highest order of seats being occupied by the plebs. The area underlying the arena was instead riddled with galleries where the animals used in the spectacles were stabled and where the scenic devices were stored; at the ends of the galleries were elevators for transporting persons and things to the surface.

The travertine exterior facade of the amphitheater had three superposed series of arches delimited by semi-columns in the three classical styles, Doric, Ionic, and Corinthian, and an attic decorated with pilaster strips, for an overall height of about 50 meters.

During the Middle Ages, earthquakes brought down certain parts of the structure; the remains were for a time transformed into fortifications controlled by the Frangipane family. The amphitheater later became an immense 'quarry' for building materials used in churches and palaces, until in 1744 Pope Benedict XIV consecrated the Colosseum to the martyrs of the Faith and issued an edict banning any further demolition. Later restoration campaigns, the first of which began in 1805, have targeted recovering the original structure.

Above, an aerial view of the Colosseum. The construction of Rome's largest-ever amphitheater, destined to become a symbol of the city, was undertaken by the Flavian emperors with the aim of providing the populace with a great permanent amphitheater after the fire that nearly destroyed the city in 64 AD.

Three images of the Colosseum and its interior, made up of a cavea and an arena.
The different sectors of seats in the cavea were occupied from lower to higher by decreasing social standing, the tiers nearest the arena being reserved for the senators.

The center of the arena was originally covered by wooden planks; the subterranean chambers, on three concentric passageways with openings connecting the different sectors, were used for storing material connected with the spectacles, from wild beasts in cages to the gladiators' weapons.

The Arch of Septimius Severus (below), with its center archway higher than those at the sides, provided the model for the Arch of Constantine (above).

THE ARCH OF CONSTANTINE

Built in 315 by the 'Senate and the People of Rome' in celebration of Constantine's victory over Maxentius in 312 in the battle of the Milvian Bridge, fought and won by the emperor, as the dedicatory inscription on the attic tells us, by 'divine inspiration', this arch may be said to be the last great monument of pagan antiquity. But it is also the ideal symbol of the beginning of the Christian era, since it was following the battle that Constantine,

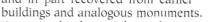

with the Edict of Milan of 313, acknowledged the right of Roman citizens to practice the Christian religion and the authority of the Bishop of Rome.

The monumental structure, with its *three openings*, is about 20 meters high and is decorated with statues and reliefs that were in part created for the occasion and in part recovered from earlier buildings and analogous monuments.

For example, the panels on the *attic* are from the Arch of Marcus Aurelius and show this emperor's triumph in 174; the interior of the center arch is decorated with two reliefs originally in the Basilica Ulpia in Trajan's Forum. This forum was also the original home of the statues of Dacian prisoners on the attic above the columns, which in turn were recovered from the Domitian's Arch. The tondi showing episodes of different types - among which hunting scenes - are from Hadrian's Arch, but the reliefs in the side strip panels, depicting the story of the emperor's triumph over Maxentius, were created specially for the arch.

Details of the Arch of Constantine, the largest of the arches erected in ancient Rome.
Many of its low-relief decoration and sculptures were taken from monuments of previous eras: for example, the eight statues of Dacian prisoners on the long sides of the attic, in pavonazzetto

marble from Asia Minor, date to Trajan's time, the eight tondi on porphyry slabs above the side archways, with hunting scenes and scenes of sacrifice, to Hadrian's reign, and the eight reliefs on the attic, showing the Return of the emperor from the campaigns against the Marcomanni and the Quadi, to Marcus Aurelius' time.
Among the decorations coeval with the building of the arch are those at the bases of the columns, the keystones of the arches, and, above all, the long frieze that begins on the long sides and continues onto the short sides to illustrate episodes from Constantine's military exploits up to the time of his triumph over Maxentius in 312 AD.

THE FORUM CHURCHES

*I*n the centuries immediately following the fall of ancient Rome, the forum area returned to being what it had always been: a stretch of pastureland broken by bogs and cane-brakes and here and there trees and shrubs - but now punctuated by traces of a glorious civilized past. And it was from here that the new Rome was to rise: or better, from those materials so suitable for the construction of buildings, palaces, and churches that were again turned to use. Thus, while many of the ancient columns of the pagan temples went to delimit the naves of the Christian churches, other structures were reused almost in their entirety, supplying, we might say, the foundations on which the new architecture, based on a different manner of conceiving both art and religion, was to develop. In about 530, Theodoric and Amalasuntha donated the remains of the Temple of Romulus and of the library of the adjacent Forum of Peace to Pope Felix IV that he might make it into the church of **Santi Cosma e Damiano**, brothers and early Christian physicians and martyrs, in counterpoint to the nearby Temple of the Dioscuri. Not much later, in the late 6th century, one of the constructions overlooking the Forum, the entranceway to the imperial palaces on the Palatine erroneously identified as the Temple of Augustus, was modified to become the church of **Santa Maria Antiqua**, which however had to be abandoned about three centuries after is founding following earthquakes and landslides; the deaconry was transferred, with the name of **Santa Maria Nuova** (better known as **Santa Francesca Romana**), to the site of an oratory built under Paul I near the ancient Temple of Venus and Rome. One of the most prestigious of the Forum's Roman buildings to be transformed into a church was the Curia, which thanks to its form was eminently suitable for such a use and which Pope Honorius I consecrated, in the seventh century, as the church of Sant'Adriano. The same Honorius exploited one of the buildings in Caesar's Forum and founded the small church of Santa Martina, which centuries later was rededicated to include the patron saint of painters as its co-titular; it is in fact better known as the church of **Santi Luca e Martina**. In the following century came the turn of the Temple of Antoninus and Faustina, which became the church of **San Lorenzo in Miranda**. With the passage of time, the medieval churches were restored and sometimes totally rebuilt, and although these actions modified the original structures in keeping with the architectural styles in vogue in this or that century. Nevertheless, the buildings remained Christian places of worship even despite the fact that from the 18th century onward the increasing interest in archaeology and Roman antiquities had in part altered their structures through restoration actions that targeted bringing their monumental pagan past to light.

The interior of the Mamertine Prison under the church of San Giuseppe dei Falegnami, with on the right the column to which Saint Peter was reputedly chained.

SAN GIUSEPPE DEI FALEGNAMI AND THE MAMERTINE PRISON

The church, placed in the care of the Confraternity of Carpenters, was built during the reign of Pope Paul III, beginning in 1597, in a style that marks the transition from the severe lines of Counter-Reformist architecture to the more decorative Baroque style. The interior gives access to the adjacent oratory with its beautiful decorations in purest Mannerist style. Underneath the church are two rooms of the ancient **Mamertine Prison**, which by medieval tradition was the site of the confinement of Saint Peter. It is said that before his escape, the saint used the water that miraculously gushed forth from the pavement to baptize the two guardians Processo and Martiniano.

The column to which the chains, today preserved in San Pietro in Vincoli, bound the first pope of the Christian Church has been venerated as a relic since the 15th century. Although the tradition would seem to have no historical foundation, the site remains one of the salient points in the pilgrimages of the faithful to Rome. The *lower* cell of the prison, probably originally a cistern, is the oldest part and in all likelihood was part of the original Tullianum Prison; the *upper* cell, trapezoidal in form, was built in 40 BC by the consuls Caius Vibius Rufinus and Marcus Cocceius Nerva, to whom we also owe the travertine **facade**. Some of Rome's most famous enemies, including Jugurtha and Vercingetorix, met their deaths in this prison.

SANTA MARIA ANTIQUA

Together with the **Oratorio dei Quaranta Martiri**, this church occupies a building of the imperial era traditionally denominated the **Temple of Augustus** at the corner of the Forum with the Palatine. Originally, the church was an early Christian basilica with a nave and two aisles built according to Byzantine canons, with an atrium and a narthex, on the ruins of which Santa Maria Liberatrice rose in the eighth century. This second church was rebuilt in the

Top: a detail of the frescoes in the church of Santa Maria Antiqua.

Center: the Temple of the Divus Romulus that forms the atrium of the church of Santi Cosma e Damiano; two small porphyry columns frame the original bronze portal on the curvilinear exterior.

Bottom: the Temple of Antoninus and Faustina with the church of San Lorenzo in Miranda.

17th century but demolished in the 20th to again bring to light the remains of the Santa Maria Antiqua we see today. The church still conserves precious frescoes from all the different eras in which the building was remodeled and redecorated. Among the most important is an 8th-century *Crucifixion* in the to the left chapel of the apse, in which the typical iconographic scheme of the evangelical episode, which over the centuries became tradition and has been repeated in innumerable versions, is already firmly established: Saint John and the Virgin at the foot of the Cross, the soldier Longinus piercing Christ's side with his lance, and the other soldier offering Him the sponge soaked in bile.

SANTI COSMA E DAMIANO

The church was built on the remains of two buildings of the imperial age, the **Temple of the Divus Romulus**, which became the atrium, and the *Biblioteca Pacis*, the remains of which are still visible. The **interior**, with the entrance on Via dei Fori Imperiali, was completely restructured in the 17th century by Bernini's pupil Arrigucci, who also created the adjacent **cloister**.
Despite its new Baroque raiment, including the beautiful gilded and painted wooden ceiling decorated by Mantegna with *Saints Cosmas and Damian in Glory*, testimony to the original appearance of the church is borne by the beautiful **mosaics** from the 6th-7th centuries that adorn the apsidal portion of the building and that were taken as a model for many later mosaic decorations in Rome. In the *Christ with Saints Peter, Paul, Cosmas, Damian, and Theodore and Pope Felix IV* that adorns the apsidal vault, the pope is carrying the model of the church, which he had built in about 530; on the triumphal arch are instead portrayed the *Apocalypse with the Mystical Lamb, Saints, and the Symbols of the Evangelists Luke and John* and, below, the *Elders of the Apocalypse*.

SAN LORENZO IN MIRANDA

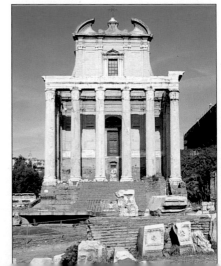

The site of the ancient **Temple of Antoninus and Faustina**, of which many significant remains are still visible, was once occupied by a church built in the 7th-8th centuries and completely restructured on occasion of Charles V's visit to Rome in 1528. Part of the work involved freeing the pronaos of the temple from the medieval superstructures and consequently reducing the size of the church, which was again remodeled by Torriani in the early 17th century. The entrance to the church is on Via dei Fori Imperiali; it is presently under the patronage of the Collegio Chimico Farmaceutico, the successor to that Collegio degli Speziali that was made titular in 1430 by Pope Martin V. In the interior, on the main altar, is the *Martyrdom of Saint Laurence* by Pietro da Cortona.

SANTI LUCA E MARTINA

Elegant, harmonious forms, a tall, graceful dome, and a marvelous **facade**, a masterpiece by Pietro da Cortona who was buried here with his family members, characterize this building of ancient foundation. In 1588, Pope Sixtus V granted the premises to the Accademia del Disegno di San Luca; Saint Luke the Evangelist thus became co-titular of the church with the early Christian Saint Martina. The academy, which stood facing the church itself, was demolished during the work for opening the route of what is today Via dei Fori Imperiali and transferred to its present home in Palazzo Carpegna in the Trevi district. In the interior of *lower* church are valuable works by da Cortona and Algardi; the balanced volumes of the *upper* church, on a Greek cross plan, are abundantly and richly decorated.

SANTA FRANCESCA ROMANA

Despite its original dedication to Santa Maria *Nova* in counterpoint to the other forum church named after Saint Mary, with the appellative *Antiqua*, this church, which rose in the ninth century near the **Temple of Venus and Rome**, is commonly known as Santa Francesca Romana, a saint much venerated by the Romans and buried in the **crypt**. The **facade** is the work of Carlo Lambardi and exhibits a decidedly Renaissance cast, with many references to Palladian architecture even though it dates to 1615. The soaring, five-story **bell tower**, with inlays in majolica tile and porphyry crosses, instead dates to the 12th century.

In the **interior**, alongside highly valuable works of art, is an important and we might say 'curious' relic: the so-called *Silices Apostolici*, stones said to conserve the footprints of Saint Peter and linked to the story of Simon Magus, who offered the saint money in exchange for the power to give the Holy Ghost with the laying-on of his hands (whence the term 'simony' for the sale of a church office or ecclesiastical preferment). Among the church's works of art are the apsidal **mosaics**, in imitation Byzantine style although dating to the 12th century, portraying the *Virgin with the Child and Saints*; the precious icon of the *Glycophilusa Madonna*, a 5th-century work moved here from Santa Maria Antiqua; and the two interesting *funeral monuments*. One is that dedicated to Pope Gregory XI, who died in 1378 after his return to Rome at the end of the exile of the papacy in Avignon. The other is to Antonio da Rio, the warden of Castel Sant'Angelo during the first half of the Quattrocento, here portrayed on horseback; this is the only example of this type of portraiture in any church in Rome.

The beautiful 17th-century facade of the church of Santi Luca e Martina (left) and the facade of Santa Francesca Romana (right).

THE IMPERIAL FORUMS AND THE MONTI DISTRICT

The area between the Imperial Forums and the lower slopes of the Monti district is the home of some of the most interesting remains of ancient Rome as well as of evocative churches and the rare surviving tower homes that in the Middle Ages constellated the entire city.
Built on the model provided by Julius Caesar, the Imperial Forums rose over a timespan of about two centuries outside of the area of the Roman Forum, which had by the time become simply too small to serve the needs of the capital of a territory that embraced almost all of the known world.
*Thus, following the Battle of Philippi and with the aim of glorifying the gens Julia to which he belonged, Augustus began building a new forum (**Forum of Augustus**) that centered, with a colonnade and two halls provided with exedrae, around the vast square in front of the **Temple of Mars Ultor** (of which conspicuous ruins remain). In the numerous niches that opened in the two exedrae stood statues of Augustus' ancestors, from the founder Aeneas to Julius Caesar, and of the greatest figures in Roman history.*
*In 69 BC, Vespasian began construction of new structures that went to make up the **Forum of Peace** (or Vespasian's Forum), of which little remains today. The vast space between Augustus' and Vespasian's forums was occupied, beginning in 81 AD, by the **Forum Transitorium**, which, begun under Domitian and completed under Nerva, included a temple dedicated to Minerva that was torn down by Pope Paul V in order to build the Fontana dell'Acqua Paola.*
*The last of the Imperial Forums to be built was the majestic **Trajan's Forum**. Work began under Trajan in 98 BC and continued under his successor Hadrian, who celebrated its conclusion with the construction of the temple dedicated to his by that time deified predecessor. The main nucleus of the forum was a large square closed in by a series of wide porticoes over which, on the northern side, there arose the broad hemicycle of **Trajan's Markets**. The markets were accessed through a mighty triumphal arch that linked the area with the adjacent Forum of Augustus. On the side opposite the arch extended the **Basilica Ulpia**, which together with the Temple of the Divus Trajanus and the two libraries (one Greek and the other Latin) delimited a quadrangular courtyard, at the center of which rose **Trajan's Column**.*
All around the Imperial Forums there grew up a densely-populated area that nevertheless, with the advent of the Middle Ages and the formation of vast bogs, the so-called Pantani, was progressively abandoned by the residents. Redevelopment began in the 16th century, when the area was included in the Monti district, called thus because it spread over the Esquiline, the Viminal and the Caelian hills. The Roman ruins were only naturally covered by the new buildings, but in the early 1800s, interest in classical antiquities began to grow and systematic archaeological excavation of the area was begun. The work went on through the rest of the century and culminated during the Fascist era in the next, with the opening of Via dei Fori Imperiali. The glories and the architectural prodigies of imperial Rome thus again saw the light, albeit as the result of some questionable demolition work.

Basilica Ulpia - This was the major building on **Trajan's Forum** and was the largest of all the ancient Roman basilicas, with its five aisles divided by grey granite and cipollin marble columns. The relief panels that made up the attic frieze were later used to decorate the Arch of Constantine.

TRAJAN'S MARKETS
(p. 94)

Torre delle Milizie - This tower, probably built by the Byzantines, was restructured in the 13th century under Pope Gregory III of the Segni counts; it later passed to Boniface VIII who armed it against the Colonna family. The series of damages suffered over the centuries reduced its height to today's 50 meters and caused a slight inclination of its vertical axis.

Forum 'Transitorium' - Called 'Transitorium' because besides uniting the Forum of Peace and the Forum of Augustus from south to north it was the place of passage between the Suburra district and the Roman Forum, this Forum completed by Nerva in 97 AD, was delimited by a portico with projecting columns and an attic, of which visible traces still remain, decorated with an entablature with friezes.

TRAJAN'S COLUMN
(p. 94)

Piazza Venezi

Torre del Grillo - This tower, dating to 1223, originally belonged to the Carboni family. In the 1600s it passed to the Marchesi del Grillo (also the owners of the adjacent 18th century palace). This was the family of Camillo, a popular figure known for the hilarious jokes and ruses he perpetrated in papal Rome.

Temple of Mars Ultor - Raised in 42 BC by Augustus to celebrate the victory at Philippi by which he also revenged the assassination of Caesar (and for this reason dedicated to Mars Ultor - the Avenger), the temple was surrounded by a high wall along which stood the other buildings of the **Forum of Augustus**.

Villa Aldobrandini - Built in 1575, this villa, with its beautiful gardens that were reduced in extension in 1876 to permit the opening of Via Nazionale, took the name of the family of Clement VIII, who in the 1600s donated the building to his nephew.

Bank of Italy Building - Built in the years spanning the turn of the 20th century to plans by Gaetano Koch.

Sant'Agata dei Goti - Testimony to the Aryan cult, this church was built in the 5th century and reconsecrated as an Orthodox temple by Gregory the Great in the 6th. Despite the 17th-century remodeling, still conserves its original three-aisled basilica-like interior with ancient columns and a 12th-century Cosmati work ciborium.

Santa Caterina da Siena a Magnanapoli - Built during the first half of the 1600s by Giovan Battista Soria on the preexisting church of the Dominican order. The single-nave interior is opulently decorated with *marblework* and *sculptures*.

SANTI DOMENICO E SISTO (p. 95)

Madonna dei Monti - With its original structure designed by Della Porta in the late 1500s, this church, which takes its name from the **miraculous** 14th-century **effigy** on the high altar, repeats on a smaller scale the structure of the Church of Gesù. The interior, graced with a great many paintings, among which the beautiful *Angels* by Orazio Gentileschi, is the resting-place of the remains of Saint Joseph Labre, a Franciscan who in the 1700s lived as a beggar in the streets of the Monti district.

House of the Knights of Rhodes - Created in the 12th century as a Basilian monastery, the building passed in the next century to the Knights of Saint John of Jerusalem, later to be called the Knights of Rhodes and later yet Knights of Malta. It was restored between 1467 and 1470, when the splendid **loggia** was added by Cardinal Barbo, the prior of the order.

Santi Quirico e Giulitta - The 15th-century portal and the Romanesque bell tower speak elegantly of this church's history until its rebuilding in rococo style in the 1700s by Raguzzini and by Valvassori. Today, it is the home of the **Museum of the Creche**.

Torre dei Conti - This imposing tower home (which was even higher before the earthquakes of 1349 and 1630) recalls the look of medieval Rome when the noble families controlled the different districts of the city. It was erected on an exedra of the Forum of Peace in 1203 by Riccardo of the Conti di Segni, brother of Pope Innocent III.

N

TRAJAN'S COLUMN

Five years after the end of the last of the two campaigns conducted between 101 and 108 AD by the emperor Trajan against the Dacians, an ancient Danubian population that occupied the territory that is today Rumania, the senate and the Roman people voted to celebrate Trajan's achievements with the erection of a column, probably designed by Apollodorus of Damascus, the architect who had planned the other buildings of Trajan's Forum. The column was raised at the center of the quadrangular courtyard on which opened the two libraries, Latin and Greek, facing each other on the short sides, and, on the long sides, the Temple of the Divus Trajanus and the Basilica Ulpia.

Set on a base decorated with reliefs depicting the Dacian weapons taken as trophies, the barrel of the *centenaria* column (called thus due to its height: 100 Roman feet or about 40 meters), is entirely covered with a spiral relief, 200 meters in length and containing more than 2500 figures, that describes the emperor's exploits, from the crossing of the Danube on a boat bridge (later replaced with a stable bridge built by the same Apollodorus of Damascus) to the many battles against the Dacian troops; from the embarkment of the Roman troops in the port of Ancona, for the second expedition, to the conquest of Sarmigethusa, the Dacian capital, to the emperor's ultimate triumph. Trajan's ashes were preserved in a golden urn interred in the base of the column. The column was topped by a bronze statue of Trajan that was lost in the Middle Ages and replaced by the *Saint Peter* installed by Sixtus V in 1587.

The height of Trajan's column, as we are reminded by an inscription on the base, reflects the height of the spur of the Quirinal hill that was excavated to make room for the buildings of Trajan's colossal Forum.

TRAJAN'S MARKETS

It was probably again Apollodorus of Damascus who created, along the side of the Quirinal hill that slopes down toward the Imperial Forums, as a sort of bulwark against possible landslides, a series of buildings set out on several levels immediately beyond the right portico of Trajan's Forum. At the lowest level, the hemicycle of the first tier exhibits a double series or superposed openings - the first rectangular, the second arched - that, respectively, allowed light to enter the eleven *tabernae* or shops on the ground floor and the floor above, a vaulted corridor that led to other *tabernae*. Above, a terrace linked the different structures and acted as the base for the second tier, along which rose several multistoried buildings linked by a road, the *Via Biberatica*, that took its name from the many watering places and the inns that provided drink to the market-goers, or, according another etymology, from *piper* = pepper, alluding to the spices that were sold here. But besides spices, the *tabernae* of Trajan's Markets also sold fruit, wine, oil, fish and miscellaneous goods that came to Rome from the distant lands of the ancient East.

SANTA MARIA DI LORETO

In this typical example of a central-plan church there coexist two different currents in 16th-century Roman architecture, one inspired by Bramantesque classicism and more firmly anchored in the Renaissance stylistic models, the other of Michelangelesque inspiration, thoroughly Mannerist in style and already looking ahead to the triumph of the Baroque.

The building - raised on the site of the Temple of the Divus Trajanus - was begun in 1507 by Antonio da Sangallo the Younger, who built the square brick base with travertine pilaster strips, probably to a design by Bramante.

The church was completed less than eighty years later by Jacopo Del Duca, a gifted pupil of Michelangelo, who added both the grandiose octagonal **dome**, topped by its unconventional *lantern*, and the *bell tower*; he also laid out the decorative scheme for the octagonal interior, with chapels in the ample niches, which was later adorned with stuccowork, frescoes, and sculptures, of note among which are the two *Angels* by Maderno and the vivid *Saint Susanna*, a 17th-century work by Duquesnoy.

SANTISSIMO NOME DI MARIA

In a certain sense, this building is the reinterpretation, in a late-Baroque key, of the adjacent church of Santa Maria di Loreto, of which it copies the central plan structure and the domed roof.

Work on this church, which began in 1736 under the supervision of Antoine Dérizet, continued under Mauro Fontana, also the author of the beautiful high altar in polychrome marbles on which stands an ancient image of the *Virgin* (13th century) originally in the Lateran oratory. The church owes its name to the Confraternita del Santissimo Nome di Maria, which commissioned its construction to commemorate Sobiesky's victory over the Turks in 1683.

SANTI DOMENICO E SISTO

This church, managed by the Dominican friars and also called San Sisto Nuovo, arose in the 16th century on the ancient Santa Maria a Magnanapoli. The name of the former church, which derives from *Banneum Neapolim* ('military encampment of the new city'), recalls the existence in this area of a fortified citadel that in the 5th century lodged the Byzantine troops come to aid the Romans in their struggle against the Lombards.

The new single-nave building was begun by Giacomo Della Porta, who set his hand first to the choir; it was restored under Urban VIII and completed by the addition of the theatrical Baroque **facade**, which, together with the **staircase** before the entrance, would seem to be the work of Vincenzo Della Greca, who was also responsible for placing Maderno's statues of *Saint Thomas Aquinas* and *Saint Peter Martyr* in the lower niches (those of the upper niches, portraying the titular saints of the church, are instead by Canini). The **interior** space is as if dilated by the prospective fresco of the *Apotheosis of Saint Dominic*, a 17th-century work by Domenico Maria Canuti and Enrico Haffner, and is further embellished by the sculptural group entitled *Noli me tangere* by Antonio Raggi and a excellent high altar built to designs by Gian Lorenzo Bernini.

Facing page: Trajan's Column topped by the statue of Saint Peter, with a detail of the frieze that decorates the shaft with the victorious exploits of the emperor Trajan against the Dacians; below right, a nocturnal view of the hemicycle of Trajan's Markets.

The church of the Santissimo Nome di Maria, center, copies the central-plan domed structure of the adjacent Santa Maria di Loreto, top. Bottom, the facade of the church of Santi Domenico e Sisto with its theatrical staircase.

Palazzo Borgia - In reality, this palace, which rises with its arch between the *Vicus Sceleratus*, the place where Tullia ran over the body of her father, Servius Tullius, with her chariot, and where the Vestals who had committed a wrongdoing were punished, did not belong to the Borgia, but to the powerful Margani family and earlier to the Cesarini family.

SAN PIETRO IN VINCOLI
(p. 98)

Santi Gioacchino e Anna ai Monti - This pleasant church with a Greek-cross plan was begun in the late 1500s and finished by Giovanni Francesco Fiori in the second half of the 1700s.

Santa Lucia in Selci - Nearly hidden among the old walls of the high Middle Ages, this small church was built in the 8th century on the ruins of the Porticus of Livia. It was subsequently rebuilt in 1604 by Maderno, who also executed the refined polychrome marble and alabaster *ciborium*. The interior contains, in addition to several paintings by Il Cavalier d'Arpino, the first entire work by Borromini, the *Landi Chapel*, which he designed around 1636.

DOMUS AUREA
(p. 97)

San Francesco di Paola - This 17th-century church, which rises above the high terraces of the Suburra (fine **view** over the Madonna dei Monti), is the work of Torriani, with interior decorations in the Berninian style added in the following century. The finest work within the church is the *high altar* by Giovanni Antonio De Rossi. Also worthy of note is the **campanile**, which can be seen behind from the churchyard of San Pietro in Vincoli. The campanile was built out of the pre-existing Torre dei Margani, one time thought to be of the Borgia family.

Ludus Magnus - This largest of the barracks for the gladiators who fought in the Colosseum, to which it was connected by subterranean corridors, was built entirely in brick during the rule of Trajan. The complex also included an inner court with a small arena where training took place.

Torre dei Capocci - Along with the nearby **Torre dei Graziani**, this 36-meter tall tower testifies to the Middle Ages, when this area was disputed by several of the most powerful families of Rome.

Palazzo Brancaccio, designed by Luca Carimini, is the last monumental patrician palace built in Rome, with strong evocations of Renaissance architecture. Today it houses the **Museo nazionale d'Arte Orientale**.

San Martino ai Monti - The original *titulus Equitii* was built by the priest Equitius, who founded it in the 4th century under Pope St. Sylvester I. Following that, Pope Symmachus had the church, dedicated to Saints Sylvester and Martin, built at this site. After numerous changes, Carlo Borromeo ordered it restructured in the 16th century, and Pietro da Cortona directed yet another restoration in the 17th century. The changes, however, did not completely alter its primitive basilican design, with its naves separated from the aisles by columns taken from the nearby Baths of Trajan. Noteworthy are the **crypt** and the **frescoes** in the left nave by Dughet, showing the *interiors of St. Peter's* and *St. John Lateran* and providing precious historical and artistic documentation about the appearance of the two basilicas before the interventions of the 16th and 17th centuries.

Sette Sale - The Seven Halls are in reality the cisterns that supplied water to the Baths of Trajan and were later used as a cemetery by the nuns of nearby Santa Lucia in Selci.

Baths of Trajan - They were probably built by Apollodorus of Damascus, also the architect of the Forum of Trajan. These baths provided the model for the other huge thermal baths of Diocletian and Caracalla, characterized by a central body surrounded by an enclosure featuring semi-circular exedra. Only scant vestiges remain of the complex.

SAN CLEMENTE
(p. 99)

THE OPPIAN HILL

*T*he Oppian hill, which is part of the populous quarter of Monti, is tied to an historical figure of ancient Rome, as notorious as he is famous: Nero. Born in Antium (Anzio) in 37 AD and killed by his own hand in Rome in 68, Nero is thought by many classical historians to be the perpetrator of the huge fire that devastated the city in 64 and destroyed, in addition to many poor neighborhoods, the Emperor's own palace, the so-called Domus Transitoria, which was connected by a long cryptoporticus to his holdings on the Oppius.

It was on this hill that Nero commanded the architects Celerius and Severus to build a palace that was even larger and more sumptuous than the previous one, and which for its richness came to be called **Domus Aurea**, or golden house. The palace, which extended over the entire Oppian hill and down the valley where the Colosseum stands today, occupied an area of 100 hectares, or twice that of Vatican City. It was decorated by the painter Fabullus in frescoes, of which remain a few suggestive traces, and by works of art of an enormous value, as well as by immense luxuriant gardens with fountains, small temples, nymphaeum and even an artificial lake. The lake later became the site of the Flavian Amphitheater, or the Colosseum, and the adjoining dwellings of the gladiators, known as the **Ludus Magnus**. The paintings of Fabullus influenced artists of the Renaissance, who had to pass through tunnels in the buried rooms of Nero's palace in order to view them. These rooms resembled grottoes, and the paintings the artists copied came to be known as 'grotesques'. At the entrance to the palace stood the colossal statue of Nero in gilt bronze, more than 30 meters high and portraying the Emperor in the likeness of the sun god. In the first half of the 2nd century, Hadrian had the statue moved by some 30 elephants near the Flavian Amphitheater, which would later give it its name of Colosseum. Excavations have uncovered almost 180 rooms of the Domus Aurea, whose exaggerated immensity was inspired by the greatness of the palaces in the East. For instance, the royal palace of the Sassanians in Persia provided the model for the so-called cenatio rotunda, a large circular triclinium, or dining room, which could turn in order to follow the path of the stars and planets. Other rooms had ceilings made of perforated ivory panels and mobiles, which sprinkled guests with perfume and flower petals. The vestibule, with its porticoes looking out over a one-mile stretch of the Via Sacra, was transformed under Domitian into a spice market. The rest of the palace was buried by Vespasian to wipe out the memory of the grim tyrant, while on its still visible ruins were built the **Baths of Trajan** and of Titus.

The Domus Aurea was also adorned with rich sculptures, including the famous group of the Laocoön, dug up in a vineyard near **San Pietro in Vincoli** in 1506 and today exhibited in the Vatican Museum. After the fall of Rome and for all of the Middle Ages, in fact, the Oppian hill was not inhabited and was planted with vegetable gardens and vineyards, the property of the two oldest tituli of the area: the previously mentioned San Pietro in Vincoli–which contains the famous **Moses** by Michelangelo–and **San Martino ai Monti**.

Another important Christian church in the area is the 4th-century **San Clemente**, which provides a remarkable example of two superimposed basilicas, an expression of two different historical periods in one fascinating compendium of art and religion. In the course of the centuries, the hill underwent very little change, just as there were few changes to the medieval urban plan. Among the few additions during that period were the **Palazzo Borgia**, the **Torre dei Capocci**, and the old tower that now serves as the campanile of the church of **San Francesco di Paola**.

Still practically intact up to the 20th century, the Oppian hill was converted into a public **park** between 1928 and 1932, with the addition of part of the gardens of **Palazzo Brancaccio**, which today houses the **Museo nazionale d'Arte Orientale** (National Museum of Oriental Art).

Via Merulana

N

SAN PIETRO IN VINCOLI

This is without doubt one of the most venerated minor basilicas in Rome, rich as it is in the memory of the first Pope of the Church, from whom it received its name. It is also called the Basilica Eudoxiana, after the wife of Emperor Valentinian III. Eudoxiana, upon receiving from her mother the chains that had bound St. Peter during his imprisonment in Jerusalem, donated them to Pope St. Leo I. When the pope set these chains with the ones that had bound the wrists and ankles of St. Peter in the Mamertine Prison, he saw the two **chains** unite to form a single piece. This relic is still kept here and the old Latin name of church, *'in vinculis'*, has remained.

The basilica, built on the site of an older edifice that had been used by Christians, was consecrated by Pope Sixtus III around the year 439, and despite the subsequent medieval and Renaissance restorations, the primitive paleo-Christian plan is still evident. This is perceivable in the rows of white marble ionic **columns** that separate the nave and aisles, and in the length of the central nave, a typical trait of the religious architecture of the period. The **portico** in front of the entrance has arcades supported by octagonal pilasters and was built in the 1400s by Baccio Pontelli or Meo del Caprino. The **interior** is the result of 18th-century restorations by Francesco Fontana, who also designed the wooden ceiling decorated by the *Miracle of the chains* by Parodi.

In the right transept is the major attraction of the church, the unfinished **Mausoleum of Julius II** by Michelangelo. The grandiose funeral monument dedicated to the Della Rovere pope was conceived by the Tuscan master as a colossal mausoleum adorned with some 40 statues and numerous reliefs and was to have been placed beneath the cupola of St. Peter's. Begun in 1513, the work was halted three years later and was never taken up again. The completed pieces were later assembled in the way they are still seen today, with the imposing figure of Michelangelo's **Moses** in the center. Flanking Moses are the statues of Leah and Rachel, symbols of the active and contemplative life, begun by Michelangelo and finished by his pupil Raffaello da Montelupo. The great master's pupils also executed the other statues, consisting of an *effigy to the Pope*, a *Virgin and Child*, the *Prophet* and a *Sibyl*. Among the other works in the church are the so-called *sarcophagus of the Maccabee brothers*, kept in the **crypt**, the fine 7th-century Byzantine mosaic of *St. Sebastian*, and the tombs of *Nicola Cusano* and of *Antonio and Piero del Pollaiolo*.

San Pietro in Vincoli, the facade with the 15th-century portico, Moses by Michelangelo, the chains that were said to have bound the Apostle Peter.

SAN CLEMENTE

One of the oldest churches in Rome, San Clemente is unique for its structure of two superimposed churches sitting atop vast subterranean grounds containing the remains of imperial **Roman buildings** and of a **Mithraic temple** from the 3rd century AD.

One of these buildings was probably the house of Clement, a freedman martyred under Domitian whose relics were kept in the church built in his honor in the 4th century. This original church constitutes the **lower basilica**, an important place of worship during the high Middle Ages and the site of many ecclesiastical councils. The lower basilica, with its central nave and two aisles, is preceded by an atrium and a narthex, both of which are **frescoed**. The **narthex** contains 11th-century wall paintings of the *Miracle of St. Clement*, with a naive but suggestive depiction of sea creatures, the *Translation of St. Cyril's body* and *St. Cyril in Glory*. The frescoes in the nave and aisles of the church are from the same period. The nave contains the *Legend of St. Alexis*, who, after leaving his family to become a hermit, returns as a servant, sleeping for years under a staircase and revealing his true identity only at the point of death. Other important frescoes include the *Legend of St. Clement*, in which the saint is depicted while he celebrates mass in the catacombs. The soldiers who surprise the saint and his faithful are blinded, and instead of carrying off Clement, they take a column.

The **upper basilica**, built by Paschal II after the original church was sacked by the Normans in 1084 and buried, shows strong contrasts with the lower church, with its rich decorations by Carlo Stefano Fontana in the most sumptuous Baroque style of the 1700s. The original structure has nevertheless been preserved in numerous instances. The *schola cantorum*, for example, preserves its white marble surface, some of it dating from the 12th century and some of it taken from the lower church. While the lower basilica is adorned with frescoes, here **Cosmatesque mosaics** dominate, as found in the fine pavement, the candelabrum, the ambones, the ciborium and the tabernacle in the high altar, dating from 1299. Particularly noteworthy are the works by the Cosmati in the **apse**, hardly altered from the 12th century, with the long marble bench interrupted by the bishop's throne decorated with mosaic highlighting. On the apse vault, above a frescoed strip, are mosaics of the *Lamb of God with the twelve companions* and the *Triumph of the Cross*.

A superb example of the Renaissance restoration is the **Chapel of St. Catherine**, with its beautiful frescoes from the late 1420s. These are attributed to Masolino da Panicale, the teacher of Masaccio, who perhaps contributed to the work. The most important scenes depict the *Crucifixion* and the *Story of St. Catherine*.

San Clemente:
the interior of the upper basilica with the elegant Cosmatesque pavement in the foreground and the schola cantorum, *in the background the ciborium and the splendid apsidal mosaics of the* Triumph of the Cross *(12th century).*

The upper basilica, the Chapel of St. Catherine, the fresco of the Crucifixion *(15th century).*

The mithraeum (3rd century) of the original lower basilica.

THE PALATINE

*T*he origins of the city of Rome are inextricably linked to this hill, where the so-called Roma Quadrata, the first nucleus of the city, was founded by the mythical Romulus on 21 April 753 BC on the site where he received favorable auspices when he sighted twelve vultures circling overhead. The site has revealed some of the most ancient traces of human settlement in the city territory: the foundations of huts dating to the 9th-8th century BC, the remains of the so-called **House of Romulus** (over which the **Temple of Cybele** or of the Magna Mater was later built), an archaic tomb, three cisterns from the same age that probably supplied water to the first inhabitants, and some blocks from the walls that are believed to have enclosed the primitive settlement. Although the origin of the name Palatine is incertain, it is probably linked to the Indo-European root pala = rise, or, according to another much accredited hypothesis, it may derive from Pales, the goddess of herding and herdsmen whose figure is traditionally linked to the founding of Rome. However that may be, it was on this hill that the first king of Rome resided, and that of royal residence was its destination even later, when it became the site of the palaces of the emperors, first among whom Augustus, who was also born here. The various dynasties that succeeded one another in leading the Roman Empire all chose the Palatine as their place of residence. Each new palace was statelier and more sumptuous than its predecessor: the **Domus Tiberiana**, begun by Tiberius and enlarged under Caligula, and Nero's **Domus Transitoria**, which after it was destroyed in the fire of 64 AD was rebuilt as part of the Domus Aurea and linked, by a **cryptoporticus**, to the buildings on the Oppian hill. The next construction projects were promoted by Domitian, who commissioned the architect Rabirius to redo the Palatine buildings: the **Domus Flavia**, designed for use for state functions, and the **Domus Augustana**, the official royal residence, the remains of which, together with those of the **Paedagogium**, a sort of diplomatic academy at which the imperial dignitaries were trained, still dominate the **Circus Maximus** below. Finally, after 191 AD, Septimius Severus began reconstruction of the palaces destroyed in the colossal fire that had devastated Rome and thus gave rise to a new, grandiose palace, the **Domus Severiana**. Other buildings were also built on the hill: many temples, like that of Apollo, commemorating the victory at Actium, built by Augustus in 36 BC and inaugurated in 28 BC, rose over time alongside other buildings for the most varied uses (stadiums, baths, nymphaea, libraries). The Palatine remained the seat of the supreme imperial authorities through the Byzantine and Othonian eras, until in the early 11th century it was provided with massive fortifications and entrusted to the Frangipane family, who made of it one of the most powerful strongholds and one of the most prestigious sites in the city: for example, it was here that Saint Francis lodged in 1223, during his last Roman sojourn.

The hill then declined in importance: many of its edifices were stripped of their precious marbles (Sixtus V, in the late 1500s, used those of the Septizodium for building Saint Peter's Basilica and the Sistine Chapel of Santa Maria Maggiore) and its slopes were turned over to vineyards and gardens. Finally, in the 19th century, following the systematic excavation campaigns that brought to light the remains of the ancient buildings, the hill became part of the Parco archeologico del Foro romano e del Palatino.

San Sebastiano al Palatino - The ancient Santa Maria in Pallara is today dedicated to the saint who according to tradition was martyred on the Palatine at the Temple of Diocletian. Of the tenth-century building, which rose on the ruins of the Temple of Elagabalus, today's church preserves only the apse and a few frescoes, while the rest of the structure dates to the 17th century.

Temple of Cybele - Built in honor of Cybele, or the Magna Mater, in 204 BC, this temple sheltered a black stone, the symbol of the goddess. Over time the temple underwent various transformations; during excavation work a splendid headless statue of Cybele, now in the *Domus Tiberiana*, was found on the site.

House of Livia - The remains of the home of the wife of Augustus constitute one of the most precious architectural monuments of early imperial Rome. The exquisite *central hall* is decorated, in the Pompeiian style, with the fresco of *Mercury Rescuing Io*.

DOMUS FLAVIA
(p. 102)

Sant'Anastasia - Built in the 4th century on the site of the *Lupercale* (traditionally, the place where Romulus and Remus were found and nursed by the she-wolf), this church was initially reserved for imperial dignitaries. It was restored first under Theodoric and again under Sixtus IV; it owes its present aspect to Luigi Arrigucci, a pupil of Bernini's, who almost totally rebuilt it in Baroque style in 1636.

CIRCUS MAXIMUS
(p. 103)

The center of ancient Rome at the moment of its greatest expansion, in the scale model in the Museo della Civiltà Romana.

San Teodoro - Set like a gem in the slope of the Palatine, this small, circular-plan church was built on the ruins of the *Horrea Agrippiana*, the ancient storehouses for foodstuffs, in the 6th century. The beautiful *mosaic* in the apse dates to this period. The church was renovated, perhaps by Rossellino, in the mid-Quattrocento, when it was provided with a cloister-vaulted dome built in accordance with the canons of Florentine Renaissance architecture.

Horti Farnesiani - These gardens, created in the mid-16th century for Cardinal Alessandro Farnese on the ruins of the **Domus Tiberiana**, owe their daring conception to architects like Vignola and Rainaldi. From the Forum, on which a monumental entrance opened, the gardens created a complicated system of plays of water (the Nymphaeum 'della Pioggia' and the Theater 'del Fontanone') and of aviaries (the 'Uccelliere') as they rose on overlapping terraces to a belvedere that became the home of the Botanical Garden in 1625.

San Bonaventura al Palatino - Built in 1675 by Clement X on the ruins of an ancient cistern from Nero's time, this church was also called San Bonaventura alla Polveriera due to the fact that a number of nearby buildings were used as weapons and ammunition depots. The facade is a 19th-century addition ordered by Cardinal Tosi.

Huts of Romulus - Some very ancient evidence of constructions from the prehistorical and the early Iron Age, the oldest in the architectural history of Rome; traditionally, the home of the founder of the city.

Palatine Stadium - The western sector of the *Domus Augustana* complex comprised the so-called Stadium, a large garden in the form of a circus, measuring 160 by 50 meters, surrounded by a two-order portico. All that remains of the center *spina* are the two semicircular extremities.

Antiquarium Palatino - Besides the interesting artefacts from the primitive settlements on the hill, this collection includes sculptural and pictorial works, dating from the Augustan age through late antiquity, that provide precious evidence of the refined artistry achieved in the decoration of the imperial palaces on the Palatine.

Domus Severiana - The construction work performed under Septimius Severus in the Palatine area following the fire of 191 AD included enlargement of the *Domus Augustana* and the building of the Severian Baths and an arresting nymphaeum, the *Septizodium*. This marvelous architectural creation, with its seven orders of superposed niches decorated with precious marbles and statues, was totally demolished in the 16th century.

DOMUS AUGUSTANA
(p. 102)

The Domus Flavia. Above, a general view of the area of the peristyle with the ruins of the octagonal fountain; below, the remains of one of the two nymphaea.

THE IMPERIAL PALACES OF THE PALATINE

The powerful ruins that today command the Palatine hill are mostly the remains of the enormous, and equally sumptuous, complex designed by the architect Rabirius for the emperor Domitian that included a series of buildings and spaces for the most varied of uses. The strictly residential portion was the **Domus Augustana**, a group of multistoried buildings with peristyles that opened with a semicircular portico in correspondence to the Circus Maximus. In the interior, rooms opulently decorated with precious marbles and paintings alternated with large courtyards adorned with prodigious fountains, statues, and small temples. Adjacent to the residence proper was the **Stadium**, reserved for private spectacles held for the emperor, who watched from a semicircular tribune. It was built during Domitian's reign and restored by Septimius Severus; Theodoric modified the structure to obtain an oval track for equestrian uses.

The western portion of the complex, known as the **Domus Flavia**, was instead used for official state functions. It was built on the remains of the ancient buildings of the republican era and over part of those of Nero's time, and included a great number of rooms arranged around a central courtyard with an **octagonal fountain**. The colossal *aula regia*, in which the emperor granted private audiences to ambassadors and important personalities, also opened on the courtyard. Adjoining the *aula regia* were two other buildings: one, the so-called *lararium*, was a private temple for the worship of the Penates, the Lares or household gods of the imperial house; the other, the *basilica*, was reserved for hearings of legal cases in which the emperor was called to participate personally. Off the other side of the peristyle opened the *imperial triclinium*, a large official banqueting hall. At its sides were two oval nymphaea, one of which is still identifiable.

THE CIRCUS MAXIMUS

Although the Circus Maximus, the first construction of its kind in Rome, was initially built of wood, the sections in masonry gradually increased in number, beginning with the *carceres*, a sort of starting-gate for the horses. The circus consisted of a long track surrounded by a *cavea* with various tiers of seats, broken, on the side adjacent to the Palatine, by the *pulvinar*, a building with a tribune on which were placed the statues of the divinities that presided over the spectacles and from which the emperor watched the contests.

The structure, which was modified repeatedly under Caesar, Augustus, Claudius, and Trajan, expanded to mammoth size until, at the height of its grandeur under Constantine, it could contain more than 300,000 spectators. In 10 BC, Augustus installed an obelisk dedicated to the Sun, from Heliopolis in Egypt, on the *spina*, the central segment decorated with templets and statues around which the horses raced. This obelisk, today in Piazza del Popolo, was later flanked by another from the Temple of Ammon in Karnak, installed and dedicated to the Moon in about 357 AD by Constantius II and much later moved to Piazza San Giovanni in Laterano.

The last race in the Circus Maximus was run under Totila in 549; after this date the structure was abandoned and fell into ruin. It was used from the Middle Ages through modern times for the most disparate functions, until in the 1930s it was freed of the superstructures that had been added over time (to the exception of the Torre della Moletta) and the entire construction was again exposed.

Above, a low relief showing the games and equestrian contests held in the Circus Maximus in honor of the god Consus, on the site of whose altar in the valley between the Palatine and the Aventine the circus was built. Legend attributes its foundation to Tarquinius Priscus (7th century BC).

Right, the ruins of the Domus Augustana and below, those of the Domus Severiana seen from the Circus Maximus.

THE BATHS
OF CARACALLA

The area in which the still-majestic remains of ancient Rome's largest-ever bath complex stand lies along the slopes of what is called the 'Piccolo Aventino', where the Sanctuary of the Bona Dea Subsaxana once stood. The goddess Bona was identified with Fauna, wife or daughter of Faunus, a divinity linked to the fertility of the land who often revealed prophecies and auspices. Only women were admitted to this place of worship at the foot of the Saxum Sacrum (hence the title of Subsaxana), the rock from which Remus had seen the six vultures before his brother Romulus' twelve and where he was later buried.

*The flattest portion of the area, excluded from Rome proper by the Servian circle but later embraced by the **Aurelian Walls**, was in practice a shallow valley delimited to the north by the Caelian heights, at the center of which was the Piscina Publica, a man-made pond used as a public bath. Construction of the **Baths of Caracalla** began on the site of this pond in 212 AD; water was supplied by a specially-built feeder of the Aqua Marcia aqueduct called the Aqua Antoniana, which branched off the main aqueduct and crossed over the nearby Via Appia and the Arch of Drusus. The monumental bath complex begun by the emperor Caracalla and completed by Elagabalus were restored under Diocletian and Theodoric and remained in use until 537, when the Goths destroyed the Antoniana aqueduct and the immense, 80,000-liter capacity **cisterns** remained dry. The main body of the building, where the bath establishment proper was located, was surrounded by a vast garden enclosed by a wall broken by porticoes and exedrae, where the accessory services were located: palaestrae for gymnastics, storerooms for unguents and perfumes, conference halls, two libraries (one Greek and one Latin, to the sides of the cistern), and a **mithraeum** (or Temple of Mithras), the largest in ancient Rome, of which there remain only few traces of the rich architectural decoration and the mosaic floors but where in the 1500s were found two of the most famous sculptures of classical antiquity: the Farnese Bull and the Farnese Hercules, both now in the Archaeological Museum of Naples but once in Palazzo Farnese.*

*The baths as such consisted of a central block comprising the three principal sections (frigidarium, tepidarium, calidarium), and a series of other service rooms (palaestrae, changing rooms, steam baths) arranged symmetrically along the sides. The entrance led into the ambient-temperature **Frigidarium**, a sort of vestibule with colossal granite columns, one of which now stands in Piazza Santa Trinità in Florence, along its sides. Next came the **Tepidarium**, on a basilica plan, with granite basins at the sides; two of these are today the fountains of Piazza Farnese. Finally, the hot bath or **Calidarium**, a circular room with a high dome 34 meters in diameter.*

*The baths were severely damaged during the barbarian invasions; after that time the area remained mostly uninhabited and the land was turned to agriculture. Places of worship soon began to be built here; the titulus of **Santa Balbina** (595) was erected on what was probably the site of an even earlier chapel built in honor of the daughter of the martyr Quirinus, martyred himself, on the remains of the home of the consul Lucius Fabius Cilone. At the same time, a short way away from the site on which Saint Peter is reputed to have lost one of his foot bandages during his flight toward the Via Appia, there was built the church of **Santi Nereo e Achilleo**.*

*Last in chronological order was **San Cesareo de Appia**, built on the Via Appia in the 7th century. With the passing of time the area did not undergo many major modifications; this state of affairs was favored by the creation, between 1887 and 1914, of the Parco di Porta Capena and the Passeggiata Archeologica, which as originally conceived would have linked the Via Appia with the Forum area; it was instead partially modified by the opening, in 1940, of Via dei Fori Imperiali, the artery leading to the nearby EUR district.*

Santa Balbina - This church, which some sources date to as early as the 4th century, was radically restructured in 1489 by Marco Barbo, nephew of Paul II, and again under Sixtus V, who replaced the columns of the portico with pillars. The interior, which gives access to the courtyard of the adjoining convent, was substantially remodeled in the 20th century. It contains many interesting elements, such as the series of large niches, alternately squared and circular, that contain valuable works of art including a marble relief of the *Crucifixion* attributed to Mino da Fiesole. In the vault of the apse are remains of *frescoes* of the school of Pietro Cavallini.

BATHS OF CARACALLA

THE WALLS OF ROME

The walls of Rome are still immensely fascinating, with the mostly preserved circuit punctuated by defensive towers, bulwarks, bastions, and numerous fortified gates. The historical circumstance that saw Rome remain a Papal city-state until 1870, in the midst of an Italy that was by then unified by the House of Savoy, explain the continued defensive role of the walls and their surprising preservation.

Although this circle mostly corresponds to the walls erected by the emperor Aurelian between 271 and 275, at least two other sets of defensive walls were built earlier: the **walls of Roma Quadrata**, raised under Romulus (8th century BC), and the so-called **Servian walls**, built according to tradition by King Servius Tullius (6th century BC), but in reality dating from the republican age (4th century BC) and erected to face the threats of the Gauls and Hannibal and of Italic and slave insurrections. The long period separating these walls from the construction of the **Aurelian walls** corresponds to the period of Rome's uncontested supremacy in the world; as that waned, it led to the need to protect the city from the growing threat of barbarian invasions.

The walls were strengthened between 401 and 402 by Honorius and Arcadius and in the 6th century by Belisarius. The inclusion of the Vatican and the Janiculum Hill by **Leo IV** (847-55) and **Urban VIII** (1623-44) extended the circuit of walls to a length of approximately 19 kilometers.

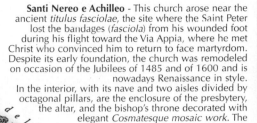

Santi Nereo e Achilleo - This church arose near the ancient *titulus fasciolae*, the site where the Saint Peter lost the bandages (*fasciola*) from his wounded foot during his flight toward the Via Appia, where he met Christ who convinced him to return to face martyrdom. Despite its early foundation, the church was remodeled on occasion of the Jubilees of 1485 and of 1600 and is nowadays Renaissance in style.
In the interior, with its nave and two aisles divided by octagonal pillars, are the enclosure of the presbytery, the altar, and the bishop's throne decorated with elegant *Cosmatesque mosaic work*. The *mosaic decoration* of the apse, dating to the time of Leo III, is of Byzantine fabrication.

Piazzale Numa Pompilio

San Cesareo de Appia - Along the urban tract of the Via Appia, this building dating to the 8th century was remodeled in late Renaissance style in the late 16th century, when the precious *Cosmatesque mosaics* that adorned the presbytery enclosure, the pulpit, the facing of the high altar, and the bishop's throne of the Lateran basilica were transferred here. The affinities with the decorations of the cloister of San Giovanni in Laterano date these works to about 1220. The mosaics that decorate the ceiling of the nave and the vault of the apse instead date to the late 1500s; they were created to cartoons by the Cavalier d'Arpino.

Aurelian Walls - Construction of this last circle of city walls was ordered by the emperor Aurelian; work began in 270 AD and continued under Aurelian's successor Probius. The walls replaced the ancient Servian Walls and also enclosed many areas theretofore excluded from the city proper. Nineteen kilometers in length, rising to an average height of nearly 8 meters, the construction had 14 main and five secondary gates, which were often flanked by cylindrical or semi-cylindrical towers, while every 100 Roman feet (about every 30 meters) stood a defensive tower on a quadrilateral plan. A guard-walk, some stretches of which were covered, ran along the top of the entire perimeter of the walls, which in certain points were crowned by battlements.

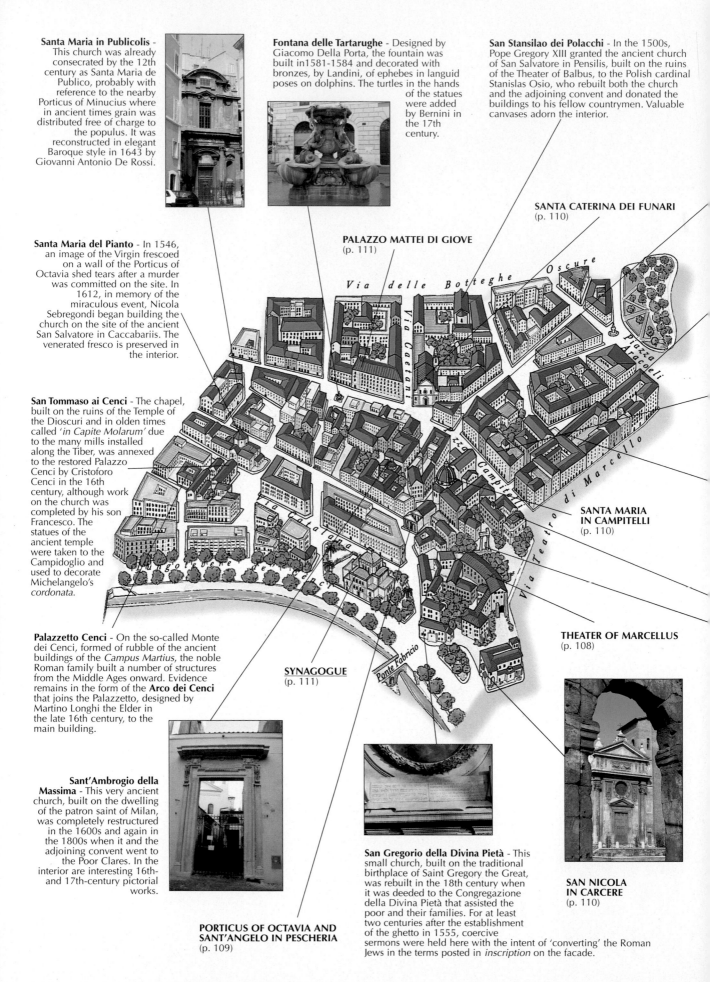

Santa Maria in Publicolis - This church was already consecrated by the 12th century as Santa Maria de Publico, probably with reference to the nearby Porticus of Minucius where in ancient times grain was distributed free of charge to the populus. It was reconstructed in elegant Baroque style in 1643 by Giovanni Antonio De Rossi.

Fontana delle Tartarughe - Designed by Giacomo Della Porta, the fountain was built in 1581-1584 and decorated with bronzes, by Landini, of ephebes in languid poses on dolphins. The turtles in the hands of the statues were added by Bernini in the 17th century.

San Stansilao dei Polacchi - In the 1500s, Pope Gregory XIII granted the ancient church of San Salvatore in Pensilis, built on the ruins of the Theater of Balbus, to the Polish cardinal Stanislas Osio, who rebuilt both the church and the adjoining convent and donated the buildings to his fellow countrymen. Valuable canvases adorn the interior.

SANTA CATERINA DEI FUNARI
(p. 110)

PALAZZO MATTEI DI GIOVE
(p. 111)

Via delle Botteghe Oscure

Via Caetani

Piazza Aracoeli

Santa Maria del Pianto - In 1546, an image of the Virgin frescoed on a wall of the Porticus of Octavia shed tears after a murder was committed on the site. In 1612, in memory of the miraculous event, Nicola Sebregondi began building the church on the site of the ancient San Salvatore in Caccabariis. The venerated fresco is preserved in the interior.

San Tommaso ai Cenci - The chapel, built on the ruins of the Temple of the Dioscuri and in olden times called 'in Capite Molarum' due to the many mills installed along the Tiber, was annexed to the restored Palazzo Cenci by Cristoforo Cenci in the 16th century, although work on the church was completed by his son Francesco. The statues of the ancient temple were taken to the Campidoglio and used to decorate Michelangelo's *cordonata*.

Via Catalana

Piazza Campitelli

Via Teatro di Marcello

SANTA MARIA IN CAMPITELLI
(p. 110)

THEATER OF MARCELLUS
(p. 108)

Palazzetto Cenci - On the so-called Monte dei Cenci, formed of rubble of the ancient buildings of the *Campus Martius*, the noble Roman family built a number of structures from the Middle Ages onward. Evidence remains in the form of the **Arco dei Cenci** that joins the Palazzetto, designed by Martino Longhi the Elder in the late 16th century, to the main building.

SYNAGOGUE
(p. 111)

Ponte Fabricio

Sant'Ambrogio della Massima - This very ancient church, built on the dwelling of the patron saint of Milan, was completely restructured in the 1600s and again in the 1800s when it and the adjoining convent went to the Poor Clares. In the interior are interesting 16th- and 17th-century pictorial works.

San Gregorio della Divina Pietà - This small church, built on the traditional birthplace of Saint Gregory the Great, was rebuilt in the 18th century when it was deeded to the Congregazione della Divina Pietà that assisted the poor and their families. For at least two centuries after the establishment of the ghetto in 1555, coercive sermons were held here with the intent of 'converting' the Roman Jews in the terms posted in *inscription* on the facade.

SAN NICOLA IN CARCERE
(p. 110)

PORTICUS OF OCTAVIA AND SANT'ANGELO IN PESCHERIA
(p. 109)

Palazzo Odescalchi Maccari - In the heart of one of Rome's most picturesque areas, a few steps from the medieval **Torre dei Margani**, stands this palace with its stupendous courtyard with ancient Roman archaeological finds arranged around a fountain and nymphaeum.

Palazzo Massimo di Rignano and **Palazzo Pecci-Blunt** - These two beautiful palaces on **Piazza d'Aracoeli** are the work, respectively, of Carlo Fontana, who rebuilt them in the late 1600s, and Giacomo Della Porta, who completed their construction about a century earlier.

Palazzo Spinola and **Palazzo Capizucchi** - Both built by Della Porta in the late 16th and early 17th century, these palaces, facing the church of Santa Maria in Campitelli, form the scenic backdrop of **Piazza Campitelli**.

Monastery of Tor de' Specchi - The small church of the Santissima Annunziata was added to the monastery, founded in 1433 by Saint Frances of Rome on the site of the ancient homes of the Crivelli family and the medieval tower from which it takes its name, in the late 1500s. The church contains a copy by Allori of the famous painting of the *Virgin* that hangs in the Florentine church of the same name. In the **interior** of the monastery is the chamber in which the saint died; the vase of balsamic ointment she used to cure the sick is on exhibit here.

TEMPLE OF APOLLO SOSIANUS, FORUM HOLITORIUM (p. 108)

N

Santa Rita da Cascia - Until the 1930s, this church was located to the left of the staircase of Santa Maria in Aracoeli. Disassembled and rebuilt on its present site, it conserves its original 17th-century architecture by Carlo Fontana; it is now deconsecrated and used as an exhibit hall.

THE GHETTO AND THE SANT'ANGELO DISTRICT

*T*hat which today is Rome's smallest neighborhood is situated on what was once the extreme southern tip of the Campus Martius, the site of the Forum Holitorium, a vast area used mainly as the fruit and vegetable market. It abounded in porticoes and sacred buildings, including the **Temple of Apollo Sosianus** and those of **Bellona**, of **Juno Sospita**, of **Spes** (Hope), and of **Janus**, which all rose in the area now occupied by the church of **San Nicola in Carcere**. The foodstuffs were brought to market by the river route and over two important road links: the first of these, corresponding to today's Via delle Botteghe Oscure, cut across most of the Campus Martius; the second ran parallel to the river along the north side of the Flaminian Circus. Built by Flaminius Nepote in 221 BC near the Temple of Bellona, this circus was demolished in Augustus' time to make room for the **Theater of Balbus** and the **Theater of Marcellus**. The work was part of a far-reaching improvement project that included demolition of the Porticus of Metellus, dating to 147 BC, and its replacement with the **Porticus of Octavia**.

Despite the state of decay into which its ancient monuments had fallen by the early Middle Ages, the area lost none of its importance and even assumed further strategic value thanks to the Ponte Fabricio, second in importance only to Ponte Sant'Angelo, that linked the area of the ancient Campus Martius with Trastevere. To protect the neighborhood, the city's most powerful families built numerous garrisons incorporating some of the Roman ruins that emerged from the soil. This is the case of **Palazzo Orsini**, at the time the fortress of the Pierleoni family, or that of the Savelli, built on the ruins of the Theater of Marcellus; or again the **'Isola Mattei'**, a complex built over the course of two centuries on the site of the Theater of Balbus.

A radical change in the life and the look of the district began in 1555, when Pope Paul IV had the large Jewish population of Rome transferred here from other neighborhoods, principally from Trastevere. In the style of the restrictive measures adopted a few years earlier in Venice, where the Jews were relegated to an area of the city called the Ghetto - because it was the site of a foundry, called gheto in local dialect - he had much of the Sant'Angelo district (named for the small church of **Sant'Angelo in Pescheria** built on the ruins of the Porticus of Octavia) ringed with high walls with gates that were locked from without from dusk to dawn. Over the centuries the homes were built higher and higher, sometimes even to ten stories, due to the limited space enclosed within the ghetto walls and the constant increase in the population forced to live there. Although a certain degree of freedom of worship and of education was granted the synagogues and the five Talmudic schools - the Tempio, the Siciliana, the Catalana, the Castigliana (where the Sephardic rite was celebrated), and the Nova - of which there remain traces only in the place names, the Jews were nevertheless forced to periodically listen to the sermons delivered in the church of **San Gregorio della Divina Pietà**. Evidence of this coercive action remains on the facade of the church in the bilingual inscription of a verse from the Bible condemning the Jewish religion as perseverance in error.

Despite the 17th-century reconstruction of the square in front of **Santa Maria in Campitelli**, the urban fabric of the district remained unchanged until the 19th century, when following the abolition of the ghetto under Pius IX in 1848 the walls were taken down and the area renovated after all-too-radical demolition work forty years later. Nor did the deportations and the extermination campaigns against Rome's Jewish community during World War II succeed in bowing the spirit or canceling out the physical presence of the Jews in this neighborhood, which still boasts a monumental **Synagogue**, a museum of Roman Jewish culture, and a number of Kosher restaurants.

RIONE · XI
S · ANGELO

Forum Holitorium. Left and below, the three columns of the ruins of the Temple of Apollo Sosianus and a detail of the architrave; above, a detail of the Theater of Marcellus.

On the facing page, a view of the ruins in Vico Jugarius and a view of the Theater of Marcellus incorporated in Palazzo Orsini.

THE FORUM HOLITORIUM AREA AND THE THEATER OF MARCELLUS

The Forum Holitorium, which at its extreme southern point touched on the sacred area on the site of today's church of San Nicola in Carcere, continued northward with its porticoes and *tabernae*, or greengrocers' shops, along the ancient Flaminian Circus.

In the northern portion stood the **Temple of Apollo Sosianus** and the Temple of Bellona, close by one another. The first was built in 433 BC to cast out the plague from the city, and was for this reason dedicated to Apollo Alexicos ('he who wards off evil'). At the time the Theater of Marcellus was built, the temple was moved a few meters; it was restored in 34 BC by the consul Gaius Sosius, hence the name. Of this building, besides the podium and the access stairs, there remain a few beautiful marble columns and a piece of the architrave that is richly decorated with bucrania and olive garlands.

The **Temple of Bellona**, of which instead scant ruins remain, was built in the 3rd century BC by Appius Claudius Caecus, who had vowed its construction during the Battle of Sentinum in which the Romans vanquished the coalition forces of Samnites, Etruscans, and Celts. Dedicated to Bellona, a goddess of war, the temple had an enclosure containing the war column against which the Fetiales, priests empowered to make alliances and maintain treaties with foreign peoples, threw their lances during the solemn ceremony that marked the beginning of hostilities.

A substantial change in the structure of the Forum Holitorium came about when the **Theater of Marcellus** was built: to make room for it, the ancient Flaminian Circus was demolished and a number of pre-existing buildings were moved. Construction was begun by Caesar near a modest building used for public representations near the Temple of Apollo Sosianus, and the theater was completed by Augustus, who dedicated it in 13 BC to the memory of his nephew Marcellus, also husband of his daughter Julia, who died prema-

turely in 23 BC. The structure, with its *scaena* backing on the Tiber and *cavea* seating about 15,000 spectators, had a semicircular **facade** with two tiers of 41 arches each, the first Doric and the second Ionian, and an attic with Corinthian pilasters.

The Theater of Marcellus hosted musical exhibitions and poetry contests; soon, however, the Romans' preference for circuses and gladiatorial games claimed an ever-increasing number of spectators and the theater was forced to close. Thus in the 4th century it began to supply construction materials for other buildings.

In the Middle Ages, the *cavea* was occupied by the Pierleoni family fortress, which when it passed to the Savelli family in the 1500s was restructured by Baldassare Peruzzi to obtain a singular palace by exploiting, as architectural elements, the 12 surviving arches of the theater. In the 1800s, the building went to the Orsini family and took the name of **Palazzo Orsini**.

THE PORTICUS OF OCTAVIA AND SANT'ANGELO IN PESCHERIA

Work in the Augustan age in the Forum Holitorium area was not limited to construction of the Theater of Marcellus and that of Balbus. Between the two, where there once stood the Porticus of Metellus, built by Quintus Caecilius Metellus in 147 BC, Octavian built a new porticus in 27-23 BC and dedicated it to his sister Octavia. It enclosed the temples of Juno Regina, which already existed and was restructured for the occasion, and of Jupiter, built entirely in marble by the Greek architect Hermodoros. Under the portico, which extended to the Library of Octavia, were housed works of art by the greatest Greek sculptors: Phidias, Praxiteles, Skopas, Lysippos. Of the structure, originally over 100 meters in length, there remains the southern propylaea with Corinthian columns and pediment, the result of restoration in 203 AD under Septimius Severus, as we are

reminded by the inscription on the architrave supporting the tympanum. From the Middle Ages until the abolition of the ghetto, it was used as a fish-market; hence name given in the 12th century to the diaconia of Sant'Angelo, founded in about 755.

The church of **Sant'Angelo in Pescheria**, of which the Porticus acts as pronaos, was the object of extensive early Renaissance remodeling in the 1400s, when it was given the pillars separating the nave from the two aisles and its trussed wooden ceiling. The second chapel on the left contains a fresco, attributed to Benozzo Gozzoli, of the *Virgin with the Child and Angels*.

The propylaea of the Porticus of Octavia.

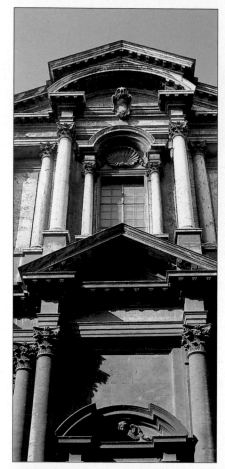

SANTA MARIA IN CAMPITELLI

This is one of Carlo Rainaldi's most interesting architectural creations, built beginning in 1662 and completed five years later. It was built to house the venerated image of the Virgin that saved the city from a serious epidemic in 1656 and replaced an earlier church a short distance away on the site of Palazzo Lovatelli. Rainaldi applied a genial perspective play both on the **facade**, made especially lively by the elegant arrangement of the columns, and in the **interior**, which repeats the theatrical exterior structure with protruding columns and cornices at the points of encounter of the nave with the transept and with the elongated apse, over which towers the congenial **dome**. The interior perspective is heightened by the sumptuous **high altar** designed by Rainaldi himself and built by De Rossi, in collaboration with Ercole Ferrata and Schor, in 1667. At its center stands the miraculous icon of the *Virgin of the Church of Santa Maria in Portico*, an 11th-century work in enameled metal.

The Chapel of the Relics contains venerated and precious liturgical objects, including the 12th-century Byzantine altar of Saint Gregory Nazienzen, decorated with precious mosaics. The fine paintings in the church include a *Virgin with Saint Joachim and Saint Anne* by Luca Giordano and Baciccia's *Nativity of Saint John the Baptist*.

SANTA CATERINA DEI FUNARI

The date of reconstruction of this church on the site of the earlier Santa Maria Dominae Rosae, and that is 1560-1564, would place it in the Counter-Reformist class, although the architecture of the building is actually more directly inspired by the classical forms of the Renaissance; for example, the well-balanced travertine **facade** by Guidetto Guidetti of Como. Of the same period is the bizarre **bell tower**, created by raising the belfry, with its unusual but gracious octagonal dome, on an earlier structure. The organization of the single-nave **interior** that belies the typical late Renaissance taste for a certain severity in form and ornament stands in counterpoint to a cohesive and quite interesting collection of paintings, all dating to only slightly later than the church itself, by some of the most talented masters of the era: Annibale Carracci, Federico Zuccari, Raffaellino da Reggio, and Girolamo Muziano.

SAN NICOLA IN CARCERE

This church, founded certainly before the year 1000 and according to some experts dating to the 7th century, is emblematic of the history of the district and, in a certain sense, of Rome itself, in which almost every monument is the result of the superposition of different eras and styles. In this case, the medieval walls enclose the remains of three republican-era temples of the Forum Holitorium rebuilt in the 1st century AD and contain architectural elements of the most disparate eras.

To the north was the **Temple of Spes** (Hope), built following the First Punic War: a line of eight of its columns encased in the side of the church is interrupted by a beautiful Gothic portal. At the center was the **Temple of Juno Sospita**, two columns of which were used for the facade of the church, built in 1599 by Giacomo Della Porta. The structure to the south, dating to 260 BC, was probably the **Temple of Janus**: six of its travertine columns are incorporated in the left wall of the church. The late-Romanesque **bell tower** exploits a pre-existing defensive tower raised in the early Middle Ages by one of the powerful Roman fami-

The facade of the church of Santa Maria in Campitelli has many tympana of the most varied forms.

San Nicola in Carcere. The facade of the church and the Roman columns along the right side.

lies that controlled the area. The **interior**, on a basilica plan, is also adorned with reused columns and capitals; some of the temple structures visible on the outside of the church penetrate to the interior side walls. Among the many pictorial works are the frescoes by Giovanni Baglione in the Aldobrandini Chapel and the *Virgin with Child* by Antoniazzo Romano, dated to about 1470.

PALAZZO MATTEI DI GIOVE

In the early Quattrocento, the area of the ancient **Theater of Balbus** (inaugurated by Lucius Cornelius Balbus in 13 BC) was partially occupied by the homes of the Mattei family. During the decades that followed, as the noble Roman family with its various branches became owners of the property adjacent to the original nucleus, their patrician homes came to occupy an entire city block, which was thus given the name of 'Isola Mattei'.
Together with the **Palazzo di Giacomo Mattei** and the **Palazzo dei Mattei di Paganica**, both early 16th-century works attributed to Nanni di Baccio Bigio, **Palazzo Mattei di Giove** is certainly the most interesting example of the building program enacted by this family, which also owned one of the largest collections of classical antiques in the city.
The palace in question was designed by Carlo Maderno in 1589 as the home of Asdrubale Mattei; it was enlarged along Via Caetani in 1613-1618 with rather severe, straight-line facades. Greater freedom in decoration and the movement of the architectural volumes was instead granted as regards the *courtyard* and the adjoining *monumental staircase*. The former is fabulously decorated with classical bas-reliefs of historical scenes inserted in sumptuous stucco cornices alternating with statues and busts on corbels. On one side is a gracious *loggia* decorated with stuccowork of classical mein and 16th-century busts of Roman emperors.
The interior, which nowadays hosts many cultural institutions, is an array of large halls frescoed by some of the greatest masters of late Mannerism and Roman Baroque: Domenichino, Pomarancio, Pietro da Cortona, and Giovanni Lanfranco.

THE SYNAGOGUE

After the demolition of the ghetto wall in 1888 and the almost total destruction of the decaying buildings it enclosed, it was only fitting that the capital's large Jewish community be given a place of worship befitting its ancient history and centuries-old culture. Thus in the early 20th century, the architects Osvaldo Armanni and Vincenzo Costa were commissioned to build the synagogue of Rome.
Although the Greek cross plan and **dome** recall the style typical of the time of Umberto I, the decoration is vaguely inspired by Assyrian-Babylonian architecture and incorporates the symbols of Judaism: the star of David, the menorah, and the Tables of the Law.
In the **interior** are elevated women's galleries along three of the four arms; in the fourth, the 'apse', is an aedicula containing the Ark of the Covenant. The building is also home to the small but interesting **Hebrew Museum** containing a collection of many liturgical objects, prints, documents, and other finds that provide a reconstruction of the life and history of Rome's Jewish population through the centuries.

The courtyard of Palazzo Mattei di Giove with the richly-decorated loggia.

The Synagogue, built in the early 20th century.

Ospedale Fatebenefratelli or **'di San Giovanni di Dio'** - Founded in 1582 and completely restructured in the 1930s, the hospital owes its name to the monks of the order of San Giovanni di Dio, who called out the invocation *"Fate bene fratelli"* (Brothers, do good) as they begged alms.

Torre dei Caetani - This tower was once part of the complex defensive system of medieval Rome, together with the homes of the Anguillara family on the Trastevere side of the Tiber and those of the Ponziani family that controlled the other end of Ponte Fabricio.

Ponte Fabricio - It was the consul Fabricius, in charge of roads in 62 BC, who replaced an ancient wooden bridge with the *Pons Fabricius*, a construction in tufa and peperino that has come down to us almost intact despite much work conducted in the Middle Ages. When, under Pope Paul IV, the Jewish community was relegated within the walls of Rome's ghetto in 1555, the bridge took the name of Ponte dei Giudei; it was also at one time called the Ponte dei Quattro Capi (Bridge of the Four Heads) on account of the two enormous four-sided Roman **herms** at the far end.

San Giovanni Calibita - Built in the 9th century on the ruins of the temple of Jupiter Veiovis, this small church was completely restructured in the mid-18th century. The remarkable **interior** is the fruit of the decorative genius of Corrado Giaquinto.

Ponte Cestio - The *Pons Cestius* was built by Lucius Cestius and was restored many times before it was completely rebuilt, using material taken from the Theater of Marcellus, by the prefect Symmachus under the emperor Gratian (375-383). The bridge was again restructured in the Middle Ages and in modern times; its present aspect dates to 1892, the year the banks of the Tiber were raised.

San Bartolomeo all'Isola - Despite the exquisitely Baroque facade of this church, its Romanesque bell tower belies its ancient origin in the 10th century. The **tower** itself nevertheless dates to only 1113, the year of the restoration promoted by Paschal II. Partially destroyed by the flood of 1557, the church was renovated at the end of the century by Martino Longhi the Elder and again in 1624 by Martino the Younger. In the interior, neither architect touched the ancient well of therapeutic waters sculpted in the 12th century, or the columns, which probably belonged to the Temple of Aesculapius.

Ponte Rotto - Originally a wooden footbridge on stone pylons, the bridge was completed by the censors P. Scipio Aemilianus and Lucius Mummius in 142 BC. It was destroyed in 1230 by a flood and rebuilt under Gregory IX with the name of Ponte Santa Maria. It was damaged and repaired repeatedly until Paul III entrusted its restoration to Michelangelo, who however failed to complete the work. Restoration was finally accomplished in 1575, but to little avail: the bridge was again severely damaged 23 years later and was never rebuilt.

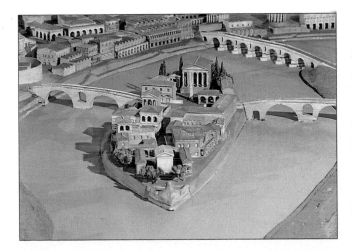

ISOLA TIBERINA

*O*ne of the most ancient of legends concerning Rome narrates how following the expulsion of the last king, Tarquinius Superbus, the Roman senate voted to confiscate and destroy all his possessions, among which his plentiful reserves of grain. The great quantity of seed, thrown into the Tiber, mixed with the silt transported by the current to create a true island in the middle of the river. However it originated, this islet of tufa was of enormous strategic and commercial importance from the very first, both as a point of crossing of the Tiber and as a river port for goods transported via the watercourse. But it was also, and above all, of great religious significance from Rome's earliest history, when it was the site of a sacred enclosure dedicated to Tiberinus, the divine personification of the river. Its importance as a sacred location was destined to increase with time. Another ancient legend narrates how the island was dedicated to the cult of Aesculapius, god of the medical art, who defeated the plague that afflicted Rome in 293 BC. A mission was sent to Greece, to the sanctuary of the god in Epidaurus, requesting his aid; Aesculapius sent his sacred serpent back to Rome. As the returning trireme plied the waters of the Tiber, the snake jumped onto the Tiber island and disappeared through a hole in the earth. The plague instantly ceased. The Temple of Aesculapius was built on the site of the disappearance of the mythical beast; around it, in later times, there were built porticoes for sheltering and caring for the ill. Moreover, in memory of the legendary trireme that brought the serpent to Rome, the island was given the form of a ship, with the bow and stern built of blocks of tufa and travertine decorated with symbols alluding to the god.

Other temples were also built on the island: one dedicated to Jupiter Veiovis and one to a faun, dating to 194 BC. Ten or so years later, the censors Marcus Aemilius Lepidus and Marcus Fulvius Nobilior ordered construction of Rome's first stone bridge, the Pons Aemilius (also called Pons Senatorius, Palatine Bridge, and, after its collapse in 1598, **Ponte Rotto**). It was followed by two other bridges linking the island to both banks of the Tiber: the **Pons Fabricius**, built in 62 BC, and the **Pons Cestius**, built in 46 BC.

Although as time went on it was partially ruined by the Tiber floods and by neglect, the island never lost its vocation as a place of healing; in fact, in the early Middle Ages a hospital was built on the ruins of the Temple of Aesculapius, near a spring believed to have therapeutic properties. Otho III ordered that there be built a church on the site: **San Bartolomeo** was initially dedicated to Saint Adalbert, bishop of Prague, and only later, when the emperor brought from Benevento the relics of the apostle martyred in Armenia that he intended to carry with him to Germany, rededicated to the latter saint. The relics remained in Rome when Otho died in 1002. The island nevertheless remained a place of healing throughout history, and in the late 1500s the Fatebenefratelli built the **Ospedale di San Giovanni di Dio** facing the church; it was pressed into service as a lazar house during the plague of 1656, and is still in use.

The Isola Tiberina in the reconstruction of ancient Rome on exhibit in the Museo della Civiltà Romana.

Santa Susanna - Built according to tradition in the 3rd century on the remains of the house in which the saint lived, the church is now the American Catholic parish. Rebuilt under Pope Sixtus IV, it was later remodeled in 1595 by Maderno, who several years later designed the beautiful **facade**, with its numerous elements a prelude to Baroque.

Fontana del Mosè - Inspired by the models of the triumphal arch and the nymphaeum, Domenico Fontana designed this fountain in 1587 to show off the so-called Acqua Felice, the aqueduct built by Sixtus V on the remains of the ancient *Aqua Alexandrina*. The large central niche holds the colossal statue of *Moses* by Sormoni and Bresciano (1588), while the works in the side niches represent, respectively, *Joshua leading the Jews across the Jordan* and *Aaron leading the Hebrew people to quench their thirst*.

Sala della Minerva - Part of one of the surviving structures of the Baths of Diocletian, the hall was made into a planetarium in 1928. At present, it houses a small section of the **Museo Nazionale Romano** dedicated to sculptures from thermal baths. Among them are the *head of a satyr* recently uncovered near the church of Santi Nereo e Achilleo and once part of the Baths of Caracalla, and the famous *Aphrodite of Cyrene*, a copy from the time of Hadrian from an original Greek statue attributed to Praxiteles and found near the Baths of Cyrene.

Porta Pia - Known for its famous 'breach' opened by the troops of the House of Savoy on September 20, 1870, which marked the taking of Rome, this gate rose near the site of the older Porta Nomentana under Pope Pius IV to mark the end of the strada Felice. Designed by Michelangelo between 1561 and 1564, the gate features a group of travertine scenes on the inside that are a prelude to the Baroque age. The external face was designed by Vespignani in the 19th century.

SANTA MARIA DELLA VITTORIA
(p.116)

Via Goito

Via XX Settembre

Via Barberini

Via Orlando

Via Torino

Via Cernaia

Via Volturno

Via Solferino

San Bernardo alle Terme - Built from a section of the Baths of Diocletian in 1598 and transformed into a building on a circular plan with a **cupola** imitating that of the Pantheon, the church contains fine statues by Camillo Mariani from around 1600.

Piazza Esedra

Viale Einaudi

Piazza dei Cinquecento

SANTA MARIA DEGLI ANGELI
(p. 116)

Via Nazionale

Via Napoli

Via D'Azeglio

Teatro dell'Opera - Built around 1880, it was restored in the late 1920s by Marcello Piacentini, who also designed the present facade.

**MUSEO NAZIONALE ROMANO
(Ex Collegio Massimo)**
(p.117)

Fontana dell'Esedra - This fountain, more properly called the **Fountain of the Naiads**, was designed by Mario Rutelli in the early 1900s. It stands in the center of **Piazza dell'Esedra**, which was set out on the remains of the large exedra of the Baths of Diocletian by Gaetano Koch at the end of the 1800s in order to provide a monumental entrance into the city along Via Nazionale.

N

Villa Torlonia - This neo-classical complex designed by Valadier in the early 1800s and carried forward by Caretti–who built the **palazzo nobiliare**–encloses **gardens** with ruins and exotic vegetation which are entered through a temple gate. There are numerous interesting structures in the gardens, such as the **medieval villa**, a **theater**, the **Casa delle Civette**, and a **Moorish greenhouse**, classic examples of the extravagant taste for the exotic and picturesque typical of the 19th century. Also in the gardens are the interesting **Jewish Catacombs**.

Sant'Agnese fuori le Mura - This building, dating from the period of Constantine, was rebuilt in the 7th century in the Byzantine style, as seen in the *matroneum* (gallery reserved for women in early Christian churches) and the apsidal *mosaics* on a gold background depicting *Saint Agnes between Popes Symmachus and Honorius I*, with the latter pope holding a model of the basilica. The saint is instead represented with the symbols of martyrdom, the sword and flame, and with a phoenix on her robe, symbol of immortality. Inside of the church is the entrance to the **Catacombs of St. Agnes**, containing the body of the saint, martyred during the persecutions of Diocletian.

Santa Costanza - An undisputed jewel of paleo-Christian architecture, the church was built in the 4th century as a mausoleum for the daughters of Constantine, Costantia and Helena. Along with Santo Stefano Rotondo and the Baptistery of St. John Lateran, Santa Costanza is the city's oldest Christian building with a circular plan. Its original structure still mostly intact, the church opens around a circular central space punctuated by coupled marble columns that set off the annular nave, or **ambulatory**. The barrel vaults are decorated with 4th-century *mosaics* in which vegetable, geometric and figurative motifs alternate with figures of animals and cupids still inspired by pagan designs. Christian motifs are instead found in the mosaics of the two side **niches**, showing *Christ giving the keys to St. Peter* and *Christ delivering the Gospel*.

MUSEO NAZIONALE ROMANO
(Museo Nazionale Romano delle Terme)
(p. 117)

Baths of Diocletian - Begun in 298 and completed in 306 along the design of the Baths of Trajan, these baths were the most grandiose of Rome. To understand the huge dimensions of the complex, it is sufficient to recall that the *Tepidarium* was transformed into the basilica of Santa Maria degli Angeli, the *exedra* into the piazza that now sits behind the basilica, and one of the *circular structures* that marked a corner of the external walls into the church of San Bernardo. In fact, the baths were able to hold about 3,000 people and covered, with its nymphaeum, gymnasiums, libraries and immense gardens, an area of almost 11 hectares.

PIAZZA ESEDRA AND THE UMBERTINE QUARTERS

*I*n ancient times, this area of the city within the Servian walls between Porta Collina and **Porta Viminale**–the latter only partially conserved near the railway station–housed the Agger, an embankment raised in the 4th century BC to reinforce the walls protecting the northern quarters of the city, which were more exposed to enemy assaults. With their defensive function no longer needed, the walls were partially demolished as early as the Imperial age and absorbed into buildings of various kinds, not the least of which were those making up the colossal **Baths of Diocletian**. The baths were built by the Emperors Diocletian and Maximian over an area of about 11 hectares and enclosed a vast number of structures, including a preserved central section that Michelangelo transformed into the basilica of **Santa Maria degli Angeli**. The other sections of the agger resisted until the late 1800s, when they were leveled during the works for expanding the capital promoted by King Umberto I of Savoy.

In the 3rd century the Servian walls were superseded by the **Aurelian walls**–still visible for long stretches despite the large-scale demolition carried out over subsequent eras. Contained within those the walls at Porta Nomentana, now called **Porta Pia**, was the **Castra Praetoria**, the barracks founded by Tiberius in 23 AD, and enlarged under Aurelius, that housed the Praetorian Guard, the personal guards of the emperor. Established a short distance from the Castra Pretoria were some of the oldest places of Christian worship and burial in the city. The basilica of **Sant'Agnese fuori le Mura** was built along Via Nomentana in 342 by Constantia, daughter of Emperor Constantine, on the spot where St. Agnes was martyred, and where the **Catacombs** of Sant'Agnese already existed. The princess and her sister were buried nearby in a circular building called the **Mausoleum of Santa Costanza**, subsequently transformed into a baptistery and then into a church.

During the Middle Ages the area remained mostly open countryside, subdivided into more or less large tracts of property owned by rich and noble families. The land was occupied by occasional farmhouses, and then later by summer cottages, and still later, starting from the 1500s, by sumptuous villas with luxuriant gardens. The area was also dotted with churches and fountains, rising at the crossroads of the main streets, as in the case of **Santa Maria della Vittoria**, **Santa Susanna** and the **Fontana del Mosè**.

The most important of the villas–located on the present site of the ex-**Collegio Massimo** (today one of the locations of the **Museo Nazionale Romano**)–was the Villa Peretti Montalto, built in the second half of the 16th century by Cardinal Felice Peretti, who later became Pope Sixtus V. The main area of the villa was the Palazzo Sistino, or Termini, built by Fontana between 1588 and 1589.

The splendid building, which served as a model for numerous villas in Rome during the subsequent Baroque period, was demolished during the construction of the **Termini Station**, begun in 1860 by Pius IX and lasting until the construction of the present facade, inaugurated in the Jubilee year of 1950. The same Pius IX launched a new urban plan for the area between the station and the historic center, which he entrusted to his minister Monsignor Francesco Saverio de Merode. The building projects of the late 1800s that aimed at converting Rome into the capital of Italy were interwoven with those of Pius IX, which had been only partially accomplished in the final years of the Papal government. The works of King Umberto I culminated the rebuilding program and created the urban fabric that is characterized by its architectural eclecticism, with constant references to Roman Classicism and Baroque. Some of these architectural solutions took advantage of existing structures and others of the vestiges from the more ancient past, an example of the latter case being Piazza della Repubblica, better known as **Piazza Esedra**, designed out of the immense exedra of the Baths of Diocletian. Along the northern edge of the city rose the so-called Umbertine quarters (Nomentana, Salario, Ludovisi), whose development however caused the destruction of villas, gardens and parks; of these survives the suggestive 19th-century **Villa Torlonia**.

Santa Maria della Vittoria, the 17th-century facade and, middle, the statue of St. Theresa by Bernini.

Left, the section facing the city of Michelangelo's Porta Pia.

The interior of the church of Santa Maria degli Angeli, built out of several imposing sections of the Baths of Diocletian.

SANTA MARIA DELLA VITTORIA

Begun by Maderno in 1608, the church replaced the previous chapel of the convent of the Discalced Carmelites and was supposed to be dedicated to St. Paul by Cardinal Scipione Borghese, who had paid for its construction.

But the 1620 victory in Prague against the Protestants by the Catholic armies led by Ferdinand II of the Habsburg, with the help of an image of the Virgin found near the castle of Pilsen and brought to the still unfinished church, led to the name being changed to Santa Maria della Vittoria. Six years later the church was completed with the **facade** designed by Giovanni Battista Storia, who took inspiration from the church of Santa Susanna near by.

The **interior**, with a single nave featuring a cupola without a drum, was decorated, according to the then prevailing Baroque taste, with an great profusion of marble, stuccoes, gold, and friezes. Contributing to the richness are also paintings by Domenichino, his last ones in Rome, located in the second chapel on the right side and portraying the figure of *St. Francis*, shown in several episodes of his life. There is also a *St. Paul rapt up to the third heaven* painted by Gherardo Delle Notti in 1620.

But the masterpiece of this church is in the Cornaro Chapel: the **St. Theresa** by Bernini. This work, as intense as it is refined in its execution, depicts the saint in mystic ecstasy transfixed by an angel, while looking on from several niches, as is from theater boxes, are the members of the Cornaro family, dressed in their 17th-century finery.

SANTA MARIA DEGLI ANGELI

The idea of transforming the monumental ruins of the Baths of Diocletian into a church that would glorify the angels and saints who, according to tradition, were forced to construct the baths, first came to a simple priest, Antonio Del Duca. He managed, however, to move the interest of Pius IV, who in 1561 entrusted the job to Michelangelo. Enthusiastic, the great master immediately accepted. Michelangelo, however, did not live to see his work completed; in only managing to salvage the ruins from which the church would rise, this work represented for him the architectural equivalent of the 'unfinished' found in many of the master's sculptures. After the death of Michelangelo, Jacopo Del Duca finished transforming the ancient *Tepidarium* and the spaces opening off of its four sides into a church on a Greek-cross plan with three entrances. The Carthusians, who were to receive the church by Pius IV, oversaw the construction of the **convent** (now the Epigraphic Section of the **Museo Nazionale Romano**), whose **cloister** was also based on a design by the Tuscan master.

Two of the three entrances were closed with the construction of the chapels of St. Bruno and Beato Albergati in the 1700s, while Luigi Vanvitelli's remodeled interior for the 1750 Jubilee had new columns set in the recesses leading to the vestibule, aligned with the remaining entrance. These added to the 14-meter high monolithic red granite columns of the **cross nave**, where numerous *altar pieces* from the Basilica of St. Peter's were placed. Other paintings went into decorating the upper sections of the church, including the *Martyrdom of St. Sebastian* by Domenichino and the *Baptism of Jesus* by Maratta (whose tomb is located in the vestibule), both in the presbytery, as well as the *Mass of St. Basil* by Subleyars, in the left transept.

MUSEO NAZIONALE ROMANO

The **Museo Nazionale Romano**, a prestigious archaeological institution founded in the late nineteenth century, brings together a great quantity and variety of precious finds and evidence of the history and the civilization of ancient Rome. Since 1997 the museum has enjoyed a new arrangement, being now split up among three main exhibit nuclei (enriched by temporary shows and exhibits) in the same number of buildings in different parts of the city.

Thus the traditional seat of the museum at **Diocletian's Baths** (called the **Museo Nazionale Romano delle Terme** and today dedicated exclusively to the epigraphical collections) has been flanked by two new exhibition centers born of the fission of the original collection and now housed in the rooms of **Palazzo Altemps**, near Piazza Navona, and of the former **Collegio Massimo**.

The second of the new centers is arranged according thematic criteria and is subdivided into sections that illustrate the phases of the historical and artistic evolution of Roman civilization from the republican through the imperial ages. The exhibit itinerary begins with a copious selection of works, above all *busts and portraits* that provide evidence of the variegated social composition of Rome from republican times through the beginning of the Empire. The central figure of imperial policy, *Augustus*, is presented in his many different roles as founder, tutelar god and defender of the homeland in a wide-ranging iconographic repertoire rooted in the personality cult typical of Greek Hellenistic art (*Portrait of a Hellenistic Prince, Portrait of Philip of Macedon*). Augustus was fascinated by this art; he collected original works and also had many copies made (the *Pugilist*, the *Caelian Athena*, the *Muse*, etc.).

The evolution in subject-matter and in iconography itself under the Flavians and in the late Empire found its highest expression in the decoration of the great imperial villas and the sumptuous homes of the aristocracy, whence come examples of celebratory statuary from the official portrait repertoire of the emperor, his family and the members of his court (the *portraits of Hadrian and his wife Sabina*, the *portrait of Antinous*, the *statue of Antoninus Pius*) but also works inspired by Greek art, symbols of the taste and of the power of the dominant class (the *Maiden of Anzio*, the *Ephebe from Subiaco*, the *Boats of Nemi*, the *Chigi Apollo*). The cult of the body and of beauty, typical of this era, is amply represented in the statues that once decorated the places consecrated to physical exercise, such as the bath establishments and the gymnasia (the *Lancellotti Discobolo*, the *Castel Porziano Discobolo*), while celebration of military might finds concrete expression in the narrative cycles and the representations of the heroic gestures of the warring armies (the *Portonaccio sarcophagus*).

As part of the reorganization of the Museo Nazionale Romano, its historical premises at Diocletian's Baths have been transformed into the **Epigraphical Department**,

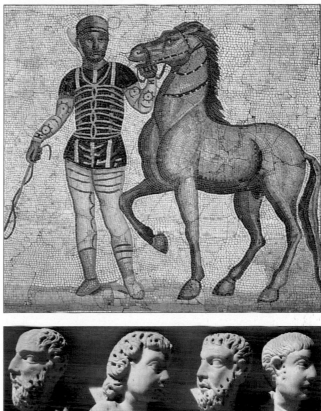

Museo Nazionale Romano delle Terme, a fresco of a tomb on the Esquiline depicting playing children (1st century).

Museo Nazionale Romano, ex-Collegio Massimo, the Auriga, floor mosaic (1st century) from the Villa of Baccano, and a detail of a marble sarcophagus with the Healing of a blind person (3rd century).

home to a rich collection of almost ten thousand inscriptions of different types; ample explanatory material and adequate figurative supports aid in deciphering and to the placing the inscriptions in their correct historical/cultural context.

PIAZZA DEL POPOLO AND THE CAMPO MARZIO DISTRICT

*O*f the ancient Campus Martius - which extended over a good part of today's city center in the flat area between the Tiber and the surrounding hills - today's district, which corresponds roughly to the northern portion of the original, has preserved the name and in some respects the landscape qualities, since it boasts ample green areas like the **Pincio** (at the time called the Collis Hortulorum or 'hill of the gardens' and today a public park).

In the classical era, the Campus Martius was used for eminently public functions; this portion in particular was the site of the barracks and the huge drill-ground reserved for training the Roman army. The monumental **Mausoleum of Augustus** (or Augusteum) was erected in early imperial times on the model of the Mausoleum of Halicarnassus and the ancient Etruscan tumulus tombs. During the 18th-century reorganization of Piazza Augusto Imperatore, the **Ara Pacis**, which had been unearthed near the church of San Lorenzo in Lucina, was installed alongside the mausoleum. The area remained practically uninhabited through the Middle Ages, to the exception of the few homes built in the 13th and 14th centuries along the stretch of the Via Flaminia that ran within the city limits, the convent adjacent **Santa Maria del Popolo**, and the hospital complex of **San Giacomo in Augusta** or 'degli Incurabili', founded in 1339 next door to the church of the same name.

A century later, during the pontificate of Nicholas V, the population of the district began to increase, above all near the river port at the Augusteum where large groups of foreigners lived, These included the Dalmatians and Illyrians who gravitated around the national church of **San Girolamo degli Illirici** (or of the 'Schiavoni', a corruption of slavoni = Slavonian), today the church of the Croatian community.

Sixtus IV launched urbanization of the area by commissioning construction, along the ancient Aurelian Walls, of **Porta del Popolo**. An authentic revolution of the urban fabric thus began. In 1509, under Pope Leo X, the vast property of the Ospedale di San Giacomo was broken up into lots and work commenced on the **Tridente**, the three streets that fanned out from Piazza del Popolo (at the time trapezoidal in form and converging toward Porta del Popolo) in the direction of the city center. In 1517, Via Leonina (today's Via Ripetta) was built alongside the urban portion of the ancient Via Flaminia (today's Via del Corso). On occasion of the Jubilee of 1525, Via Clementina (today's Via del Babuino), named for Clement VII who financed the work, was laid out on the other side of the Via Flaminia, under the Pincio; it was completed in 1543. The same year saw the creation of Via Trinitatis, an artery linking the Tiber and the Pincio that cut across the streets making up the Tridente; it was here that at the end of the century **Palazzo Borghese** was built. Other streets were laid out parallel to Via Trinitatis: by the end of the century, the district had thus taken shape as a sort of grid dotted with monumental private homes, such as **Palazzo Rondinini**, and religious buildings, like **Sant'Atanasio** and the adjoining Collegio Greco. The theatrical prospective of the Tridente was improved in the centuries that followed: Gregory XIII had a fountain installed at the center of Piazza del Popolo; in 1589, Sixtus V replaced it with the **Flaminian Obelisk**. Following the reorganization of Piazza del Popolo commissioned by Alexander VII for the entry into Rome of Queen Christina of Sweden in 1665, the building industry flowered and produced a number of masterpieces of Baroque architecture, like the twin churches of **Santa Maria di Montesanto** and **Santa Maria dei Miracoli**, on the square itself, and the **Church of Gesù and Maria**, built near the monastery of the Discalced Augustinians. All three churches were designed by Carlo Rainaldi. Further into the century, urban reorganization in the district centered mainly on renovation of the Ripetta river port, which was demolished in the 20th century to permit raising the banks of the Tiber. The new, theatrical layout given by Valadier to **Piazza del Popolo** and his **Passeggiata del Pincio**, which offers one of the most beautiful panoramic views over the city, were instead inspired by the neoclassical style that had taken hold by the early nineteenth century.

SANTA MARIA DEL POPOLO (p.121)

Piazza del Popolo - The present layout of the square is the 19th-century work of Giuseppe Valadier, whose intent it was to integrate architecture and landscape. He exploited the natural slope of the Pincio and remodeled the earlier trapezoidal form of the square, at the center of which rose the **Flaminian Obelisk**, an Egyptian granite monolith from the time of Rameses II, brought here from the Circus Maximus where it had been placed by Augustus. The two hemicycles of the square were decorated with fountains with allegorical statues: *Neptune and Two Tritons* toward the Tiber, and the *Goddess Rome between the Tiber and the Aniene Rivers* on the side toward the Pincio.

Palazzo Rondinini - This 18th-century palace, an enlargement of the home built by Flaminio Ponzio for the Cavalier d'Arpino, once housed a rich collection of art, which was dispersed in the 1800s. It included the famous *Rondanini Pietà* by Michelangelo, today in Milan.

MAUSOLEUM OF AUGUSTUS (p.120)

ARA PACIS AUGUSTAE (p.120)

San Rocco - The church was built in 1499 by the Confraternity of Boatmen on the site of the 11th-century Chapel di San Martino that once dominated the Ripetta river port. It was rebuilt in Baroque style by Giovanni Antonio De Rossi in the second half of the 17th century. Today's facade, of Palladian inspiration, is instead a 19th-century work by Valadier. Among other significant works in the interior is the interesting *Virgin with Saints Rocco and Anthony Abbot Healing the Plague-Stricken*, by Baciccia.

San Giacomo degli Illirici - Built in the mid-15th century under Sixtus IV on the site of the 13th-century Chapel of Santa Martina as the national church of the Illyrian refugees in Italy, the building was reconstructed in 1588 by Martino Longhi the Elder in a style preluding the major architectural works of the Counter-Reformist era.

Santi Ambrogio e Carlo al Corso - In 1472, Sixtus IV donated the church of San Nicolò de Tofo to the Lombard community, who originally dedicated it to Saint Ambrose. Two years after the canonization of Saint Charles Borromeo in 1612, reconstruction work began to plans by Onorio Longhi, who was succeeded by Martino Longhi the Younger. In 1668, Pietro da Cortona added the dome, and thus completed the main building; the monumental facade designed by Cardinal Omodei was added twenty years later.

In the **interior** is the only *deambulatorium* in Rome, inspired by that of the Cathedral of Milan. The beautiful *Saints Ambrose and Charles in Glory* by Maratta, on the high altar, conceals a precious reliquary containing the heart of Saint Charles Borromeo.

PORTA DEL POPOLO
(p.118)

**VILLA GIULIA AND THE ETRUSCAN
MUSEUM** (p.122)

**GALLERIA NAZIONALE
D'ARTE MODERNA**
(p.123)

Passeggiata del Pincio - In 1834, as a complement to the square beneath and inspired by French neoclassical models, Valadier laid out what might be called Rome's first public park. He exploited the slope of the hill to create tiers, decorated with allegorical statues, that lead to the 'Pinciana Terrace'. From here, avenues adorned with statues, columns and marble busts set out through the extensive park behind. To one side is the **Casina Valadier**, a reworking, in a neoclassical key, of the earlier Casino Della Rota, built over a cistern of the ancient *Horti Aciliani*.

Santa Maria di Montesanto - Begun to designs by Rainaldi in 1662 as part of the restructuring work of the square commissioned by Pope Alexander VII, construction of the church was taken up again by Bernini and Fontana about a decade later. They set it apart from its 'twin' by building a twelve-sided dome and an elliptical-plan interior.

Santa Maria dei Miracoli - Carlo Rainaldi's architectural creation of 1675, the 'twin church' of the adjacent Santa Maria di Montesano, replaced a 16th-century chapel. It was modified, however, by Fontana, who completed it in 1681 on a circular plan and with an octagonal dome. It is also called the 'Artists' Church' because it is often used for the funerals of show-business and theater personalities.

Sant'Atanasio This Greek Catholic church was built in 1580-1583 by Giacomo Della Porta. To the harmonious facade framed by twin bell towers corresponds an equally harmonious interior reflecting the artistic suggestions and the particular demands of the form of the religion for which the church was designed and taking concrete form in the **iconostasis** (what we see today is the 19th-century renovation) and in the triconch plan of the apse.

Accademia Nazionale di Santa Cecilia - In 1935, the ancient 17th-century convent of the Ursuline nuns was transformed into a **conservatory of music** among the world's most important, with a vast library and a celebrated **concert hall** adapted from the adjoining church of Santi Giuseppe e Orsola.

Church of Gesù e Maria - The design for this church, completed in the second half of the 17th century by Carlo Rainaldi, was originally designed by Maderno, who intended adapting the architecture to the sober nature of his patrons, the mendicant order of the Discalced Augustinians. Rainaldi maintained the severity of the exterior, but gave vent to his Baroque imagination in the interior, decorated on commission from Giorgio Bolognetti, who transformed the church into a sort of huge family chapel.

Palazzo Borghese - The form of this grandiose building, created in the early Seicento for Cardinal Camillo Borghese to designs probably by Vignola, recalls a harpsichord; hence the popular nickname. When it was enlarged toward the Tiber by Flaminio Ponzio in 1612-1614, it was consequently dubbed the 'keyboard'. The beautiful courtyard is dominated by a singular Baroque nymphaeum, populated with statues, known as *Venus' Bath*.

San Giacomo in Augusta - Carlo Maderno completed construction of this church, which had been begun by Francesco da Volterra for Cardinal Salviati on occasion of the Jubilee Year 1600. The interior, on an elliptical plan, is surmounted by an elliptical dome; this may be said to be the first example, at least in Rome, of a Mannerist interpretation of the Pantheon.

The Ara Pacis Augustae. A general view of the enclosure; bottom, a detail of the frieze of the Procession.

Left, an aerial view of the Ara Pacis and the Mausoleum of Augustus.

THE ARA PACIS AUGUSTAE AND THE MAUSOLEUM OF AUGUSTUS

Consecrated in 9 BC to celebrate the return of peace following the Gallic and Spanish campaigns, the altar was originally erected, by order of Augustus, on the Via Flaminia, today's Via del Corso, near the famous *Horologium Augusti* and what is now the site of the church of San Lorenzo in Lucina, in the *Campus Martius* area that at the time was dedicated to the glorification of the emperor. The altar was unearthed during archaeological excavations conducted in the late 1930s and moved to a pavilion built specially to house it. The Ara Pacis consists of a rectangular enclosure decorated on all four sides by a lower band of elegant decorations in the form of acanthus branches, and by a series of reliefs. Those to the sides of the entrance show the *Lupercale*, the grotto in which the she-wolf nursed Romulus and Remus, and the *Sacrifice of Aeneas to the Penates*; on the opposite side are found, in correspondence to the first two reliefs, *Peace* and the *Goddess Rome*. In the relief of the *Procession for the Consecration of the Altar* that runs along the short sides, the figures of the emperor Augustus and his family are clearly identifiable. Inside the enclosure, which is decorated on the inner face with bucrania and garlands, is the altar as such; it was originally adorned with female figures and scenes of the annual sacrifice. Facing the Ara Pacis is the **Mausoleum of Augustus**, ordered built by the emperor as the tomb of the Julian-Claudian dynasty in 27 BC, the year in which he was proclaimed *Augustus* by the Roman senate following the successful Egyptian campaign. Originally, this was a structure consisting of concentric circular tiers planted with cypress trees, at the center of which rose a colossal column topped by a gilded bronze statue of the emperor. A cell in the column held Augustus' ashes, while his family members were buried in the ring immediately surrounding it. The entrance to the mausoleum was flanked by two **obelisks**, which today stand one on the Esquiline in front of Santa Maria Maggiore and the other on the fountain in Piazza del Quirinale.

A view of Piazza del Popolo.

*Santa Maria del Popolo. From top to bottom:
Chigi Chapel, Jonah and the Whale by Lorenzetto;
Della Rovere Chapel, Pinturicchio's fresco of the Nativity;
the spired bell tower and the octagonal dome, examples
of the Lombard Renaissance style in Rome.*

SANTA MARIA DEL POPOLO

An outstanding example of Roman Renaissance religious architecture, the church of Santa Maria del Popolo was totally rebuilt by order of Pope Sixtus IV in 1472-1477 on an 11th-century building erected by Pope Paschal II in gratitude to the Virgin for having interceded, in 1096, in the liberation of the Holy Sepulcher. The first construction was financed by the people of Rome; hence the name by which the church is known today. But another, more evocative legend relates that it was built with the declared aim of driving out Nero's ghost, which hovered near one of the poplar trees (in Latin, *populus*) in which the area abounded, near which was laid the first stone of the building. There is some truth in the second version, since the site on which the church now rises was that of the Mausoleum of the Domizii, where the notorious emperor was buried.

The medieval building, which passed, with the adjoining convent, to the Augustinians in the 13th century and then to the Lombard Congregation, was reconstructed by Andrea Bregno and his followers in accordance with the dictates of the Po Valley religious architecture of the time. This style is clearly evinced by the brick **bell tower** with its typically Lombard forms, and the octagonal **dome**, the first of this type to have been built in Rome. In the early Cinquecento, under Pope Julius II, Bramante somewhat modified the 15th-century structure: he remodeled the choir and built the Chigi Chapel to Raphael's designs. About a century later, Bernini modified the Renaissance structure with new decoration of the **facade** and substantial transformation, in a Baroque key, of the interior. He added a number of chapels, among which that of the Cybo family, designed by Carlo Fontana. The **interior** of the church is a veritable museum of 13th- through 17th- century art. When he re-

built the church, Bregno also created the *high altar* and a number of interesting *funeral monuments* in the various chapels; the original altar has now been moved to the sacristy and replaced with the 17th-century altar, where is found the oldest work in the church, the 8th-century panel painting of the *Madonna del Popolo*, once believed to be the work of Saint Luke.

The Cinquecento is represented by the beautiful *frescoes* that decorate the vault of the choir, in which are found two *funeral monuments* by Sansovino that are commonly considered among the artist's finest works. Raphael, after having styled the project for the **Chigi Chapel**, also supplied the cartoon for the *mosaics* that decorate its dome and that dominate from above other extremely valuable works like Sebastiano del Piombo's vivid *Nativity of the Virgin*, Lorenzetto's *Jonah and the Whale*, and *Abacuc and the Angel* by Bernini. The latter artist also left his mark on the decoration throughout the church, with many statues of saints - among which a sublime *Saint Barbara* - designed by him but actually sculpted by Antonio Raggi.

In the **Cerasi Chapel** in the left transept are two masterpieces by Caravaggio: the *Conversion of Saint Paul* and the *Crucifixion of Saint Peter*, painted by the master in 1601-1602.

VILLA GIULIA AND THE ETRUSCAN MUSEUM

One of the most fanciful realizations of architectural Mannerism is the Villa Giulia, built for Pope Julius III with the collaboration of such famous names in the artistic panorama of the mid 1500s as Vasari, Ammannati, and Vignola. Standing in the area called the Vigna Vecchia, against the walls of the city, Villa Giulia is an admirable example of integration of plays or architectural spaces and volumes into the spectacular cornice of environmental green that from the Monti Parioli slopes down to the Tiber. The various structures develop around the **central courtyard** and two smaller courts, in turn linked by the **garden**, which acts as a coordinating element for the entire complex.

The villa as such is attributed to Vignola and characterized by a sober two-story

Interior of the church of Santa Maria del Popolo. Sacristy, the marble altar by Andrea Bregno and the dome of the Chigi Chapel with its mosaic decoration on Raphael's cartoons.

Villa Giulia. The nymphaeum with the Fontana dell'Acqua Vergine.

Villa Giulia, Etruscan Museum. Bronze mirror (3rd cent. BC).

Villa Giulia, Etruscan Museum. An Attic amphora with a pattern inspired by the episode of Achilles and Ajax playing dice during a lull in battle.

facade, with two projecting portions, animated by pilaster strips, Doric columns, and lateral niches. At the rear of the building, Ammannati's **loggia** overlooks the first courtyard, designed by Vignola, which gives access to the garden and the central courtyard. From here, two flights of stairs lead to the ideal center of the entire complex, the **nymphaeum**. This is a structure on three levels with two series of overlaid loggias, with below the **Fontana dell'Acqua Vergine**, a work by Vasari and Ammannati decorated with river gods and caryatids. A third courtyard, unfinished at death Julius III's and remodeled in the 18th century, concludes the charming arrangement of the open spaces of this interesting suburban villa, one of the few left untouched by the expansion of Rome under Umberto I and in contemporary times.

Villa Giulia was chosen in 1889 to house the rich collection of Etruscan antiquities and relics of the Italic civilizations that flourished between the Iron Age and the beginning of Roman hegemony in the territory between the lower Tiber valley and Tuscany. The finds on display in today's **Etruscan Museum** are arranged according to topographical criteria based on the place of discovery: from Vulci to Veii, from Cerveteri to the territory of *Falerii Novi*, from Palestrina to Umbria. The rich tomb furnishings that testify to the high artistic level attained by Etruscan civilization are highlighted: the **Husband and Wife Sarcophagus**, from the 6th century BC, is certainly one of the most evocative pieces of evidence regarding the cult of the dead of this civilization, and, together with the *Ficoroni Cist* and the elegant household goods found in the *Tomb of the Warrior* and in the *Barberini* and *Bernardini Tombs*, one of the major attractions in the museum.

Much space is dedicated to Greek and Etruscan-Italic ceramics; outstanding among them are the items in the *Castellani Collection*, which contains examples of this art form arranged in chronological order from the 8th century BC through the Roman era.

GALLERIA NAZIONALE D'ARTE MODERNA

This gallery, which contains a vast series of collections of works representing the most important and prolific artistic movements of the 19th and 20th centuries, was transferred in 1914 to the **Palazzo delle Belle Arti**, built on occasion of the Exposition of 1911.

The arrangement of the works follows the chronological development of Italian art, beginning with *Neoclassicism* (Appiani, Canova, Bartolini) and *Romanticism* (Hayez, Induno). A space apart is reserved for the landscape painters, especially those of the *Sorrento School*, who used warm luminous tones to represent the landscapes of southern Italy.

The *Neapolitan School*, which also flourished in the mid-1800s, is instead represented by works with a clear Realist cast: historical and genre paintings (Camarano, Toma) and sculptures of historical and cultural figures of the Italy of the times (Gemito). The northern schools of the second half of the nineteenth century are also given ample breathing space with important series of the works of the *Naturalists* (Delelani, Ciardi) and above all of the currents more directly influenced by the contemporary French artistic movements such as *Impressionism* and *Divisionism* (Corcos, De Nittis, Segantini, Morbelli). A separate section is instead dedicated to the peculiarly Italian - and in particular Tuscan - phenomenon of the *Macchiaioli*, with the works of the most important exponents of this pictorial current, such as Fattori, Signorini, Cecioni, and Lega.

There are also many works by those foreign masters to whom 19th- and 20th-century Italian art is in more than one way indebted (Rodin, Van Gogh, Monet, Degas, etc.); besides its intrinsic value, this section provides the visitor with a yardstick for obtaining a better understanding of the tightly-woven mesh of artistic interchange among the various European countries. Much space is also dedicated to the so-called 'historical avant-garde' movements, from *Symbolism* to *Futurism* (Balla, Boccioni, Severini) and from *Cubism* to *metaphysical painting* (Morandi, Carrà, De Chirico), and to the principal artistic movements of the postwar period, from *Surrealism* and *abstract art* to *informal art* (with Burri and Fontana) and the experimental installations of *kinetic art* (Mari, Alviani, Munari), to more contemporary currents, with works by both Italian and foreign artists (Calder, Tinguely, Pollock).

Galleria Nazionale d'Arte Moderna. An early example (1947) of the infinite variety of effect and expression achieved by Jackson Pollock with his 'poured painting' technique.

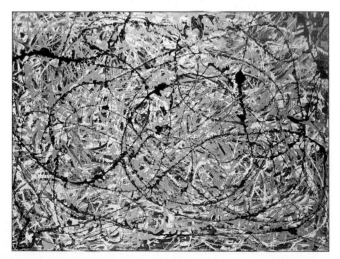

MONUMENTAL ROME

CASTEL SANT'ANGELO AND THE PONTE DISTRICT,
PIAZZA NAVONA AND THE PARIONE DISTRICT,
CAMPO DE' FIORI AND THE REGOLA DISTRICT,
THE JANICULUM, THE PANTHEON AND
THE PIGNA DISTRICT, MONTECITORIO AND
THE COLONNA DISTRICT, THE QUIRINAL AND
THE TREVI DISTRICT,
PIAZZA BARBERINI AND THE LUDOVISI DISTRICT,
PIAZZA DI SPAGNA, TRASTEVERE,
THE CAELIAN HILL, THE VIA APPIA ANTICA

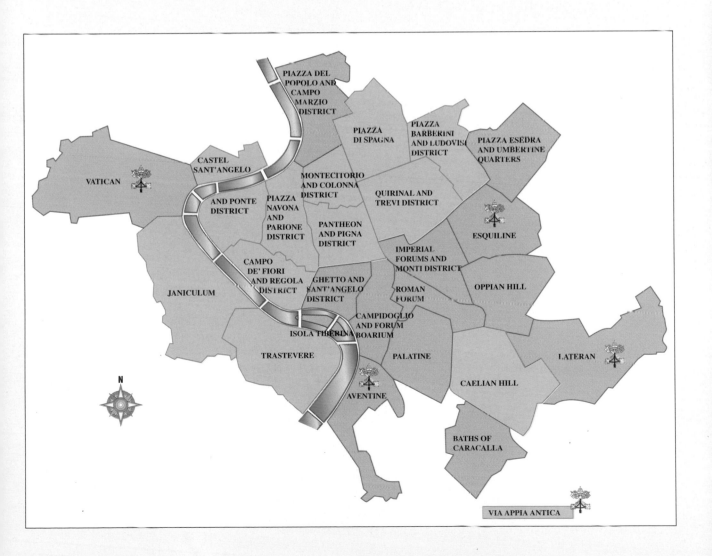

CASTEL SANT'ANGELO AND THE PONTE DISTRICT

*T*he densely-populated district that corresponds to the western portion of the ancient Campus Martius owes its name to **Ponte Sant'Angelo**, built by the emperor Hadrian as the Pons Aelius to provide access to his mausoleum - today's **Castel Sant'Angelo**, which by a strange twist of fate is now, with its neighboring buildings, included in the Borgo district. The area, which was densely populated as far back as the 2nd century BC, was cut through by a closely-knit mesh of streets that included the Via Recta that ran along what is now Via dei Coronari to the stretch of the Via Flaminia within the walls (today's Corso). A third axis linked the Pons Aelius to the Pincio. In the part overlooking the bend in the river, the district was protected by a stretch of the Aurelian Walls in which sidegates opened onto docks along the river used for loading the goods produced by the area's many crafts enterprises, including numerous tanning establishments.

Due to its economic importance, the district never depopulated, even in the early Middle Ages; it is rather the only district of Rome to have remained uninterruptedly inhabited from the time of the birth of the city through modern times. In the Quattrocento, its prestige grew when the papal see was transferred from the Lateran to the Vatican Palace; the area became the object of a large-scale urban development program promoted by Sixtus IV and continued by his successors. The system of streets in the area was reorganized with the opening of the Via Papalis (today's Via dei Banchi Nuovi and Via del Governo Vecchio) and improvement of Via Peregrinorum (today's Via dei Banchi Vecchi) along which the crowds of pilgrims streamed to visit Saint Peter's Basilica, especially during the Jubilee years.

These 'public' works spurred a surprising reprise of private construction, above all in the area closest to Ponte Sant'Angelo, where over the course of the centuries a populous colony of Florentines had settled; their number was destined to increase even further in the 16th century, when Leo X Medici was elected to the papal throne. Under the banner of the fleur-de-lis of Florence were grouped mainly bankers and moneychangers whose establishments were concentrated in the 'Banchi' area. The community enjoyed legal independence and had its own tribunal, constituted in 1515, as well as its own church, **San Giovanni dei Fiorentini**.

The increasing importance of the area led Pope Julius II to launch new urban improvement works with the aim of linking the district with Saint Peter's and the Trastevere port area: that is, the economic, religious and commercial centers of the city. Thus the pope commissioned the Via Giulia to create a direct link to the Vatican, and promoted construction of a series of buildings destined to house administrative functions: the mint, better known as the **Palazzo del Banco di Santo Spirito**, the Old Chancery - today's **Palazzo Sforza Cesarini**, seat of the Papal Chancery - and the monumental Palazzo dei Tribunali, on Via Giulia, begun by Bramante in 1508 but never completed. Although the area's vocation for banking and administration was reflected in the preponderance of moneychangers' shops that served the many foreign pilgrims visiting the holy city, there was also a thriving crafts industry that catered to those same visitors.

Nowadays, however, the old-time sellers of wreaths, medals, and sacred objects in **Via dei Coronari** have been replaced by antique dealers. The opening of **Corso Vittorio Emanuele II** and the raising of the banks of the Tiber in the late 1800s changed the fabric of the district, but it has nevertheless preserved a charm all its own and many monuments of unexpected beauty.

Ponte Sant'Angelo - The name of the bridge, built in 133 by Hadrian, was changed to Ponte Sant'Angelo in the Middle Ages, after the miraculous apparition of the Archangel Michael to Pope Gregory the Great in 590. The bridge was originally equipped with a defensive tower; in the mid- 15th century Pope Nicholas V decided to have it covered (to plans by Alberti) to provide shelter for the pilgrims visiting Saint Peter's Basilica. The eight statues of evangelists and patriarchs installed in 1536, on the occasion of Charles V's visit to Rome, gave Bernini the cue for the **statues** of angels set on the parapets in 1668.

Banco di Santo Spirito - Probably designed by Bramante and originally built as the seat of the mint, this building was restructured by Antonio da Sangallo the Younger in 1521-1524.

SAN GIOVANNI DEI FIORENTINI (p. 130)

Palazzo Sacchetti - Although at length attributed to Antonio da Sangallo the Younger, it would seem that this palace was actually built in 1552 by Antonio Lippi - over the house belonging to the Florentine architect - for Cardinal Ricci. It is clearly inspired by the nearby Palazzo Farnese; the beautiful garden, with its nymphaeum visible from the Lungotevere, was a later addition.

San Biagio degli Armeni - This small, pretty 18th-century church, officiated according to the Armenian Catholic liturgy, is also known by the name of 'Pagnotta' because of the ancient custom of distributing, on Saint Blaise's Day (3 February), small loaves (*pagnotte*) of blessed bread.

Casa dei Mutilati - The style of this typical expression of the taste in monuments, informed by Rationalist principles, in vogue in the Fascist era is further emphasized by the inclusion of many grandiloquent elements recalling ancient Rome.

CASTEL SANT'ANGELO
(p. 128)

Piazza Adriana

Piazza Cavour

Palazzo di Giustizia - More often called simply the **Palazzaccio**, this mastodontic edifice in eclectic style, built by Calderini at the turn of the twentieth century, is the seat of the Court of Cassation.

San Salvatore in Lauro - This church, already standing in the Quattrocento (to which time date the adjacent cloister and adjoining rooms), is Renaissance in structure despite its having been rebuilt by Mascherino in 1591. The single-nave interior, of Palladian inspiration, is marked out by travertine columns along the perimeter walls. The facade dates to the 1800s.

Lungotevere Castello

Ponte Umberto

Palazzo Lancellotti - Rebuilt by Francesco da Volterra for Cardinal Scipione Borghese in the late 1500s and completed by Maderno. Domenichino added the monumental portal. The interior is decorated with allegorical frescoes by Guercino.

Ponte Sant'Angelo

- Tevere

Lungotevere Tor di Nona

Torre dell'Orologio ai Filippini - The portion of **Palazzo dei Filippini** toward Monte Giordano was renovated by Borromini in 1647-1649 with an aerial structure that exploits alternating concave and convex surfaces and terminates in a bell cage in wrought-iron scroll work. The clock tower was decorated with a mosaic of the *Virgin of Vallicella* to a design by Pietro da Cortona.

Via dei Coronari

Corso Vittorio Emanuele II

Via Giulia

Corso Vittorio Emanuele II

CHIESA NUOVA
(SANTA MARIA IN VALLICELLA)
(p. 131)

Chiavica Vecchia

Oratorio dei Filippini - The hall in which Saint Philip Neri organized his first *Sacre Rappresentazioni* of recitation of passages of the Holy Scriptures alternating with polyphonic musical pieces - the musical term 'oratorio' derives from these services - was rebuilt, beginning in 1637, by Borromini, who was also the author of the rooms in the adjoining **Convent of the Oratorians of Saint Philip Neri** that open off three courtyards. Currently only certain of the rooms are occupied by the monks, while the rest host prestigious cultural institutions including the **Biblioteca Vallicelliana**, the first library in Rome to have been opened to the public.

Oratorio del Gonfalone - Falling within the competence of the nearby church of Santa Lucia del Gonfalone, which replaced Santa Lucia Vecchia, the oratory is a true masterpiece of Roman Mannerism.

Castel Sant'Angelo. An aerial view of the fortress and a view of the walls.

Left, the Mausoleum of Hadrian and a detail of fragments of entablatures.

Below right, the bronze statue of the Archangel Michael placed on the summit of Castel Sant'Angelo in the 1700s.

CASTEL SANT'ANGELO

The massive fort that reflects in the waters of the Tiber, known as Castel Sant'Angelo, was originally the **Mausoleum of Hadrian**, designed and built by the emperor in 130 AD as his final resting place and the tomb of the members of the Antonine dynasty. The building consisted of a quadrangular base with an entrance in the form of a triumphal arch, which gave access, through a long corridor and a spacious vestibule (both still visible), to the overlying structures; the whole was topped by a gilded bronze sculptural group of a quadriga driven by the emperor. The overall effect was that of a gigantic Etruscan-style tumulus tomb, on the model of the Mausoleum of Augustus. The burial chamber at the center, in which were preserved the urns containing the ashes of Hadrian and his family members (and which later sheltered those of his successors through Caracalla), was accessed through a **helicoidal gallery** that despite later drastic remodeling is still recognizable.

Under Aurelian, the mausoleum became part of the defensive system raised to protect the *Pons Aelius*, today's **Ponte Sant'Angelo**, while still continuing to play its original role as a place of burial. In the meantime some of its original structures had been dismantled and reused in the construction of new buildings. This was the fate of the Parian marble rustication that sheathed the exterior, the colossal bronze peacocks, now in the Cortile del Belvedere in the Vatican, and the marble columns of the imperial sacellum, used to decorate the Basilica di San Paolo.

In about 520, Theodoric, who had momentarily moved the capital of his empire to Rome, transformed the building into a prison - a function it continued to carry out until 1901 (with such famous historical 'guests' as Cellini and Cagliostro). It also continued to operate as a fortress, to which use it was consecrated from the time of the Gothic War that bloodied the city for a long period. Some decades after the end of the conflict, in 590, the plague struck Rome. The then-pope Gregory the Great, as he crossed the bridge to the mau-

Castel Sant'Angelo. An image of the walls and two spaces within the fortress.

Below, Castel Sant'Angelo from the bridge decorated with the statues, designed by Bernini, alluding to the Passion of Christ.

soleum/fortress, saw atop it the Archangel Michael sheathing a flaming sword. He took the vision as a sign that the epidemic would soon cease, and from that moment on the structure took the name of Castel Sant'Angelo. It was only later, in 1544, that the episode was commemorated with the installation of the marble statue of the *Archangel Michael* by Raffaello da Montelupo in the place the apparition had been seen. The original angel was replaced, in 1752, by the bronze copy by Verschaffelt.

During the Middle Ages, the fortress became especially important for defense of the Vatican. In the ninth century, Pope Leo IV made it an integral part of that system of walls that delimited the area known as the 'Leonine City' and by which it was linked to many other buildings, including the nearby Vatican Palace. In the 13th century, under Pope Nicholas III, an overhead corridor was added along this stretch of the walls. Known as the **Passetto** or the **Borgo Corridor**, the passageway was restructured and perfected in the following centuries to permit the popes to reach Castel Sant'Angelo quickly in case of danger. The first pope of the modern age, Alexander VI, had Giuliano da Sangallo reinforce the castle with construction of a

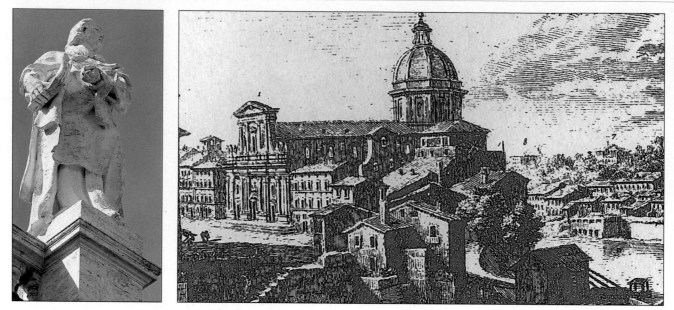

San Giovanni dei Fiorentini. One of the statues decorating the top of the facade, and the church in an 18th-century engraving.

San Giovanni dei Fiorentini. A partial view of the travertine facade crowned with statues.

four-sided surrounding **wall** with four octagonal corner **towers** named for the four evangelists, a series of new bastions, and a wide moat. A few years later, under Julius II, the marble **loggia** overlooking the Tiber was added; Paul III, fearing a Turkish invasion of the coasts of Latium, commissioned Antonio Sangallo the Younger to completely renovate the defensive installations and to enlarge the papal apartments in the castle. The rooms were decorated by Perin del Vaga and his studio in the mid-16th century with cycles of frescoes inspired by the *History of the Church* (**Sala Paolina**), and with figures from classical mythology (**Camera del Perseo, Camera di Amore and Psyche**).

But for the most part, the aspect of Castel Sant'Angelo is still that of a fortress built for defense, with its armed bastions complete with batteries of cannon, the **Armory** of Clement X built by Bernini and later transformed into the Chapel of the Condannati (prisoners awaiting execution in the **Courtyard of the Angel**), the so-called **Oliare**, large rooms and silos used to store foodstuffs for use in case of siege, and the parapet walk, which still today offers the visitor a full view of the Vatican and indeed of much of Rome.

SAN GIOVANNI DEI FIORENTINI

In the early Cinquecento, the Florentine community based in the Ponte district of Rome, with its many banks and the luxurious palaces of its most important members, began to feel the need for a church worthy of representing its wealth and standing. Thus the decision to build a magnificent temple dedicated to Saint John the Baptist, the patron saint of Florence, at the end of that Via Giulia that had been opened by Pope Julius II as part of the urban renovation work carried out in the area a short while before. The decisive stimulus to construction of the church was the election of Pope Leo X, of the Florentine Medici dynasty. In 1519, the pope called for plans; the contest was won by Sansovino, who began work on the church but was soon replaced by Antonio da Sangallo the Younger. Work was interrupted in 1527, when the Sack of Rome spread death and ruin in the district, which was particularly hard-hit by looting and wilful destruction. In 1559, Michelangelo presented designs for a central-plan church, but they were rejected in favor of Sansovino's original design, on the basis of which Della Porta resumed work in 1583. His successor Maderno completed the **dome** in 1620.

At this point there remained only the **facade**, for which another contest was called by Clement XII, a member of the Florentine Corsini family whose coat-of-arms adorns the tympanum of the center portal. The commission was won by Alessandro Galilei, also the author of the facade of San Giovanni in Laterano, who completed the majestic and austere front decorated with statues and reliefs by Della Valle and other artists. Of note in the **interior** is the presbytery, on which some of the most important exponents of Roman Baroque worked. It was begun by Pietro da Cortona, to whom we owe the gilded coffered ceiling, and was completed by Borromini, who is buried here. Borromini also created the *Falconieri family monuments* and the *aedicula of the high altar*, home to Antonio Raggi's masterful *Baptism of Christ*.

Santa Maria in Vallicella, also known as Chiesa Nuova. The facade is inspired by that of the neighboring Church of Gesù.

CHIESA NUOVA

The name Chiesa Nuova (New Church) alludes to the 16th-century renovation of the original building, traditionally attributed to the time of Gregory the Great, although the church nevertheless also conserves its ancient denomination of **Santa Maria in Vallicella**, which in turn alludes to a slight depression in the terrain that was later leveled. The 'new' church, like the adjacent oratory by Borromini, is linked to the figure of Saint Philip Neri, the founder of important humanitarian institutions, among which the Confraternita della Santissima Trinità dei Pellegrini e dei Convalescenti, and a zealous apostle of Catholicism. In recognition of Neri's deeds, Pope Gregory XIII granted him the church in 1575; the future saint immediately embarked on reconstruction, entrusting the work first to Matteo da Città di Castello and then to Martino Longhi the Elder. The church was consecrated in 1599 but was completed only early in the following century with the erection of the **facade**, inspired by that of the nearby Church of Gesù, and the decoration of the **interior**, work on which continued on into the 18th century. The frescoes in stuccowork frames by Fancelli and Ferrata that adorn the ceiling of the nave, the dome, and the vault of the apse are all by the hand of Pietro da Cortona, who between 1647 and 1665 decorated the three parts with the *Vision of Saint Philip Neri*, the *Assumption of the Virgin*, and the *Triumph of the Holy Trinity*, respectively. Three other masterpieces, this time by Rubens, depict the *Virgin and Child* and two groups of *Saints* in the high altar chancel.

The **chapels** also abound in important works of art. The Chapel of Saint Charles Borromeo, built by Rainaldi for the Spada family, is home to a splendid 17th-century altarpiece by Maratta, while across the nave the Baroque Chapel of Saint Philip Neri by Onorio Longhi, in which the relics of the saint are preserved, is sensationally adorned with precious marbles, inlays of semi-precious stones and mother-of-pearl, gilded bronzes, and stuccowork. The sacristy gives access to the **Rooms of Saint Philip**, on two floors, that were superbly decorated during the 1600s. The rooms abound in curios and mementos recalling the saint; in the chapel is an interesting work by Guercino depicting *Saint Philip with an Angel*.

Santa Maria in Vallicella. A detail of the center portal framed by two pairs of columns and topped by the arched fronton.

PIAZZA NAVONA AND THE PARIONE DISTRICT

A bounding in monuments since ancient *times (it was here that Domitian's Stadium and Odeion and Pompey's Theater rose), the Parione district owes its name (an augmentative of the Latin* paries = wall) *to the remaining walls of one of the aforementioned constructions, which in later centuries provided the foundations for the new buildings of modern-day Rome.*

Differently from other areas of the city, the population of the Parione district never decreased significantly; quite the contrary, in the 1300s it was one of the most densely inhabited areas in all Rome. Its period of greatest splendor, however, began only a century later, with the Renaissance. The reign of Sixtus IV saw a long series of urban development and building projects that began with the creation of two new thoroughfares, Via Papalis and Via Florida, laid out in such a manner as to permit more orderly carrying out of the religious processions and the papal ceremonies and more rapid movement of the pilgrims visiting Saint Peter's. Above all, during the papal investiture ceremonies, the new route made it easier for the pope to move from the Vatican to the Basilica di San Giovanni in Laterano, of which he took symbolic possession as Bishop of Rome.

In the two centuries that followed, the district, with its renewed urban fabric, began to attract the attention of the noble families, who began to choose it as the site of their sumptuous homes. At the same time the transfer of the Capitoline market to Piazza Navona attracted a great many craftsmen, who established their workshops in the streets off the square. There still remain evident traces of the crafts vocation in the many ateliers that dot the district and in street names that recall the crafts of old: Giubbonari (tailors), Chiavari (locksmiths), Baulari (trunk-makers), etc. Behind Piazza Navona, where the Parione district blends into the outskirts of the Ponte and Sant'Eustachio districts, certain of the many colonies of foreigners in Rome built their churches and hospices for sheltering their fellow countrymen: **Santa Maria dell'Anima**, *the church of the Germans (including the Flemish and the Dutch), the Spanish San Giacomo degli Spagnoli (today* **Nostra Signora del Sacro Cuore**), *the French* **San Luigi dei Francesi**, *the Portuguese* **Sant'Antonio dei Portoghesi**, *and the Lorrainers'* **San Nicola dei Lorenesi**. *The 'international' importance acquired by the district determined the construction of a great many hotels and inns offering lodging to both pilgrims and the political figures linked to the Roman Curia, which here had its* **Chancery**.

When Piazza Navona was remodeled in the 17th century, the district took on a look that only further development actions in the 19th and 20th centuries, culminating in the opening of Corso Vittorio and Corso Rinascimento, succeeded in partially altering.

Piccola Farnesina - Probably designed by Antonio da Sangallo the Younger and built in 1523 for the Breton abbot Thomas Le Roy, the palace owes its name to the fact that the French fleurs-de-lis making up the decoration were mistaken for the lilies of the Farnese family coat-of-arms. The building was remodeled in the 19th century by Enrico Guy, who nevertheless preserved its original style. Today, the palace houses the **Museo Barracco**, with its precious works of ancient statuary.

SANT'ANDREA DELLA VALLE
(p. 139)

Palazzo Pamphili - Built in 1650 to plans by Rainaldi, as part of the complex work of reorganizing Piazza Navona undertaken by Innocent X Pamphili. The rooms in the interior, which today host the Embassy of Brazil, are decorated with beautiful frescoes by 17th-century artists.

Teatro Argentina - Inaugurated in 1732, this was one of the most important theaters of papal Rome. It was here that Rossini's *Barber of Seville* made its debut performance in 1816. The building was remodeled a number of times during the 19th century.

SANT'IVO ALLA SAPIENZA
(p. 138)

Palazzo della Sapienza - The 16th-century Palazzo della Sapienza was until 1935 the seat of the *Studium Urbis*, the Roman university founded by Pope Boniface VIII in 1303. The building was begun to plans by Guidetti and Pirro Ligorio in 1562 and completed in the early 17th century. Today it is home to the **Rome State Archives**.

Nostra Signora del Sacro Cuore - Probably built by Rossellino for Rome's Spanish community on occasion of the Jubilee of 1450 and initially named for Saint James, this church was restructured by Antonio da Sangallo the Younger. Although it still conserves some of its Renaissance features, its original plan was later completely revolutionized by the opening of Corso Rinascimento, which deprived it of its transept.

SANT'AGNESE IN AGONE
(p. 135)

PALAZZO MADAMA
(p. 137)

PALAZZO DELLA CANCELLERIA AND SAN LORENZO IN DAMASO (p. 137)

Palazzo Massimo alle Colonne - The innovative **facade** in flat rustic work with a Tuscan colonnade follows the curve of Domitian's Odeion over which it was built in 1536 by Baldassare Peruzzi when he restructured the Massimo family palace that had been severely damaged during the Sack of Rome in 1527. The finely-decorated interior contains Daniele da Volterra's, *Scenes from the Life of Quintus Fabius Maximus*, the legendary ancestor of the family that for centuries was entrusted with superintendency of the papal post office.

San Pantaleo - Valadier's sober neoclassical facade introduces the genial 17th-century **interior** by De Rossi: a single space with a frescoed barrel-vaulted ceiling, two side chapels, and a deep apse.

Palazzo Braschi - Seat of the **Museo di Roma**, a rich collection documenting life in the city from the Middle Ages through the modern era. In the 18th century the palace belonged to Pius VI, who had it rebuilt on the site of 15th-century building.

Pasquino - One of the famous '**talking statues**' to which the Roman people traditionally posted brief satyric verses ridiculing those in power, called *pasquinades*. The statue is actually one figure from a Roman sculptural group of *Menelaus Supporting Patrocles*, found in 1501 and installed in its present location by order of Cardinal Oliviero Carafa.

Santa Maria dell'Anima - The church of the German community (as well as of the Dutch and the Flemish) was built in the early 16th century in a neo-Gothic style inspired by the 'hall churches' typical of northern European tradition. The Renaissance **facade** has been attributed to Sansovino, who is certainly the author of the sculpture, over the main portal, of the *Virgin between Two Souls in Purgatory* from which the church takes its name.

SANTA MARIA DELLA PACE (p. 136)

PALAZZO ALTEMPS (p. 136)

Sant'Apollinare - Rebuilt to plans by Fuga in the mid-18th century, this church, which originated in the 7th century on the ruins of the site used for the *Agoni Apollinari*, is noteworthy mostly on account of its size. The interior, with works of considerable artistic value, is nevertheless very harmonious.

Sant'Antonio dei Portoghesi - The church of the Portuguese nation was built in accordance with a clearly Baroque conception that emerges especially in the facade, of Iberian inspiration. The building is nevertheless the work of Italian architects, among whom Martino Longhi the Younger and Carlo Rainaldi, author of the beautiful lowered dome.

PIAZZA NAVONA (p.134)

Sant'Agostino - Although it conserves many Gothic elements such as the flying arches of the left side and the high cross vaults of the nave, the architecture reflects the forms of the early Renaissance, inspired above all by the theories of Alberti. The church was built for the Augustine order by Jacopo da Pietrasanta between 1479 and 1483. The **interior** is home to some sensational artistic treasures: Caravaggio's *Madonna dei Pellegrini*, Raphael's *Isaiah*, the venerated statue of the *Madonna del Parto* by Sansovino, and the beautiful *high altar* by Bernini.

SAN LUIGI DEI FRANCESI (p.138)

Corso Vittorio Emanuele II

Via di Parione

Piazza S. Luigi de' Francesi

Via della Scrofa

Via di Monte Brianzo

Lungotevere Marzio

Piazza Navona. The facade of the church of Sant'Agnese in Agone and that of the adjacent Palazzo Pamphili; in the foreground, the Fontana del Moro.

Some remains of Domitian's Stadium; below, the stadium in the scale model of ancient Rome in the Museo della Civiltà Romana.

PIAZZA NAVONA

If this square is one of the most famous in the world, it is justly so thanks to the theatrical air created by the sumptuous monuments facing on it and the fountains that decorate its center. The square has in fact always been a space for games and spectacles, and it was so even before Domitian chose the site for his **Stadium**, inaugurated with the *Agoni Capitolini* in 86 AD. The Stadium was a colossal structure in travertine and brick, with an arena delimited by steep tiers of seats supported by two orders of wide arches. It was 276 meters long and 56 meters wide, and for almost four centuries hosted an infinite series of athletic meetings. Even after its decline began in the 5th century, the arena, then known as the *Campus Agonis* (Games Field), continued to be the site of games, jousts, festivals, and spectacles of every type; beginning in 1477 it was also the home of the city market, transferred here from the Campidoglio. The role played by the site throughout history also determined its name. 'Navona' is a corruption of the Latin expression *in agone*, used to describe the square in the Middle Ages.

And while it preserved the form and the dimensions of the ancient Stadium, of which some remains are still visible today, the square meanwhile began to acquire its characteristic look. In the 13th century its perimeter was constellated by a long line of tower-homes belonging to the most important Roman families; little remains today of these constructions, which during the Quattrocento were replaced by sumptuous patrician residences like **Palazzo Orsini** and **Palazzo De Cupis**, and by the church of San Giacomo degli Spagnoli, today known as **Nostra Signora del Sacro Cuore**. The square was paved during the papacy of Inno-

Piazza Navona. The Fontana dei Quattro Fiumi by Bernini and two detail views.

cent VIII, and in the 16th century Gregory XIII installed the **Fontana del Moro** and the **Fontana del Nettuno**, both by Giacomo Della Porta. The fountains take their names from the statues that currently adorn the basins: respectively, the *Moor Fighting a Dolphin*, a 17th-century work by Antonio Mari, and the 19th-century *Neptune Fighting an Octopus*. In the early 17th century the series of buildings that delimited the square acquired new, prestigious architectural elements, such as **Palazzo Millini** and **Palazzo Pamphili**. It was a member of the latter family, Giovanni Battista (who became pope in 1644 with the name of Innocent X) who gave Piazza Navona its present aspect, and to do so he employed the talents of the most celebrated architects of the age: Bernini, Borromini, Pietro da Cortona, and Girolamo and Carlo Rainaldi. The latter was commissioned to build the church of **Sant'Agnese in Agone**, which was, however, completed by Borromini. And of the same architect the pope initially commissioned the **Fontana dei Quattro Fiumi** (Fountain of the Four Rivers) as an ornament for the center of the square, but in the end gave the nod to Bernini's more fanciful and theatrical

sketch of a rock rising at the center of the pool, with on it exotic plants and animals, surmounted by an obelisk against which stand out the allegorical representations of the four greatest rivers on Earth as symbols of the four

known continents (Asia, Europe, America, and Africa): the *Ganges*, by Purissimi; the *Danube*, by Raggi; the *Rìo de la Plata* by Baratta; and the *Nile*, portrayed by Fancelli with her face covered because at the time the sources were yet unknown.

The legend that grew up around the rivalry between the two greatest Baroque architects recounts that the *Nile* is shown blindfolded as not to have to observe Borromini's facade of Sant'Agnese, and that the extended arm of the statue of the *Rìo de la Plata* alludes to its imminent collapse. The legend, of course, has no historical foundation whatsoever, since Bernini completed the fountain in 1651, a year before work began for the construction of the church.

SANT'AGNESE IN AGONE

In 1652, as part of the works undertaken for reorganizing Piazza Navona, Innocent X decided to restructure the ancient church of Sant'Agnese, founded by Pope Damasus on the site on which the saint, exposed naked on the pillory but miraculously covered by her own hair, met her death as a martyr. And since the pope's main intention in the work was to give the square a 'face-lift', when he commissioned Carlo and Girolamo Rainaldi to rebuild the church he also required that they invert its original orientation.

After about a year from the start of the work, supervision of the project was turned over to the Ticinese Borromini, who while keeping the Rainaldis' Greek cross plan modified the

135

Sant'Agnese in Agone. The facade with the twin bell towers and the soaring dome; in the foreground, the Fontana dei Quattro Fiumi with the obelisk.

Santa Maria della Pace. The upper portion of the facade; bottom, Bramante's Renaissance cloister.

design of the **facade** to obtain an imaginative concave front that emphasized the slender, soaring **dome**, the interior of which was frescoed by Baciccia and by Ciro Ferri. In 1657, supervision of the work returned into the hands of Carlo Rainaldi; he was succeeded by Baratta and Del Grande, who built the twin **bell towers** to plans by Borromini.

In the **interior**, decorated with gilded stuccowork and precious marbles, are many valuable works of art. The underlying area reveals the ancient history of the site: in the subterranean vaults some traces of Domitian's Stadium are still visible, as are the remains of the original church with 13th-century frescoes and Algardi's last work, a marble bas-relief showing *Saint Agnes Led to Martyrdom*.

SANTA MARIA DELLA PACE

In the 15th century, on the site of today's church, there stood the small medieval oratory of Sant'Andrea de Aquazariis, which obtained considerable notoriety in 1480 when an image of the Virgin began bleeding prodigiously after having been struck by a stone. Sixtus IV thus decided to rebuild the church and to dedicate it to Saint Mary of Virtue, but he died before completion of the work. It continued under Innocent VIII, who gave the church the name it bears today.

Finally, in 1656, Pope Alexander VII Chigi ordered its restructuring. Pietro da Cortona created the two-order **facade**, deftly inserted into the plays of concave and convex surfaces that surround it, and added a singular semicircular **pronaos**, on the architrave of which is an inscription in Latin, reading "To the people, may the mountains bring peace and the hills justice," alluding to the Chigi coat-of-arms, with its six-peaked mountain.

In the striking **interior** is the harmonious **Chigi Chapel**, built to plans by Raphael and frescoed by the artist with the images of four *Sibyls*, and other no-less-interesting chapels including that of the Cesi family designed by Antonio da Sangallo the Younger, who also designed the **dome** of the church, built by Jacopo Ungarino in 1524, and the Pozzetti Chapel, frescoed by Baldassare Peruzzi. To the side of the church is the elegant **cloister** on two superposed orders, built in 1500-1504 for Cardinal Oliviero Carafa, that was Bramante's first commission in Rome.

PALAZZO ALTEMPS

It was count Girolamo Riario, nephew of Pope Sixtus IV and the husband of Caterina Sforza, who in the late 15th century commissioned the architect Baldassare Peruzzi to build a massive palace with a simple Renaissance **facade** and a Doric-style **courtyard** adorned with ancient statues. The work continued even after the palace passed into the hands of the cardinal of Volterra, Francesco Soderini, and in 1568 to Cardinal Marco Sittico Altemps. The latter owner commissioned Martino Longhi the Elder, who is also the author of the tall panoramic tower with its loggia on the roof and belvedere, to complete the construction. Cardinal Altemps revealed himself as a great collector of ancient art, and in this activity he was favored by his friendship with Pope Clement VII, whose candidacy to the papacy he had promoted. As a sign of his gratitude, Clement VII presented the Altemps family with a precious relic: the body of his far-off predecessor Saint Anicetus. This relic, a unique case of private burial of a pope, was moved to the palace **chapel**, frescoed with scenes of the saint's life and martyrdom by Ottavio Leoni and Pomarancio.

The precious **Altemps Collection** of ancient statuary suffered a quite different fate. It was broken up in the eighteenth and nineteenth centuries, when the palace became the property of the Spanish Sacred College, and only 16 pieces survived; these are today on display in the building, now a section of the **Museo Nazionale Romano** inaugurated in December 1997, together with two analogous collections: the **Boncompagni Ludovisi Collection** and the **Mattei Collection**, both transferred here from the Museo delle Terme. The former of these, the largest and the most prestigious, was begun by Cardinal Ludovico Ludovisi, who collected examples of ancient statuary to adorn his villa built around 1621 between the Pincio and the Quirinale on the site of the ancient *Horti Sallustiani*. Other statues that came to light during the work for construction of the villa were added to the collection: the so-called *Acrolito* and the *Galatian Killing his Wife* (found together with the *Dying Galatian*, which is now in the Capitoline Museum); later there were added the *Ares*, the *Athena*, and the *Large Ludovisi Sarcophagus*. The restoration and integration of these priceless marbles was entrusted to sculptors of the caliber of Bernini and Algardi, who with their master's touch returned statues like the *Hermes Loghios*, the *Dadophoros*, and the *Bathing Aphrodite* to their original splendor.

Palazzo Altemps. The busts of Marcus Aurelius and Demeter; left, the bust of Mars Ultor with helmed head.

Below, the 17th-century facade of Palazzo Madama, home of the Senate, and the building in a period print.

PALAZZO MADAMA

In imperial Roman times, the site of today's Palazzo Madama, the prestigious home of the Senate of the Republic, was that of Nero's Baths.

In the 12th century, it was under the control of the Crescenzi family, who built on it a tower that is now incorporated into the Senate building. In 1478 Sinulfo, Bishop of Chiusi and treasurer of Sixtus IV, purchased an extensive property bordering on that of the Crescenzis, on which he had built a palace that later passed to the Medici family. Margherita of Austria, who married duke Alessandro in 1533, resided in the palace during her stays in Rome; the building thus acquired the popular epithet of 'Madama'.
During the pontificate of Sixtus V, Cosimo II de' Medici

commissioned Cingoli to restore the building, but his plans were concretized only in 1649 by Cardi and Marucelli, who created the splendid **facade**, in Florentine Baroque style, on three levels with three different motifs for the window decoration, surmounted by an elegant cornice.

PALAZZO DELLA CANCELLERIA AND SAN LORENZO IN DAMASO

In 1517, Cardinal Raffaele Riario - responsible for the construction of this palace, begun in 1485 by a group of architects that included the young Bramante - deeded the building to the pontifical domain. It thus became the seat of the Papal Chancery, although its role changed various times through the centuries.
The severe, monumental exterior of the palace, with its rectilinear travertine **facade** faced on the ground floor with rustic work, with arched windows and two elegant portals, is counterbalanced by the sumptuous **interiors**.
The smaller of the two portals on the facade, built by Vignola in the 16th century, leads in to the church of **San Lorenzo in Damaso**, founded by Pope Damasus in 380 and later absorbed by Cardinal Riario's palace and completely rebuilt at the time of its construction.

Caravaggio's canvas of The Calling of Saint Matthew *in the church of San Luigi dei Francesi, Contarelli Chapel.*

SAN LUIGI DEI FRANCESI

The national church of the French community in Rome was begun in 1518 and completed in 1589, thanks above all to the generosity of Caterina de' Medici, who made available the many family properties in the area. The travertine **facade**, built by Domenico Fontana to plans by Della Porta, opens into a three-aisled **interior** entirely faced in stuccowork and precious marbles in the 18th century by Antoine Derizet and dominated by Natoire's fresco, on the vault, of the *Apotheosis of Saint Louis*, the saint and king to whom the church is dedicated.

But it is in the side chapels, with their frescoes and paintings by the greatest masters of the Roman Seicento, that the most important of the church's artistic treasures are preserved. In 1614, Domenichino decorated the Chapel of Santa Cecilia with some of his most successful frescoes, but it was above all Caravaggio who made this church famous, with the works preserved in the **Contarelli Chapel**.

The decoration of the chapel was begun by the Cavalier d'Arpino in 1591 and completed in 1600 by Merisi, who created the three canvases depicting the *Calling* and the *Martyrdom of Saint Matthew* and *Saint Matthew and the Angel*. The first version of the latter painting was judged to be indecorous; a second version was painted by the master in 1602 and hung in the chapel the same year. The incriminated first version, which found its way into the Prussian royal collection in Berlin, was destroyed in the bombings of World War II.

SANT'IVO ALLA SAPIENZA

In 1642, the Palazzo della Sapienza, seat of the Roman university, acquired one of the most singular and equally most emblematic creations ever born of the genius of Borromini. The courtyard of the *Studium Urbis*, which at the time terminated in a concave facade, was completed by the

Sant'Andrea della Valle. The 17th-century dome and octagonal tambour with large windows.

Sant'Ivo alla Sapienza. The lanternino designed by Borromini and topped by the stucco-decorated spiral scroll.

Sant'Andrea della Valle. Above, the funeral monument to Pope Pius II Piccolomini; below, a view of the interior illuminated by wide windows.

addition of an attic on which the architect from Ticino erected the multifoiled lantern of the **dome** and decorated the intersection with tambours bearing the coat-of-arms of the Chigi family. The church was completed under Pope Alexander VII Chigi in about 1600.s completed. Over the lantern there rises the tiered 'cap' of the dome, then the *lanternino*, and finally, surrounded by travertine torches, the stucco-decorated 'scroll' that terminates in a flame from which a tiara, a globe, and a wrought-iron cross rise.

SANT'ANDREA DELLA VALLE

Together with the Gesù and the church of Sant'Ignazio, Sant'Andrea della Valle is an emblem of the Counter-Reformist spirit. It is the most important church of the Theatine monks, that religious order that more coherently than any other incarnated Tridentine orthodoxy. It was in fact a member of the order, Father Grimaldi, who continued the work begun in 1591 by Olivieri and who supervised construction until, in the early 17th century, he was replaced by Maderno, who completed the original structure by raising, in 1622, the enormous **dome** that is second in height only to Saint Peter's. But completion of the **facade** had to wait for Rainaldi, who built it in collaboration with Carlo Fontana to plans by Maderno, inspired by the facade of the Church of Gesù although accentuating the Baroque elements.

The same is true for the **interior**, a huge single nave with a short transept and six communicating side chapels. In the vestibule are two *funeral monuments* transferred here from the Old Saint Peter's Basilica in 1614: both are to Piccolomini popes, Pius II and Pius III, and were created by Andrea Bregno and Sebastiano di Francesco Ferrucci, respectively. The importance of this church nevertheless derives primarily from the many precious works of art that adorn its interior.

Santo Spirito dei Napolitani - The church of the Neapolitan community was completely restructured in the early 17th century by Domenico Fontana and Ottaviano Mascherino, and completed in the following century by Carlo Fontana. In the interior, besides the *Martyrdom of San Gennaro* by Luca Giordano, are the tombs of the last Bourbon rulers of Naples, Francis II and Maria Sophia, who lived as exiles in the nearby Palazzo Farnese. The interior was restored, like the facade, by Antonio Cipolla.

Palazzo Ricci - Built in the late Quattrocento, this palace changed hands many times before it was purchased by Giulio Ricci in 1577. It owes its notoriety to its frescoed facade, the work of Maturino da Firenze and Polidoro da Caravaggio, illustrating episodes from the *History of Rome*. Large portions of the frescoes are still intact today.

San Girolamo della Carità - Built over the home of the matron Paola, who had offered hospitality to Saint Jerome in 382, the church was flanked by a hospital and a convent by order of Pope Martin V. It was here that Saint Philip Neri founded his institute.
In the mid-17th century the building was rebuilt in Baroque style and given a new facade, the work of Carlo Rainaldi. In the interior, the elegant play of polychrome marbles and the harmonious forms of the **Spada Chapel** illustrate the genius of its creator, Borromini.

PALAZZO FARNESE (p. 142)

CAMPO DE' FIORI (p. 143)

SANT'ELIGIO DEGLI OREFICI (p. 145)

Santa Maria di Monserrato - The church, built to a sketch by Antonio da Sangallo the Younger, is dedicated to the Virgin of Montserrat in Catalonia, recalled in the 18th-century group of the *Virgin and Child Cutting Stone* on the facade. The name Montserrat indicates a stone quarry. In 1817, Ferdinand VII of Spain decided to close San Giacomo degli Spagnoli in Piazza Navona and to make Santa Maria the Spanish national church, which it still is today, and to bring to it a number of works of art, including Sansovino's statue of *Saint James*.

Santa Brigida - The patroness of Sweden to whom the Scandinavian national church is dedicated lived in Rome, in the adjacent convent, from 1354 until her death in 1358. In 1393, the year of her canonization, Boniface IX commissioned the building of the church; it was often renovated and in the 18th century finally rebuilt as we see it today.

Palazzo Falconieri - The facade of this building, today the home of the Hungarian Academy, stands out for its singular pilaster strips in the form of caryatids with female torsos and falcons' heads, allusive to the coat-of-arms of the Falconieri family. Like the rear loggia overlooking the Tiber, they were designed by Borromini in 1646.

San Salvatore in Onda - Even following many renovations, this small basilica from the early Middle Ages still exhibits a pre-Romanesque structure with ancient columns and a crypt built over a 2nd-century building. The name derives from the frequent flooding to which it was subject.

Santa Maria dell'Orazione e Morte - The church, built on the site of the hermitage of Cardinal Odoardo, is a masterpiece by the genial Ferdinando Fuga, who designed the splendid domed *elliptical* structure. The winged skulls that act as corbels on the center portal and the macabre marble slab in the facade over the offertory box allude to the tasks of the pious confraternity for which it was built.

Santissima Trinità dei Pellegrini - Today's church rises on the site of the ancient San Benedetto in Arenula, granted by Pope Paul IV in 1558 to Saint Philip Neri, the founder of the Confraternita dei Pellegrini e dei Convalescenti that managed the adjacent hospice. It was enlarged beginning in 1603, and in the same year Paolo Maggi began work on the church, which was completed in 1723 with the erection of the facade by Francesco De Sanctis, also the designer of the Spanish Steps. The interior houses exceptional works of art, including the *Holy Trinity* by Guido Reni, who also frescoed the interior of the lantern.

Santa Maria della Quercia - This small church originated in the 14th century and owes its name to the cattle dealers from Viterbo, whose patron was the Virgin of the Oak. In 1523 they were absorbed by the Confraternity of Butchers, which in 1727 commissioned Raguzzini to reconstruct the church in its present rococo style.

Santa Barbara dei Librai - Known in the Middle Ages as Santa Barbara in Satro, the church was granted to the Confraternity of Booksellers in 1306 by Clement V. In 1608, a member of the congregation, the Florentine printer Zanoni Massotti, had it rebuilt to plans by Passeri.

SAN CARLO AI CATINARI
(p. 145)

PALAZZO AND GALLERIA SPADA
(p. 144)

Santa Maria in Monticelli - This church, of very ancient origin, was rebuilt under Paschal II in 1101. Witness of its Romanesque past is today borne by the **bell tower** and the apse with a fragment of the mosaic that once decorated it. The Baroque facade is an 18th-century work by Matteo Sassi.

San Paolino alla Regola - Built over the house in which Saint Paul stayed during his Roman apostolate and renovated in 1684 by Bergonzoni, when the lively yet harmonious facade by Sardi and del Cioli was also added. Alongside the church are the 13th-century **Case di San Paolo** (in the photo) that give us an idea of the look of the district in the Middle Ages.

CAMPO DE' FIORI AND THE REGOLA DISTRICT

*T*he name of the district derives from renula or arenula, the ancient term for the sand banks formed by the Tiber along its left bank in this area of the city. Since earliest times, the economic and social life of this area of Rome has been conditioned by its close relationship with the river. The district arose in the southern portion of the Campus Martius *near the Forum Boarium, the Forum Holitorium, and the Portus Tiberinus,* the major landing for the boats that plied the Tiber, and it was here, in fact, that the Navalia, the boatyards, were installed. But there were also important places of worship like the Temple of Neptune, and porticoes and crafts workshops. This intimate relationship with the Tiber continued on into the Middle Ages, when the river became the driving force for the mills that processed the great quantities of grain laid in in the nearby storehouses.

The area thus increased in population, and the homes of those craftsmen who had their shops in the area began to rise near the churches and the monasteries, which had theretofore been rather isolated. Many of the street names reflect this crafts vocation. In the midst of the modest dwellings of the common folk were built the great homes of the titled Roman families, like the Cenci, the Savelli, and the Salomoni, who disputed control of this important area of the city. In the mid-15th century, Renaissance palaces began to replace the medieval buildings and a new urban structure began to emerge.

At the beginning of the following century, the opening of **Via Giulia** and the construction of **Palazzo Farnese** sparked a true urban revolution characterized by the construction of sumptuous patrician residences like those of the **Falconieri**, the **Ricci**, and the Capodiferro families; many were set in luxuriant gardens on the Tiber.

The closeness of Saint Peter's, made more accessible by the new Via Giulia, sparked the building and/or enlargement of hospices maintained by the national churches for foreign pilgrims to the Holy City, who were particularly numerous during the Jubilee years. Thus, alongside the church of **Santa Brigida** in Piazza Farnese there rose the hospice of the Swedes, while the Spaniards and the English were offered hospitality at the churches of **Santa Maria di Monserrato** and of **San Tommaso**. Another powerful stimulus to construction and restructuring of the hospices was provided by the confraternities, some of which were formed of members of crafts corporations or guilds, like the butchers, who had (and have) their headquarters in **Santa Maria della Quercia**, or the goldsmiths, based in **Sant'Eligio degli Orefici**. But there were also confraternities established for humanitarian and charitable aims, like that of **Orazione e Morte**, based at the church of the same name, whose members' task was to provide burial for abandoned corpses, or Saint Philip Neri's Confraternita dei Pellegrini e Convalescenti that managed the hospice for pilgrims and convalescents at **Santissima Trinità dei Pellegrini**.

The proximity of the district to the river was not always idyllic: civil and religious buildings were damaged from time to time by floods, and frequent restoration was a necessity; for this reason, the banks of the Tiber were raised in the 19th century. Despite this improvement, which together with the work that followed when Rome was made capital of Italy caused a substantial upset of the topography, the area still has managed to conserve picturesque corners where time seems to have stopped.

CAMPO DE' FIORI R.VI

PALAZZO FARNESE

The elegant and compact Palazzo Farnese, which due precisely to its compactness has earned the popular epithet of 'Farnese Cube', stands in the heart of the Regola district. The well-balanced facade, designed by Michelangelo, commands **Piazza Farnese** below, with its two **fountains** by Girolamo Rainaldi. The marble lilies from which the water falls into the marble-and-granite basin repeat the heraldic irises, symbol of the Farnese family, that run along the string-courses of the building: the stylistic coherence thus created between palace and piazza is practically unique.

The complex story of the construction of Palazzo Farnese began in the second half of the 15th century, when Cardinal Alessandro Farnese bought a building from the Augustinian fathers. Together with adjoining structures purchased later, it formed the nucleus of his future residence near the Via Giulia, then under construction, which provided him with easy access to the Vatican. In 1523, Antonio da Sangallo the Younger finally set his hand to the actual building of the palace. But the cardinal, who had in the meantime been elected pope with the name of Paul III, soon came to see the original plans as obsolete.

At the death of Sangallo in 1546, another Tuscan architect took over the work. Michelangelo made radical changes to the original plans and completed Sangallo's building in sumptuous forms more congenial to the status of his patron; he crowned his creation with a rich cornice, and, taking his inspiration from the neighboring Theater of Marcellus, built the **gallery** along the first floor in the **courtyard**. When Vignola took over the work, he added the back wing with its two **loggias**, complementing which Della Porta, who completed the building in 1589, built a third. In the meantime, the interior was being decorated by a veritable host of artists, among whom Zuccari, the Caraccis, and Domenichino, with some of their best works. In the early 1600s, as the start of an unfinished but ambitious project that called for bridging the Tiber to link Palazzo Farnese and Villa Farnesina alla Lungara, the Via Giulia **archway** was built between the superb palace and the retreat of Cardinal Odoardo, replaced in the following century by the church of Santa Maria dell'Orazione e Morte. When the Farnese family died out in the 18th century, the property was inherited by the Bourbons, who carried off to their royal palaces in Naples and Caserta a goodly part of the Farnese furnishings and statuary. It was thus that the famous *Farnese Hercules*, which with other masterpieces stood in the courtyard, reached what is still its home in the Archaeological Museum of Naples. After having served as the residence of the last king of Naples, Francis II, and of his wife Maria Sophia, exiled to Rome after the annexation of the Kingdom of the Two Sicilies to the Kingdom of Italy, in 1870 the palace was rented to France and is still the seat of that country's Embassy.

*Piazza Farnese.
One of the two fountains decorated with the Farnese iris and a corner of Palazzo Farnese showing Michelangelo's cornice.*

Church of Santa Maria dell'Orazione e Morte. The plaque of the offertory box, the proceeds from which were once spent for giving Christian burial to the bodies of the unknown dead.

Campo de' Fiori. Right, the flower market.

Campo de' Fiori. Above, three images suggesting the typical atmosphere of the district: a devotional medallion of the Virgin, the monument to Giordano Bruno, and the buildings lining the square, with the picturesque restaurants, shops, and wine-sellers.

CAMPO DE' FIORI

The special atmosphere that makes Campo de' Fiori one of Rome's most authentic milieus changes hour by hour, just as its colors and the sounds that invade the fascinating space, bounded by picturesque small buildings and charming shops, make spectrum shifts according to the time of day. In the morning, the brightly-colored **market** fills the square with the voices of the hawkers who sing the praises of their wares: fruit and vegetables, meats and cheeses, clothing and household goods. But in the late morning, as the last of the vendors' stalls are carted away, silence falls as though by magic and the feel of Campo de' Fiori becomes almost intimate, with the only sounds the discreet footfalls of Roman and foreign passers-by. At dusk, especially in summer, the square comes alive again, with visitors attracted by the typical **cafes**, **taverns**, **restaurants**, and **wine-shops** that face on it and the streets off it, while strolling musicians fill the air with their music.

In the past, however, the spectacles and pastimes were of quite a different kind: although Campo de' Fiori was the theater of festive events such as horse-races, jousts, and tournaments, it was also the site of executions, including that of the philosopher **Giordano Bruno**, who was accused of

heresy and burned at the stake in February of the year 1600, as the 19th-century monument by Ettore Ferrari, at the center of the square, reminds us. And it was so even despite its poetical name, which traditionally derives from the flowers that grew on the site when it was no more than a meadow sloping down toward the Tiber - that is, before Pope Eugenius IV had it paved in the mid-1400s. Another tradition has the name deriving from Flora, the mistress of that Pompey who built his grandiose theater, adjoining the Temple of Venus Victrix, on the site that is now the square.

Over the centuries homes and palaces, but also hotels, inns, and taverns, were built lining the square: for example, the Hostaria della Vacca and that 'della Fontana', both managed by Vanozza Cattanei, the mistress of Pope Alexander VI Borgia. They are still recognizable thanks to the signs that attracted customers, the forerunners of the picturesque stopping-places that still today offer hospitality to both the Roman and the tourist to the city.

The Campo de' Fiori marketplace in an 18th-century print: on the far right, the side of Palazzo Pio Righetti, and at the center the fountain at which the animals sold in the market were watered.

PALAZZO AND GALLERIA SPADA

The very **facade** of this palace, today the home of the Council of State and one of the most important art museums in the city, surprises the visitor. It owes its architectural affiatus and the imaginative design of the decoration to some of the most farseeing architects of the time: Bartolomeo Baronio was followed by Giulio Mazzoni in the construction of this singular building commissioned in the mid-16th century by Cardinal Girolamo Capodiferro. To Mazzoni we owe the interesting decoration of the courtyard and the facade, which consists in four superimposed orders that alternate three rows of windows of differing sizes and complex decorative apparatuses with simple, flat rustication from the first floor up. The facade at the first floor lev-

el features eight niches containing the **statues** of illustrious figures in the history of ancient Rome: Trajan, Pompey, Quintus Fabius Maximus, Romulus, Numa Pompilio, Marcellus, Caesar, and Augustus; at the mezzanine level above, instead, is a series of garlands with cherubs and caryatids and medallions depicting a dog standing near a burning column and a scroll with a Latin motto, the emblem of Cardinal Capodiferro. On the last floor, crowning the building, the windows alternate with eight panels bearing inscriptions relative to the exploits of the eight historical figures that appear in the niches on the *piano nobile*. Mazzoni employed the same extraordinary imaginativeness in the decoration of the **courtyard**, which is adorned with elegant reliefs of a *Battle of Centaurs* and *Scenes of the Hunt* as well as with statues of the *Olympian gods*. Following the death of Cardinal Capodiferro, in 1559 the building passed to his mother and his nephew Pietro Paolo Mignanelli and then, in 1632, to Cardinal Francesco Spada, who commissioned Borromini to carry out renovation. Borromini, in collaboration with Maruscelli and Della Greca, made a number of fantastic modifications to the original structure.

The most sensational was the creation of the so-called **Prospective Gallery**, a corridor nine meters in length that thanks to peculiar architectural sleights of hand appears instead to be thirty-seven. Borromini, in developing an original idea by the Augustinian friar Giovanni Maria di Bitonto, in fact created a singular play of perspective by building a slightly inclined floor with a series of arches and columns that decrease in size and height from the near to the far end of the corridor so as to create the illusion of greater length. The illusion is so effective that the statue of *Mercury* set at the end of the gallery, as the focus of the perspective, seems much larger than it actually is.

The **Galleria Spada**, which contains the works of art collected by Cardinal Bernardino Spada, is instead of a completely different nature. Here, works by the most important painters of the seventeenth century are exhibited in accordance with the tried-and-true criterion of the seventeenth-century private picture gallery: Titian, Mattia Preti, Baciccia, Guercino, Guido Reni, Annibale Caracci, Rubens, Solimena, and Orazio and Artemisia Gentileschi are only a few of the artists represented here.

Palazzo Spada. The stucco decoration of the street facade and the walls of the courtyard; the porticoed courtyard.

SAN CARLO AI CATINARI

This church, commissioned by the Barnabiti fathers in honor of Saint Charles Borromeo shortly after his canonization, owes its name to the many tinsmiths' shops that were situated in the vicinity in the early 17th century, when construction of the church began, and that produced mainly *catini*, or basins and bowls.

Built according to a plan showing the strong influence of late Renaissance architecture, the church, by Rosati - also the author of the tall **dome**, Rome's third highest - was completed in 1638 with the erection of the **facade** by Gian Battista Soria.

The works of famous 17th-century artists decorate the interior with superb compositions immortalizing episodes from the life of the dedicatory saint. On the inside facade, Gregorio and Mattia Preti painted two frescoes of *Saint Charles' Crusade against Heresy* and *Saint Charles Giving Alms*, and in the facing vault of the apse Lanfranco depicted *Saint Charles in Glory*; the **choir** was decorated by Guido Reni with a beautiful *Praying Saint Charles*, and finally, on the high altar, the work of Martino Longhi the Younger, is Pietro da Cortona's depiction of *Saint Charles leading a procession in Milan to ward off the plague*.

Domenichino painted the four *Cardinal Virtues* in the pendentives of the dome in about 1630, and toward the end of the century Antonio Gherardi, who had previously worked on the decoration of Santa Maria in Trivio, completed the theatrical ornamentation of the Chapel of Saint Cecilia with imaginative, elaborate plays of color and perspective.

Palazzo Spada. Borromini's column-lined Prospective Gallery.

SANT'ELIGIO DEGLI OREFICI

This small jewel of Roman Renaissance architecture, the headquarters of the Confraternity of Goldsmiths, is one of the rare surviving works by Raphael in the guise of architect. Although it clearly shows the influence of Bramante the design of the building is Raphael's alone, and the artist from Urbino personally supervised the start of its construction in 1516. The work was brought to completion by Baldassare Peruzzi, who took over as site manager at Raphael's death in 1520. The **facade** of the small Greek-cross church, with its graciously airy, small hemispherical **dome**, was seriously damaged in the following century and was rebuilt by the able late-Renaissance architect Flaminio Ponzio, who created a simple, well-proportioned frontage in perfect keeping with Raphael's original plan.

The small church of Sant'Eligio degli Orefici, designed by Raphael in the full flower of the Renaissance.

The same absolute economy of form also dominates in the **interior**, which Raphael probably expected to decorate himself. Its surprisingly elegant simplicity lends harmonizes well with the works by Romanelli and Taddeo Zuccari that adorn the walls.

The late-Renaissance facade of the church of San Carlo ai Catinari.

THE JANICULUM

*T*he verdant heights of the Janiculum hill (Gianicolo in Italian) derive their name from Janus, who in antiquity had a temple here. The hill, prevalently composed of yellow sand, was also called Mons Aureus (Hill of Gold), preserved in the name of the church of St. Peter Montorio, which stands where an ancient although unfounded tradition claims that St. Peter was martyred. The hill was sparsely populated even in Roman times, with the exception of several villas with gardens that reached to the Tiber, such as those of the poet Martial and of Caesar, whose marvelous gardens were left to the Roman people in his last will and testament. The Janiculum was placed inside of the protected city with the construction of the **Aurelian walls**, whose only passage here was through the present **Porta San Pancrazio**, through which one of the busiest of the Roman consular roads, the **via Aurelia**, ran. Below the ridge of the hill ran another important road that bordered the river and passed through Porta Portuense (now Porta Portese), reaching the maritime ports of Claudius and Trajan. Part of the route, also called via sub Janiculo, was incorporated into the via Santa, begun by Sixtus IV for the Jubilee of 1475 and linking the Vatican with the so-called Ripa Romea or Ripa Grande, the river port on the Tiber where the pilgrims disembarked to visit the tomb of St. Peter. The road also connected the Ponte Santa Maria, or Sanatorio, with the present Ponte Rotto, which provided a rapid linear route to the Boarium Forum and from there to the Jubilee basilicas of St. John Lateran and Santa Maria Maggiore.

At the beginning of the 1500s, using some of the roads built under Sixtus, Julius II had Bramante plan a circuit that ran parallel to the banks of the Tiber, with Via Giulia on the left bank and **Via della Lungara** on the right. The meeting points of the two routes were to be Ponte Sisto and Ponte Giulio, or the Sixtus and Julius bridges, although the latter was designed but never built. Via della Lungara, which was straighter than the previous Via Santa up to **Porta Settimiana**, connected the Trastevere with the Borgo rione. From there the roads split again, climbing the sides of the hill, at times narrowing into the sharply turning lanes, along which stood only occasional houses.

Apart from these changes, the area continued to maintain its suburban character. It was dominated by vast green areas in the midst of which, between the 15th and 16th centuries, rose up splendid buildings such as **Villa Farnesina**, **Palazzo Corsini alla Lungara**, **Palazzo Salviati** the panoramic **Villa Lante** and **Villa Aurelia**, and the churches of **San Pietro in Montorio**, with its famous **Tempietto by Bramante**, and **Sant'Onofrio**. In the 1600s, Urban VIII reinforced the western side of Janiculum, which had proved to be a weak point in the defense of the city during the sack of Rome in 1527, thus strengthening the defensive line between the head of the ponte vaticano composed of the Città Leonina and Castel Sant'Angelo, and the Aurelian Walls, which marked off the Trastevere precinct.

Janiculum remained unchanged during the following century, when the **Botanical Gardens** of Rome were established there. In the 1800s, the hill was significantly altered, first under Pius IX with the opening of the present Via Garibaldi, which linked the area more directly with Trastevere. After that, when Rome became the capital of Italy, development continued with the construction of the **Passeggiata**, a broad avenue, and of the **Janiculum Terrace**, which provides one of the most breathtaking **views** of the city. In 1849 the hill was the scene of battles between French troops, coming to the aid of the Papal State, and of the Roman Republic troops, under the command of Garibaldi, who has a **monument** dedicated to him on the terrace.

Faro del Gianicolo - The square beneath the light tower, donated by Italians living in Argentina, offers the most complete **panorama** of Rome.

Sant'Onofrio al Gianicolo - The church and convent were built in the mid-15th century on a pre-existing oratory built by the hermit Nicola da Forca Palena. The **convent** has a stupendous 15th-century **cloister**, whose lunettes were frescoed with *Stories of St. Onophrius* by 17th-century masters. The lunettes of the portico depicting *Stories in the life of St. Jerome* are instead by Domenichino. To the left rises the Oratory of the Madonna del Rosario, with its fine Baroque facade. The interior of the main church, with a single nave, contains the *funerary monument to Torquato Tasso*, who died in the adjoining convent, beautiful frescoes in the apse depicting *Stories of Mary*, of uncertain attribution, and works that are attributed to Peruzzi, in the upper part, and to Pinturicchio, in the lower section.

Villa Lante - The villa was built on the remains of the villa of Martial by Giulio Romano for Baldassarre Turini between 1517 and 1527. After several decades, the villa began to change ownership frequently. During the 1800s, when it was converted into a novicate, the *frescoes* by Polidoro da Caravaggio and Giulio Romano were removed. Today they are kept in Palazzo Zuccari. The building currently houses the Embassy of Finland.

Monument to Anita Garibaldi - This 1932 monument pays homage to the memory of Anna Maria Ribeiro da Silva, the first wife of the illustrious leader of the struggle for Italian statehood, to whom she bore three children. After fighting by his side in 1849 at Porta San Pancrazio against French troops, she died shortly thereafter, weakened by her efforts and not yet 30 years old. The remains of Anita are kept under the statue.

Monument to Giuseppe Garibaldi - Gallori's 1895 monument to the Hero of two Worlds was placed here to dominate the **Janiculum Terrace** and commemorate the strenuous defense of the Roman Republic, created by Mazzini, against French troops. One of the best views of the city, which unfolds at the foot of the hill in all of its grandiose and monumental beauty, can be enjoyed from here.

Palazzo Salviati - The palace, created for Filippo Adimari, secret counsel to Leo X, was the work of Giulio Romano, who built it in 1520 with an airy loggia along the facade facing gardens and a harmonious chapel in the style of Bramante. The building passed to Cardinal Salviati in the middle of the century and was enlarged by Nanni di Baccio Bigio to its present form. Today it houses military institutes.

Villa Farnesina - Baldassarre Peruzzi designed this villa for banker Agostino Chigi in the early 1500s in the typical style of Roman Classicism. In 1590 it was bought by the Farnese family, who had planned to join it, with a bridge over the Tiber, to their palace on the opposite bank. In the 1800s, when the embankments of the Tiber were being restored, the villa lost part of its gardens and the river-front loggia, which was attributed to Raphael. Raphael also drew the cartoons for the frescoes of the *Loggia of Psyche* and of the fine wall painting of *Galatea* on a chariot pulled by dolphins. Other frescoes in the villa are by masters of the 1500s, including Peruzzi, Sebastiano del Piombo, Giulio Romano and Sodoma.

PALAZZO CORSINI ALLA LUNGARA
(p. 148)

Porta Settimiana - The gate was rebuilt on the site of a *posterula* of the Aurelian walls by Pope Alexander VI in 1498 with corbels and Ghilbelline merlons and restored three centuries later by Pius VI.

Orto Botanico - Rome's Botanical Gardens, started in the 1600s atop the hills of the Janiculum, were moved in 1883 to the gardens of Palazzo Corsini, after having occupied for a short time the gardens of Palazzo Salviati. The presentation of several plant environments is interesting and, together with the *Serra Corsini*, a greenhouse containing orchids and Euphorbiaceae, and with the *Serra Storica*, with its tropical plants, the gardens offer an exhaustive panorama of the main European and exotic species.

SAN PIETRO IN MONTORIO AND THE TEMPIETTO OF BRAMANTE
(p. 149)

Porta San Pancrazio - This gate replaced the Porta Aurelia during the restoration work of Urban VIII, who had the fortified walls around the Janiculum built. The present appearance is due to Vespignani, who restored the previous 17th-century structure after the damages inflicted by the French artillery in 1849. The building houses the **Museo Garibaldino**.

Villa Aurelia - Built for Cardinal Girolamo Farnese in 1650 from one of the towers of the Aurelian walls, it was rebuilt in the mid-1800s after the damages caused by the artillery of the French army, coming to the aid of the Papal State against the troops of Mazzini's Roman Republic.

Bosco Parrasio - This small wooded section of the Janiculum was donated by the King of Portugal, John V, to the Academy of Arcadia, established in 1690 by Giovanni Maria Crescimbeni from the academy created by Queen Christina of Sweden and the literati who frequented the salon of Palazzo Corsini. The Academy enjoyed great prestige during the 18th century, thanks especially to Metastasio, who was its most important member.

Fontana dell'Acqua Paola - In the early 1600s, to celebrate the restoration of the Trajan Aqueduct promoted by Paul V, Flaminio Peruzzi and Giovanni Fontana designed this spectacular Baroque fountain, inspired by the antique triumphal arches of the Forum. The Romans call it the **'Fontanone'** (big fountain) because of its impressive size.

PALAZZO CORSINI ALLA LUNGARA

The palace was originally a suburban villa built for Cardinal Raffaello Riario, nephew of Pope Sixtus IV, on Via della Lungara (at the time the Via Santa) that linked the building with the Forum Boarium area and with San Giorgio al Velabro, of which church the cardinal was the prelate. Construction work begun in the late 15th century continued under Julius II with the enlargement of the original structure. By the 17th century, the villa consisted of a main building with only nine windows on two floors and secondary facade overlooking the gardens (today's **Botanical Gardens**) that rose with the hill to the Casino dei Quattro Venti, probably built for the Riario family by Mattia De' Rossi and destroyed in 1849. The palace knew one of its moments of greatest importance when from 1659 onward it hosted queen Christina of Sweden, who having attracted a conspicuous court of men of letters and artists, founded the first Roman Academy. Following her death in 1689, the institute took the name of Arcadia and moved to the nearby **Bosco Parrasio** on the slopes of the Janiculum.

The year 1736 marked a turning point in the life of the building. It was purchased by the Corsini family following Lorenzo Corsini's election as Pope Clement XII and chosen as the Roman residence of the noble Florentine family, who transferred their well-stocked library and precious art collection here. Ferdinando Fuga was commissioned to enlarge and restructure the villa, and when the scaffolding came down it had been transformed into a three-story palace with 21 windows. Fuga also designed the **facade**, which already tended toward Neoclassical essentiality with its massive stone pilaster strips and crowning balustrade, and a carriageable vestibule with a monumental **staircase**. The Corsini family took special interest in the **gardens**, which they enhanced with new plants, statues, and plays of water, but above all, they were great collectors of art and of books, beginning with Cardinal Neri, nephew of Pope Clement XII, who set aside the two new wings built by Fuga for the **Biblioteca** and the **Galleria Corsini**. The latter, still structured as though it were a private picture gallery, contains mostly works marking the transition from Baroque to Classicism and juxtaposes, in an ideal artistic itinerary, *Saint John the Baptist* by Caravaggio and the works of his most illustrious followers (Orazio Gentileschi, Gerard Seghers, etc.) with the works of 18th-century painters of Classical and Neoclassical inspiration (Maratta, Pannini, Batoni), and also contains many works by Neapolitan artists and by the so-called 'primitives' (Andrea di Cione, Beato Angelico), added to the collection in the 1800s. The palace is the home of the prestigious **Accademia Nazionale dei Lincei**.

Palazzo Corsini alla Lungara, the neo-classical facade and a view of the interior.

A view of the Botanical Gardens

The gardens on the Janiculum.

SAN PIETRO IN MONTORIO AND BRAMANTE'S TEMPIETTO

The pontificate of Sixtus IV, which promoted many urban and public works at the foot of the Janiculum hill and in the adjacent Trastevere area, was sealed, so to speak, with the construction of a church between 1481 and 1500 by Ferdinand II of Aragon that became both a symbol of the Faith and of the magnificence of its patrons. The **church** and **convent** of San Pietro in Montorio rose on the spot where an ancient and unfounded tradition held that the first pope of the Church was martyred (in reality St. Peter was crucified in the Stadium of Nero, next to St. Peter's in the Vatican).

The complex, built on the site of an earlier 9th-century church, was designed by Baccio Pontelli in the most complete respect of Renaissance architectural dictates. It nevertheless displays the enduring Gothic influence, traceable in the rose window of the simple **facade** of the church. The facade, to which the staircase was added in the 1600s, is attributed to the school of Andrea Bregno.

The **interior**, with its single nave with cross and domical vaults also showing the influence of Gothic architecture, is characterized by numerous side chapels, originally niches, that contain artistic masterpieces of immense value. The first chapel to the right of the entrance holds an intense *Flagellation of Christ*, done in 1518 by Sebastiano del Piombo from a probable design of Michelangelo, while the fourth chapel on the same side contains the *Conversion of St. Paul* by Vasari, whose self-portrait is the man dressed in black on the left side. Until 1809 the apse contained the *Transfiguration* by Raphael, since moved to the Vatican Galleries and substituted by a copy of the *Crucifixion of St. Peter* by Guido Reni, whose original is also in the Vatican. The works carried out during the Baroque period are best and most completely represented by the fine **Raymondi Chapel** of Gian Lorenzo Bernini.

But the jewel of San Pietro in Montorio is undoubtedly

The facade of San Pietro in Montorio, with its double stairway.

the **Tempietto of Bramante**, built by the architect from the Marches between 1508 and 1512 in the first cloister of the convent (rebuilt in the first half of the 16th century), above the supposed hole in the ground made by the cross of St. Peter.

Sacred tradition and the ideals of classical antiquity induced Bramante to choose a circular plan for his harmonious creation, the quintessence of architecture and idealized space typical of the Renaissance. The structure is articulated by Etruscan columns and a hemispheric cupola; a surrounding circular courtyard was designed by Bramante to grace the small temple, but it was never executed. The interior encloses two overlapping spaces: the upper area, redesigned during the Baroque period and containing a 16th-century *statue of St. Peter* by the Lombard school; and below, the crypt–reached by a double ramp of stairs by Bernini–with the hole made by the cross on which the saint was erroneously said to have died.

The Tempietto of Bramante, a pure expression of the artistic conceptions of the Renaissance.

THE PANTHEON AND THE PIGNA DISTRICT

*I*n ancient times, the vast flat area now occupied by this district and then known as the **Campus Martius**, entirely delimited by the major bend of the Tiber and the Capitoline, the Quirinal and the Pincio hills, belonged to the Tarquin dynasty. Following the expulsion of the last of the Tarquin kings, Tarquinius Superbus, the area became state property and in the republican era was the object of a far-reaching urbanization project. Beginning in the 2nd century BC, there rose new important places of worship, civic buildings, porticoes, and theaters alongside the ancient temples dedicated to the most important Roman divinities, among whom Mars, who lent the area his name.

In the late 1st century BC, Pompey stimulated much construction activity, and many important remains from that time are still visible (the **Curia**, the **Porticus**, and the **Theater**) in the area around Largo Argentina. In the imperial age, there followed a grandiose urban renovation project promoted by Augustus and his son-in-law Marcus Vispanius Agrippa. Agrippa was responsible for the construction of the oldest public baths in Rome, known as the Baths of Agrippa and built in 25-19 BC north of the Largo Argentina sacred area. To complete the opus, he also had the **Pantheon** and the **Basilica of Neptune** built, and enlarged the Saepta Julia, the vast porticoed square built under Caesar and used for public assemblies and troop musters. The enormous bronze **pinecone** that gives the district its name was found among the ruins of the Baths of Agrippa. Originally part of a fountain, the **pigna** is now in the Vatican in the courtyard of the same name.

Work in the area continued under Domitian, to whom we owe the so-called Iseo Campense, or the Temple of Isis and Serapias, built near the Saepta Julia. It provides important evidence of the introduction of the Egyptian cults to Rome. The temple was destroyed in the 16th century, but supplied much building material reused in later constructions, among which the **obelisk** in Piazza del Pantheon. Emperor Hadrian was responsible for the restoration of many monuments in the area (Pantheon, Basilica of Neptune) and for the raising of new buildings near Trajan's Arch, which had been installed by his predecessor in the space in front of the Pantheon; the arch was known in the Middle Ages as the 'Arch of Pity'.

At that time, the area still abounded in ruins and was densely populated: unlike other areas of Rome, it was never totally abandoned, but had rather continued to develop while still following the topography of the ancient city. Thus, on the sites of the ancient buildings there were built churches and palaces, while a great number of more modest dwellings rose over time and hid the structures that had survived plunder of their materials for construction elsewhere. Profound transformations of the urban fabric of the district began in the 16th century, when the area became the nerve center of the Society of Jesus, or the Jesuit order: certain of the streets and squares were enlarged, as often as not to the detriment of the ancient monuments of the classical age. This is the case of what are today **Via di Torre Argentina**, **Piazza del Gesù**, and **Piazza del Collegio Romano**, around which at the end of the century there began to rise the sumptuous buildings that are still the area's cause for pride. Transformation proceeded gradually through the two centuries that followed, and by and large respected the peculiar nature of the area, which not even the wholesale demolition of the 19th century succeeded in altering substantially. The exception to this rule is represented by certain actions that targeted bringing to light the monuments of antiquity hidden beneath later superstructures.

Palazzetto Venezia - This building rose, in successive stages, on the site of the *Viridarium*, the porticoed garden designed by Alberti and built for Paul II in the mid-15th century. In about 1500 there was installed the bust known as **Madame Lucrezia**, one of Rome's 'talking' statues (on which, in the dark of night, the Roman people used to post bills with salacious verses deriding the government). It is actually a fragment of a statue from the *Iseo Campense*.

CHURCH OF GESÙ (p. 154)

Santa Marta - The church rose on the ruins of the Temple of Minerva Chalcidicea adjacent to the monastery, which was partially demolished to permit enlarging the square. It was renovated by De Rossi and Fontana in the late 1600s.

Basilica of San Marco - Saint Mark pope had this church built in 336 in honor of Saint Mark the Evangelist. It was radically renovated in the mid-15th century for cardinal Pietro Barbo, the future Pope Paul II. Inspired by the architectural style launched by Leon Battista Alberti, the typically Renaissance **facade** was built with material taken from the Colosseum and the Theater of Marcellus.

Via di S. Marco

PALAZZO VENEZIA (p. 155)

PALAZZO AND GALLERIA DORIA PAMPHILI (p. 156)

Collegio Romano - Built by Pope Gregory XIII in 1582 for Saint Ignatius Loyola, as an educational institution for the future members of the Society of Jesus. Besides the Library, the building also housed the Kircher Museum - named after Athanasius Kircher, its most important curator - and an astronomical observatory.

Sante Stimmate di San Francesco -
Built on the site of the earlier 13th-
century church of the Quaranta
Martiri di Calcarario, it was
restructured in the early 18th century
in late Baroque style. The facade was
inspired by Santa Maria in Via Lata.

Largo Argentina Archaeological Area -
This ancient sacred area of the republican era,
at the center of the *Campus Martius*, includes
the remains of the **Hecatostylum**, a porticus of
100 columns, and of four temples. Among these
are the original circular **'Temple of Present-Day
Fortune'** that housed a colossal marble statue of
the goddess, the remains of which are now in
the Capitoline Museums.

Palazzo Altieri - Built for Cardinal Altieri in the mid-1600s by Mattia and
Giovanni Antonio De Rossi, and enlarged following the election of Pope
Clement X, another member of the Altieri family. Of note the *court of honor*
and the elegant Baroque decoration of the *interiors*.

Basilica of Neptune - This basilica, built
behind the Pantheon by Agrippa in 25 BC,
was a temple dedicated to the sea god in
remembrance of the naval battles won by the
consul. It was restored by Hadrian. Remains
of the columns and the marble frieze
decorated with dolphins and tridents, the
attributes of Neptune, are still visible.

PANTHEON
(p. 152)

Sant'Eustachio This church
was founded by Constantine
on the site of the martyrdom
of the saint, recalled by the
stag's head crowning the
porticoed facade. It was
restructured in 1196, when
the Romanesque **bell
tower** was built, and
drastically
remodeled in the
1700s.

Via delle Botteghe Oscure

Largo di Torre Argentina

Piazza del Gesu

P.d. Pigna

pl e b i s c i t o

Piazza della Rotonda

Via del Seminario

P. d. Collegia Romano

Via del Corso

Pantheon Fountain - As
designed by Della Porta
in the second half of the
16th century, this
fountain was devoid of
the **obelisk** of Rameses
II. Originally in the *Iseo
Campense*, the obelisk
was ordered erected
here by Clement XI,
who had it transported
from the nearby
Piazza San Macuto.

Santa Maria in Via Lata -
Today's church, restored on
occasion of the Jubilee of
1650 and adorned in 1658
with its splendid Baroque
facade, by Pietro da
Cortona, rises on the site of
a very ancient deaconry
founded by Pope Sergius I
in the 7th century.
Interesting remains of the
earlier structure are visible
in the cellars. The high
altar, attributed to Bernini,
preserves a precious icon
of the *Virgin* dating to the
7th century.

Burrò - In 1727,
Filippo Raguzzini
invented a highly
theatrical solution for the
square before the church
of Sant'Ignazio involving
use of three small rococo
buildings staggered like flats
in a stage setting. The name of
the square is a corruption of the
French *bureaux* = offices.

SANT'IGNAZIO DI LOYOLA
(p. 155)

SANTA MARIA SOPRA MINERVA
(p. 153)

'Pulcin della Minerva' - This
curious monument, so-called
because the obelisk (from the
ancient *Iseo Campense*) is, with
its 5 meters height, the smallest
in Rome, was designed by
Bernini, who also designed
the small elephant sculpted
by Ercole Ferrara in 1667.

THE PANTHEON

The Pantheon is, naturally, one of the symbols of Rome, but it is also and above all one of the points of reference for the architecture of all times, a constant source of inspiration and a model that has been imitated countless times over the centuries. Conceived as an *Augusteum*, or sacred site dedicated to the deified emperor Augustus, and then, as the name implies, as the *Temple of All the Gods* protectors of his family, it was built in 27 BC by Augustus' son-in-law Marcus Vispanius Agrippa. Agrippa's statue, together with that of his powerful relative, originally occupied one of the two niches at the sides of the entrance portal. The building was damaged during the fire of 80 AD and was restored by Domitian and by Trajan; it was later totally rebuilt in 118-125 by Hadrian, to whom the plans of the present building are attributed.

The temple thus changed form and orientation, from a simple four-sided structure to a complex construction defined by the association of a cylindrical body surmounted by a hemispherical dome of equal diameter and height and preceded by a rectangular **pronaos**. The pronaos is in turn measured by 16 monolithic columns in grey and pink granite, topped with Corinthian marble capitals; it is crowned by a pediment with a **tympanum**, which was originally decorated with a bronze frieze. Bronze also sheathed the ceiling of the pronaos, but it was ordered removed in 1625 by Pope Urban VIII Barberini for use by Bernini for the Baldacchino of Saint Peter's and for casting the cannons of Castel Sant'Angelo. The populace commented this act with the famous pasquinade: *Quod non fecerunt barbari fecerunt Barberini* ("What the barbarians didn't do, the Barberinis did").

The structure of the **rotunda**, which is linked to the pronaos by a rectangular brick structure faced in marble, reveals a complex cosmic symbolism in the *seven niches* in the drum, one for each of the planetary divinities (Venus, Mars, Jupiter, Saturn, Uranus, Neptune, and Pluto), and the five orders of *lacunars* in the interior of the dome; over it all there opens the *oculus*, symbol of the disk of the Sun and the only source of illumination for the building.

The **dome**, the largest ever created in masonry, is built of an especially light agglomerate of mortar and chips of travertine that are replaced higher up with gravel and pumice.

When it was donated in 608 by the emperor Phocas to Pope Boniface IV, the temple was transformed into the church of Santa Maria dei Martiri, and despite the transformations it underwent over the course of the centuries the structure remained virtually unaltered down through our times. After 1870, when the two small bell towers at the sides (the so-called 'donkeys' ears' commissioned of Bernini by Urban VIII) were demolished, the Pantheon was transformed into the memorial chapel of the kings of Italy, whose tombs began to flank the previously-installed *Tomb of Raphael*, decorated with the famous *Madonna del Sasso* painted by Lorenzetto in 1520 on commission from Raphael himself.

Pantheon. The ruins of the Basilica of Neptune with a view of the exterior of the dome, a view of the interior, and the pronaos.

SANTA MARIA SOPRA MINERVA

The only church in Rome to have conserved its original Gothic floor-plan, Santa Maria sopra Minerva rose in the 13th century on what at the time were believed to be the ruins of the ancient Temple of Minerva Chalcidicea (actually buried under the nearby church of Santa Marta). Despite the heavy 19th-century restoration work which partially altered its forms, the building, with its three beautiful portals that during the Renaissance were added to the plain **facade**, is stylistically attributable to architects of Tuscan origin or training.

But this church is also linked to Tuscany for other reasons. It is the home of the **Carafa Chapel**, a true gem of 15th-century art created through the collaboration of a number of Tuscan artists: Giuliano da Maiano was the author, together with Mino da Fiesole (whose is also the *Tomb of Francesco Tornabuoni* near the entrance) and Verrocchio, of the splendid arch over the entrance, while Filippino Lippi frescoed the walls with the *Triumph of Saint Thomas* and the *Miracles of the Crucifixion* and painted the panel of the *Annunciation* over the altar. Tuscany is also recalled by the two *funeral monuments* created by Antonio da Sangallo the Younger in memory of the two Florentine popes, Leo X and Clement VII (in the choir, which was specially altered to host them in 1536); and by the *sarcophagus* containing the relics of Saint Catherine of Siena under the high altar. The small oratory dedicated to the saint and the chamber in which she died are in the **sacristy**, which is decorated with 15th-century frescoes.

Another work by another great Tuscan artist is the *tombstone of Fra' Beato Angelico*, sculpted by Isaia da Pisa in 1455; the *Risen Christ* (1520) against the left pilaster of the presbytery is attributed to Michelangelo.

The floor plan and a cut-away drawing of the Pantheon.

The interior of Santa Maria sopra Minerva.

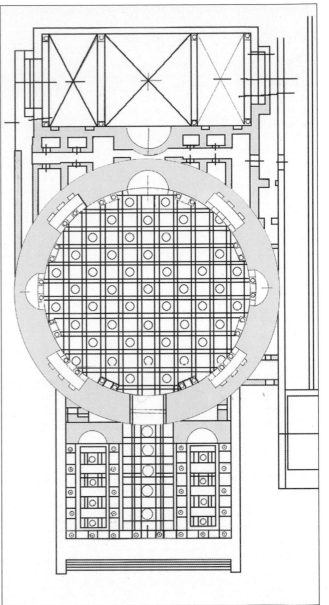

Piazza della Minerva. The 'Pulcin della Minerva'.

Church of Gesù. The Altar of Saint Ignatius, a masterpiece of Baroque art.

CHURCH OF GESU'

Emblem of the spirit of the Counter-Reform, the Gesù unites formal rigor, inspired by that orthodoxy confirmed by the Council of Trent, with a taste for the pomp and the spatial dramatization typical of the Baroque. Following the building of the church, which began in 1568, the latter style supplied a worthy decorative complement to the straightforward and weighty structure of the church itself, designed by Ignatius Loyola.

Twenty or so years earlier, the founder of the Society of Jesus had received the small church of Santa Maria della Strada (or 'degli Astalli') from Pope Paul III. He decided to enlarge it with financing provided by Cardinal Alessandro Farnese: Vignola drew up the plans for the church itself; the massive yet anything but ungracious travertine **facade** is instead the work of Giacomo Della Porta. For the **interior**, in line with the new liturgical needs dictated by the Council of Trent, Vignola designed a single nave, with side chapels, intersected by a transept of equal width and with a hemispherical dome, which was later adorned with frescoes by Baciccia. In 1679, the same artist also decorated the **vault** of the nave with the spectacular *Triumph of the Holy Name of Jesus*, an admirable example of the illusionistic perspective painting typical of the Baroque that is accentuated by the dilation of the paintwork beyond Raggi's gilded stucco cornice to invade the vault and even the structural ribbing of the church. The side chapels, although simple, contain valuable works; the showpiece is the Chapel of Saint Ignatius, a work by the Jesuit Father Andrea

Church of Gesù. The austere travertine facade by Della Porta.

Palazzo Venezia, a fine example of Renaissance civil architecture.

Pozzo, in which the body of the saint is entombed. This grandiose late 17th-century Baroque work culminates in the **Altar of Saint Ignatius**, which is set off by a profluvium of decoration that ranges from the gilded bronze of the reliefs showing *Scenes from the Life of Saint Ignatius* to the lapis lazuli that constellate the columns and the niche that shelters the silver-sheathed *statue of the saint*, a copy of the original by Pierre Legros. Alongside the church stands the **Casa Professa**, in 1543 the seat of the Society of Jesus and the site of Saint Ignatius Loyola's death in 1586.

SANT'IGNAZIO DI LOYOLA

A magniloguent monument to Counter-Reformist orthodoxy, this church, dedicated to the founder of the Society of Jesus, sanctified by Pope Gregory XV four years prior to the construction of the church (1626), echoes the at once simple and spectacular forms of the nearby Church of Gesù.

By order of the pope who had canonized Saint Ignatius, this church replaced the earlier Santissima Annunziata, which had become too small for the needs of the well-attended Collegio Romano where the Jesuit friars were trained. One of their number, Father Orazio Grassi, designed the three-aisled structure in which the center nave nevertheless greatly preponderates; the **vault** of the nave was frescoed by another Jesuit, Father Andrea Pozzo, with the *Glory of Saint Ignatius*, an authentic masterpiece of illusionistic prospective composition.

PALAZZO VENEZIA

In about the mid-15th century, Cardinal Pietro Barbo began work for the construction of his residence around the medieval Torre della Biscia. Work continued even after the cardinal was elected to the papal throne with the name of Paul II, and the palace, suitably enlarged in a style that in many respects presaged that of the Renaissance, became the papal palace. During the pontificate of Paul II, the building, which had incorporated in its architectural fabric the adjoining Saint Mark's Basilica, the facade of which was redesigned by Alberti, underwent considerable modification: the wing which was to become the Palazzetto Venezia was added along Via del Plebiscito, and in the **interior** there was created the famous *Sala del Mappamondo*, probably decorated by Mantegna, which hosted Mussolini's cabinet during the Fascist era.

In the early 16th century, Cardinal Lorenzo Cybo expanded and modified the Pauline layout with the creation of the so-called *Cybo Apartment*, which between 1564 and 1797 was home to the titular cardinals of San Marco. During the same period the palace was the property of the Republic of Venice, which used it as the residence of its ambassadors and further altered the original fifteenth-century structure. Still further remodeling was carried out during the two centuries that followed, until in 1924, after lengthy restoration of questionable value, the building became a museum and, from 1929 onward, the seat of the Gran Consiglio of the Fascist government.

Today's **Museo di Palazzo Venezia** overflows into the rooms of the adjoining Palazzetto Venezia, which communicates with the main building through the so-called *Passetto* or *Corridor of the Cardinals*, an ancient guard-walk modified in the 1700s, and houses rich collections of applied art, including pieces from the former Kircher Museum. Terra-cotta and pottery, porcelain, bronze and silver objects, church ornaments and vestments, wooden sculptures, paintings, weapons, ivory, crystal, tapestries, and *objets d'arte* of the most disparate types, both Italian and foreign, fill the numerous rooms and offer the visitor an exhaustive panorama of the evolution of the arts from the Middle Ages through the eighteenth century.

Museo di Palazzo Venezia. Saint Anne with the Virgin and Child, a polychrome wooden statue by the 16th-century German school.

PALAZZO AND GALLERIA DORIA PAMPHILI

Today's palace originated as a primitive 15th-century building, the dwelling-place of the prelates of the adjacent church of Santa Maria in Via Lata, completely rebuilt in 1489, to plans attributed to Bramante, by Cardinal Giovanni Santoro. The cardinal was soon forced to relinquish his property to the duke of Urbino, Francesco Maria Della Rovere, nephew of Pope Julius II, who however was in residence only rarely.

In 1573, one of his successors began a series of acquisitions of the surrounding properties which from then until the end of the century increased the surface area over which the coming expansion of the original building was to extend in the two centuries that followed.

In 1601, after the enormous holding had passed to Cardinal Pietro Aldobrandini, construction of the two wings on the larger **courtyard** was begun. But in 1657, still under construction, the palace again changed hands and became the property of the Pamphili, the family of Camillo, the nephew of the then Pope Innocent X and husband of princess Olympia, the last descendant of the Aldobrandini family.

In 1659, taking their cue from the restructuring work then going on in Piazza del Collegio Romano, the facade of the palace facing on that square was completed in accordance with plans by Antonio Del Grande, a pupil of Borromini. The work on the Via Lata side continued in the years that followed, as did the decoration of the magnificent reception halls, in the Baroque style then very much in vogue. The Via del Corso side had to wait until 1730 before it was finally completed thanks to Gabriele Valvassori, who in a little under three years created the highly-decorative rococo **facade** and the monumental **Galleria** on a four-armed plan. It was here that the works of art in the family collection begun by Innocent X, which included his masterful portraits by Velasquez and by Bernini, were arranged.

Further work on the palace was begun in the mid-1700s, following the passage of the property to the Doria Pamphili heirs, and it continued into the next century. At the same time, beginning in 1732 and for some decades thereafter, numerous artists and craftsmen were engaged in the decoration of the vast interiors, which began with the ceiling of the Galleria, frescoed by Milani with motifs inspired by the *Battle of the Giants* and the *Stories of Hercules*. The work continued into the apartments, where the ceiling of the throne room was frescoed by Tommaso Agricola with the *Sacrifice of Iphigenia* and the ballroom was embellished with paintings by Nessi, to the chapel, and to the grandiose Salone Aldobrandini, which in 1838 was added to the Galleria.

The Salone became the home of many works of art by great Italian and foreign masters. The original nucleus of the collection contained, among others, works by Caravaggio (for example, the celebrated *Rest on the Flight into Egypt*) and artists of the Emilian school (Parmigianino, Correggio). The Olimpia Aldobrandini inheritance added to this nucleus a number of masterpieces by painters of the Venetian school, including Titian, Tintoretto, Bellini, and Bassano; it is instead to Cardinal Benedetto Pamphili that we owe the group of works by the Flemish masters; with the advent of the Doria family, the collection acquired works by Sebastiano del Piombo, Bronzino, Lorenzo Lotto, and the so-called 'primitive' painters.

An 18th-century print showing the church of Santa Maria in Via Lata and Palazzo Doria Pamphili along Via del Corso. The origins of the church date back to an ancient diaconia on the medieval Via Lata. The street was straightened in the 15th century to become Via del Corso.

Galleria Doria Pamphili. Caravaggio, Rest on the Flight into Egypt.

Santa Maria in Aquiro - This austere church typical of the Counter-Reform was begun by Pietro da Volterra in 1590 on an existing foundation deeded to the Confraternita degli Orfani in 1540 by Paul III. Work continued under the direction of Maderno and was completed only on the 17th century, the era to which the two side bell towers also date.

Palazzo Capranica - Built for Cardinal Domenico Capranica in 1451, the palace originally had but one floor and a side tower; its windows exhibit both Gothic and Renaissance elements. The building, which embraced the preexisting Chapel of Sant'Agnese, hosts one of the oldest theater spaces in all of Rome. It is today a shell used as a movie house.

Santa Maria Maddalena - The construction of this church was begun on a 14th-century nucleus in 1621 by Grimaldi and continued by Carlo Fontana, who in 1673 added a **dome**, and by Giovanni Antonio De Rossi, who made further modifications near the end of the century. The **facade** - a fine example of Roman rococo with incredibly lively architectural forms adorned with niches, statues, and excellent stuccowork - was added only in 1735 by Giuseppe Sardi. The **sacristy** in the interior is a lovely example of the *rocaille* style, with a profusion of decorative carvings and frescoes and perfectly-preserved coeval ornaments and vestments.

Palazzo della Borsa - The building was raised around the remains of the **Temple of Hadrian**, built in memory of the emperor, deified in 145 AD, by his son Antoninus Pius. In 1695, the Roman building was transformed by Carlo and Francesco Fontana into the Dogana di Terra (land customs office); 20th-century restoration exposed the eleven columns of the ancient temple.

Palazzo Wedekind - Once the seat of the Vatican Post Office, the palace was rebuilt in 1818 by Pietro Camporese, who for the realization of the long portico surmounted by a terrace used 11 Ionic columns from the excavations at Veii.

PALAZZO CHIGI
(p. 161)

OBELISK OF PIAZZA MONTECITORIO
(p. 161)

COLUMN OF MARCUS AURELIUS
(p. 161)

Fountain of Piazza Colonna - Commissioned of Della Porta to adorn the square in 1576, the fountain was partially modified in the 19th century, when the four obelisks, from which the jets of water originally spouted, were replaced by sculptural groups.

San Lorenzo in Lucina - This church - founded in the 4th century on the site of the dwelling of the Roman matron Lucina - underwent far-reaching restructuring in the 17th and 18th centuries, although it still preserves many medieval elements.
Enlarged under Sixtus III, it was totally rebuilt under Pope Paschal II (1099-1118), when the **portico** and the Romanesque **bell tower** were added. Later work was carried out by Bernini, who designed the **Fonseca Chapel**, and by Carlo Rainaldi, to whom are attributed the Chapel of the Blessed Sacrament and the high altar, decorated with a famous *Crucifix* by Guido Reni.
In the full-blown 1800s, Giuseppe Sardi provided the church, from which many of the Baroque decorative elements had been removed during the preceding century, with a splendid **baptistery**, a fine example of rococo architecture and ornamentation. Recent archaeological excavations under the church have brought to light the remains of the colossal sundial called the *Horologium Augusti*, the gnomon of which is the obelisk now standing in Piazza di Montecitorio.

San Salvatore alle Coppelle - Set in one of the most suggestive corners of old Rome, this little church, which was founded in 1195 and remodeled during the 18th century, still possesses its Romanesque *bell tower* and a number of curious, ancient stone plaques with inscriptions directing the innkeepers of the area to report any customers who took ill in their establishments.

Santa Maria in Campo Marzio - This church, attached to the Benedictine monastery of **Saint Gregory Nazianzen** founded by Pope Zachary in the 8th century, was built with the collaboration of Della Porta, Maderno, and Peparelli, and restructured in typically Baroque style in the late 18th century by Giovanni Antonio de' Rossi.

PALAZZO DI MONTECITORIO
(p. 160)

Palazzo di Firenze - Built in the 1500s and restructured by Julius III, this palace went in 1561 to the Florentine Medici family (hence the name), who commissioned Ammannati to build the interior facade and that facing on the garden.

Palazzo Ruspoli - Ammannati was the author of this building, begun in about 1560, with its typically severe, late Renaissance **facade**. Martino Longhi the Younger is instead responsible for the *monumental staircase* that gives access to the *gallery*, finely decorated with Mannerist frescoes and with busts from the classical era.

MONTECITORIO AND THE COLONNA DISTRICT

*I*n ancient times, the Colonna district included a part of the vast flat area known as the Campus Martius, *object in imperial times of a program of urban redevelopment; in particular, that in correspondence to the urban tract of the Via Flaminia, today's Via del Corso. Here, in the Augustan era, in the area immediately adjoining the monumental area of the Baths of Agrippa that runs to the Pantheon, were the vast gardens that Augustus had dedicated to the glorification of the Empire and the gens Julia, of which he was a descendent. Testimony of this period is borne by the Ara Pacis, at the time set near what is now the church of San Lorenzo in Lucina (and now near the Mausoleum of Augustus); close by was the Horologium Augusti, a colossal sundial designed by Mecenate in 10 BC: an open area of considerable size paved in travertine formed the face of the dial; the marks and letters and numbers were inlaid in bronze, and an obelisk (the same now standing in front of Palazzo di Montecitorio) acted as the gnomon, its huge shadow marking the hours.*

*In the Antonine age the area acquired monuments designed to commemorate the emperors of that dynasty. There thus arose, in chronological order, the Temple of Matida, the **Temple of Hadrian**, the Antonine Column, the **Column of Marcus Aurelius**, from which the district later took its name (column = colonna), and around it, an area reserved by this emperor for the funeral celebrations for his father Antoninus Pius. Far from the two poles delimiting the development of the city on the Middle Ages, the Tiber and the Capitoline, this area with its eminently monumental and celebratory character was gradually overrun by vegetation and used as a 'quarry' from which construction materials were pillaged, and as a dump for rubble and earth removed from other, developing areas of the city. The low rise created by the accumulation of waste materials was called the Mons Acceptorius (roughly, 'receiving mound'); the name Montecitorio derives from the Italian Monte Accettorio. With time, the lonely site was recognized as the perfect place for the foundation of hermitages and small monasteries.*

*As early as the 7th century, there existed here a convent of Eastern nuns who had fled Byzantium with the relics of Saint Gregory Nazianzeno; their retreat was the original nucleus of the Benedictine convent of **Santa Maria in Campo Marzio**. Both **San Lorenzo in Lucina** and the small church of San Biagio de Monte, later demolished to create space for **Palazzo di Montecitorio**, date to just as remote an era. At the time, the 'mount' in question was the site of the towers from which the Colonna family controlled the area until papal power was established over the city.*

*In the 1300s, the population of the district began to increase gradually and the extensive expanses of green began to be constellated with homes, but another century and a half were to pass before the area underwent intense urban development. This period began in 1457 with the construction, on the slopes of the Monte Accettorio, of the mighty building erected by the **Capranica** family; construction of other, smaller palaces with painted facades and of churches, such as that of **Santa Maria in Aquiro**, began shortly thereafter and continued throughout the Cinquecento.*

*But the face of the district was changed above all by popes Gregory XIII and Sixtus V, who promoted alacritous development work, and change continued into the 17th and 18th centuries with **Palazzo Chigi** and **Palazzo di Montecitorio**, construction of the squares known as **Colonna**, **Montecitorio**, and **Maddalena**, and rebuilding of churches and convents. The intricate grid of streets and alleyways marked out by buildings of different kinds (of which **Via delle Coppelle** is a excellent example), was profoundly modified after 1870, when Palazzo di Montecitorio was selected as the seat of the Chamber of Deputies and doubled in size.*

PALAZZO DI MONTECITORIO

After the Colonna towers and until 1536, the artificial rise of Montecitorio hosted a small building owned by the Gaddi family, next door to the church of San Biagio. It went to the cardinal of Santa Severina in 1603, then to the Somaschi friars, and finally, in 1653, became the property of prince Nicolò Ludovisi, nephew of the then-reigning Pope Innocent X.

To Bernini, who had already worked for him in Piazza Navona, the pope proposed creating a sumptuous residence on the site. The Baroque architect took the peculiar lay of the land into account when he designed a broad, circular space to be bounded by a long, slightly convex **facade** divided into five sections, of which the center portion was to be projecting and the others gradually receding. Bernini's plans, which also called for the unification of Piazza Colonna and Piazza di Montecitorio and the installation in the latter of Trajan's Column to balance Marcus Aurelius' in the former, were never brought to completion due to financial crises within the Ludovisi family. At the death of Nicolò, in 1664, the palace was in fact still incomplete, and so it remained for about thirty years, until in 1694 Pope Innocent XII commissioned the architect Carlo Fontana to again take up work and to demolish the adjacent medieval homes and the church of San Biagio in order to adapt the structure to house the Papal Tribunal of Justice. Fontana thus finished the palace, which took the name of Curia Innocenziana (by which it was known until 1870), in substantial harmony with Bernini's original plans. He nevertheless "personalized" his coork by inserting, in the center of the facade, a **portal** with three openings surmounted by a balcony and decorated with two bas-reliefs on the themes of *Justice* and *Charity* on the two lesser doors.

Crowning the same portion of the facade, Fontana replaced Bernini's balustrade with statues with a raised portion incorporating a clock and a vaulted **bell tower**; he took greater liberties, instead, with the inner courtyard. In 1871, the palace became the seat of the Chamber of Deputies, and to adapt it to its new function its volume was 'doubled' with the addition of an adjoining portion, in order to make way for which the entire block behind the ancient seat of the Curia was demolished. The author of these works was Ernesto Basile, who completed the task amidst not a few difficulties and debate.

Bernini's facade of Palazzo Montecitorio, today the home of the House of Deputies, with the obelisk of Psammetychus II at the center of the square.

The Column of Marcus Aurelius. A detail of the long, spiraling low relief and, right, a full view of the column with the statue of Saint Paul at its top.

THE OBELISK OF MONTECITORIO AND THE COLUMN OF MARCUS AURELIUS

The aspect to be given to Piazza di Montecitorio and Piazza Colonna was a centuries-old question that had often been debated and a final solution just as often put off. In the first case, the proposed solutions had been many; the last, advanced by Clement XI in the 18th century, called for re-erecting the Antonine Column, until that time preserved in the courtyard of the nearby Convento della Missione, at the center of a semicircular space. The plan was rejected; then, in 1792, Pio VI charged Giovanni Antinori with the task of setting up at the center of the square the **obelisk of Psammetychus II** - the gnomon of the *Horologium Augusti*. For its restoration, the architect made use of the porphyry of the Antonine Column; fittingly enough, with the addition of a perforated bronze globe, the gnomon, now column, again performed its original function and marked the hours on the paving stones of the square.

We might say that the circumstances leading to the creation of Piazza Colonna were instead entirely the opposite: the square was constructed, by order of Sixtus V, around the preexisting **Column of Marcus Aurelius**. On the model of Trajan's Column, it had originally been raised by the emperor on the ancient Via Flaminia, now Via del Corso, to commemorate the two campaigns against the Quadi, the Marcomanni, and the Sarmatians, brought to victorious conclusions between 172 and 175 AD and described in the long frieze that spirals around the shaft. In 1589, the pope had the column detached from its original base and restored; a bronze statue of *Saint Paul* gazing in the direction of the Vatican was placed at its top.

PALAZZO CHIGI

The reconstruction of Piazza Colonna promoted by Pope Sixtus V extended to influence the buildings making up its sides. The first to decide to follow the plans of the pope was Giovan Battista del Bufalo, a collector of antiques and owner of many of the medieval homes on the square. In 1548 he began demolition of the old buildings and later proceeded with construction of a palace designed by Matteo da Città di Castello. Although still incomplete in the late 16th century, the building nevertheless aroused the interest of the Aldobrandini family, who purchased it with the intention of enlarging it to produce a residence worthy of their family status. The task was entrusted to Giacomo Della Porta and Carlo Maderno, who during the pontificate of Clement VIII Aldobrandini started to shape the new residence, beginning at the corner between the square and the Corso. But work was suspended for financial reasons and the building was put up for sale as was. In 1659 it was purchased by the Chigi family, the owners of the surviving medieval buildings on the square. Felice Della Greca was commissioned to continue the work; he expanded the building by completing the wing on the Montecitorio side and created a superb enclosed **courtyard** decorated with precious stuccowork. A fountain was installed at its center in the eighteenth century. Della Greca was also the author of the monumental **staircase**

Piazza Colonna. A detail of the Column of Marcus Aurelius, built in imitation of Trajan's Column.

Below, the two facades of Palazzo Chigi - on Piazza Colonna and Via del Corso - in an 18th-century print, and the facade on Piazza Colonna as it appears today.

adorned with antique statues that leads to the first floor of the building. The palace underwent extensive restructuring and renovation in the mid 1700s on occasion of the wedding of Sigismondo Chigi. It was then that Stern created the lavish decoration of the *Salone d'Oro*, in which was installed the *Sleeping Endymion*, a masterpiece by Baciccia. In the two centuries that followed, Palazzo Chigi became the Austrian Embassy and then, under Fascist rule, the first seat of Mussolini's cabinet before it was transferred to Palazzo Venezia in 1927; since the 1960s, Palazzo Chigi has been the home of the Presidency of the Council of Ministers.

Galleria dell'Accademia di San Luca - This collection of valuable works of art by Italian and foreign masters, among whom Raphael and Van Dyck, is located in the Baroque Palazzo Carpegna, construction of which is attributable in part to Borromini.

FONTANA DI TREVI
(p. 166)

Santi Vincenzo e Anastasio - The church - which stands across from the Fontana di Trevi - was commissioned in about 1650 by Cardinal Mazzarino. It shows the mark of the Baroque genius Martino Longhi the Younger, above all in the elaborate **facade**, with its two superposed orders and stands of columns that earned it the nickname of 'cane-brake'.

Santa Maria in Trivio and Santa Maria in Via - These two churches, both of ancient origin and both dedicated to the Virgin, represent two profoundly different models for Roman art between Mannerism and the Baroque.

Oratorio del Santissimo Crocefisso - A small jewel of Roman Mannerism built in the mid-16th century by Giacomo Della Porta. The interior of the oratory is decorated with fine frescoes of the *History of the Cross* and the miraculous events linked to it.

Santa Croce e San Bonaventura dei Lucchesi - Rising on the ruins of an earlier church dedicated to Saint Nicholas, today's building, which in the 1500s belonged to the Capuchin friars and a century later became the church of the community from Lucca, is a Baroque work by Bernini's celebrated pupil Mattia De Rossi. The interior, for the decoration

of which two masters from Lucca, Coli and Gherardi, were called in, is on a single-nave plan and lavishly adorned with gilded stuccowork and interesting paintings.

San Marcello al Corso - Tradition has it that the church of San Marcello rose in the year 418 on the site of the ancient *Catabulum*, the grandiose imperial Roman post-house where the pope and saint was condemned by Maxentius to serve as a stable hand. The basilica was destroyed by fire and in 1519 was rebuilt to plans by Jacopo Sansovino, who also turned it around, placing the apse where the entrance originally opened. The late-Baroque **facade** is instead the work of Carlo Fontana (1682-1686).

Santi Apostoli - Of early medieval origin, founded in the 6th century by the general Narsetes following the Gothic War, and originally on the Byzantine model, this basilica was modified many times over the centuries. Radical rebuilding was promoted in 1421 by Pope Martin V, on occasion of the construction of the adjacent Piazza Colonna. Of this operation there remain the **portico** and the loggia above it; the original structure of the latter was modified during later restoration. Between 1701 and 1714, Francesco and later Carlo Fontana, his father, were commissioned to restructure the building both inside and out. Today's neoclassical **facade** is by Valadier (1827).

Palazzo Odescalchi - This building was long taken as a model for Baroque residences, and was imitated even outside of Italy. Three great architects contributed to its creation: Maderno, who began construction, Bernini, who took over in 1664 and designed the **facade**, and Vanvitelli, who modified the structure of the palace a century later and added new architectural elements.

Palazzo Colonna - The noble Colonna family, who resided on the site from medieval times forward, descended from the Tuscolo counts, whose violent resistance to papal power resulted in Boniface VIII's demolishing the original buildings. The palace, rebuilt in the Quattrocento by Pope Martin V, a member of the Colonna family, was rebuilt anew in 1730 by Niccolò Michetti and finely decorated by artists of the time. In the halls of the palace hang paintings by Italian and foreign masters collected by various members of the family and today on public exhibit in the **Galleria Colonna**.

PALAZZO DEL QUIRINALE
(p. 164)

SANT'ANDREA
AL QUIRINALE
(p. 165)

PIAZZA
DEL QUIRINALE
(p. 165)

N

THE QUIRINAL AND THE TREVI DISTRICT

*A*ccording to tradition, the name of this hill derives from that of the god Quirinus, a warrior divinity venerated by the Sabines, the first people to inhabit the height; following their meeting and fusion with the Latins who occupied the Palatine, they gave rise to the first agglomerates to rise outside the walls of Roma Quadrata. Under Numa Pompilio, the god was given a temple alongside an older place of worship, dedicated to Semo Sancus, another god of Sabine origin, on the site of today's church of **San Silvestro al Quirinale**. A great number of other sacred buildings were built later: the temples of Salus, of Pudicitia Plebeia, of Fortuna Primigenia, and of Venus Erycina; in the imperial age, Domitian added a temple dedicated to the gens Flavia, and Caracalla erected the great Temple of Serapias. The rest of the hill was occupied by prestigious buildings, not a few of which were the residences of the patrician families. In 326 AD, following demolition of a number of these, Constantine built an enormous bath complex, the ruins of which capped the hill through the Middle Ages until 1603, when they were removed to make room for **Palazzo Pallavicini-Rospigliosi**. Among these suggestive ruins were found the two colossal statues of the **Dioscuri** with their mounts that today adorn Piazza del Quirinale and that earned the hill the nickname of 'Monte Cavallo' (horse hill).
All around there rose only suburban villas set amidst fields and vineyards. One of these, a property of Cardinal Ippolito d'Este, attracted the attention of Pope Gregory XIII, who in 1574 enlarged the structure to create a summer residence as an alternative to the lower and less well-ventilated Vatican, and so began construction of **Palazzo del Quirinale**.

The area that spread out below the slopes of the hill was instead densely populated. Beginning in the Middle Ages, homes had grown up around two principal nodes: the church of the **Santi Apostoli** and the three roads that led to the Fontana dell'Acqua Vergine where the **Fontana di Trevi** was built in the 18th century. The name of the district, like that of the famous fountain, alludes to this trivium (meeting of three roads). Development continued into the modern era thanks above all to the initiatives of two popes, Pius IV and Sixtus V, who launched a series of road-building, hydraulic, and urban redevelopment projects. These culminated in the construction, in about 1563, of the Strada Pia linking the district to the Vatican, and, in 1589, of the Acqua Felice aqueduct, the branches of which supplied water to the many fountains on the Quirinal and the nearby Esquiline hill; at the same time, alongside the homes and shops there began to rise churches of great artistic value and the new, sumptuously-appointed residences of noble families like the Odescalchi and the Colonnas. The latter family had resided near the Quirinal for centuries, and by the time of Sixtus V's great improvements their palace had become the fulcrum of the entire district. It was enlarged during the 17th and 18th centuries. In 1870, the urban renewal work commissioned to make Rome the capital of Italy brought about many changes that had important repercussions on the urban fabric of the area; nevertheless, the ancient look of the district has been preserved practically unaltered in the area around the Fontana di Trevi, which not without reason is today one of the symbols of the city.

Palazzo delle Esposizioni This 19th-century building on Via Nazionale, with its somewhat grandiose neoclassical lines, is an important exhibition space as well as home to cultural initiatives of all kinds.

San Vitale - Following its consecration in the 5th century, this church of very ancient origin has undergone much remodeling over time. The original three-nave structure was modified to a single-nave plan by Sixtus IV in 1475. The same pope also added a *portico* and a rich *portal*. The church was later completely restored in severe Counter-Reformist style under Clement VIII, who donated it to the Jesuits.

Palazzo della Consulta - The building owes its present princely aspect to renovation under Clement XII, who commissioned Ferdinando Fuga to peform the work between 1732 and 1734. The classical, late-Baroque compositional scheme devised by the Florentine architect includes a massive central building with a majestic **facade** with large windows and pilaster strips and an ornate portal decorated with the allegorical statues of *Justice* and *Religion*, a clear allusion to the building's use destination. But the most genial element in Fuga's design is undoubtedly the aerial, twin-ramped **staircase** on the inner courtyard.

Palazzo Pallavicini-Rospigliosi - The palace, with its unadulterated late-Renaissance forms, is flanked by a hanging garden. The ceiling of the **Casino**, or summerhouse on the grounds of the palace, is 'opened' by Guido Reni's celebrated fresco, *Aurora*.

San Silvestro al Quirinale - Already standing in the 11th century and partially reduced to permit the nineteenth-century widening of the street on which it stands, the main body of this church is in the finest style of the mature Cinquecento. The single-nave interior boasts a beautiful coffered *ceiling* and interesting side chapels containing many valuable works of art. The most important is the *Bandini Chapel*, with its 17th-century paintings by Domenichino and sculptures by Algardi.

Villa Colonna - The villa, surrounded by extraordinary gardens with a *monumental entrance* dating to the 1800s, was built in about 1618 on the site of the ancient Temple of Serapias. It is linked to Palazzo Colonna by a series of arches over Via della Pilotta.

Palazzo del Quirinale. Two details of Bernini's facade with the papal window and Maderno's portal.

Piazza del Quirinale. The Dioscuri with their horses and the obelisk at the center of the square.

PALAZZO DEL QUIRINALE

In 1583, Pope Gregory XIII, who had acquired the habit of spending his vacations on the Quirinal at the villa of Cardinal Ippolito d'Este, commissioned the architect Ottavio Mascherino to build a new summer residence on the same site. Work began the following year at the rim of the hill with a small palace (*palazzetto*) with a double loggia embraced by two avant-corps, a singular **helicoidal staircase**, and a panoramic **tower** (raised in 1723 by the addition of a small vaulted bell tower).

Mascherino's plans also called for complete restructuring of the building on the corner of Piazza del Quirinale and the Strada Pia, today Via del Quirinale. But it was Gregory XIII's successor Sixtus V who carried the work forward, entrusting its continuation to Domenico Fontana, who had begun reorganizing the square itself in 1586.

A year later, Fontana began construction of two long **galleries** linking the Gregorian *palazzetto* and the remodeled corner building and delimiting a vast inner courtyard on which the large, luxurious rooms designed to host the pope and his court were to face. Sixtus V lived in the palace and died there. At his death, however, work slowed down: of the two planned galleries only one was completed, and Domenico Fontana's brother Giovanni wholly dedicated his energies to the vast **gardens**, which he provided with a sophisticated irrigation system linked to the Acqua Felice aqueduct and an array of refined waterworks, such as the **Fontana dell'Organo** built during the papacy of Clement VIII.

In the early 17th century, Pope Paul V gave the grandiose palace its more or less final arrangement when he commissioned Flavio Ponzio to complete the second gallery, that facing the gardens; the architect added a raised volume at the center to support the monumental **grand staircase** to the *Sala del Concistoro* (in the 19th century transformed into the Reception Hall) and to the *Sala Regia*. Construction was supervised by Maderno, who in 1617 also created the *Pauline Chapel* (in addition to the *Chapel of the Annunciation* built by Ponzio and frescoed by Guido Reni) and the beautiful **entrance portal** with its tympanum decorated with the *statues of Saint Peter and Saint Paul*.

During Urban VIII's time, Bernini added the **papal window** over the portal. Under Alexander VII, he designed the so-called **Manica Lunga** or 'Long Sleeve', the seemingly-interminable wing of the building that delimits the gardens along Via del Quirinale (then the Strada Pia), where the many servants to the papal court were lodged; it was completed by Ferdinando Fuga in 1730. Bernini also designed the **Coffee House** installed in the gardens for Benedict XIV in 1743. When Rome was proclaimed capital, the palace became the residence of the royal family; today, it is the seat of the Presidency of the Republic.

PIAZZA DEL QUIRINALE

The summit of the hill to which the two statues of the **Dioscuri**, Castor and Pollux (imperial-age copies of Greek originals attributed, as an inscription on the pedestal tells us, to Phidias and Praxiteles), were transported from the nearby ruins of the Baths of Constantine, began to assume coherency from both the planning and the architectural points of view during the pontificate of Sixtus V. In 1586, the pope commissioned Fontana to level the terrain and set the carefully-restored statues at the center of the square in such a manner as to continue the prospective play of the Strada Pia, the axis linking the Vatican and the Quirinale. Despite the many projects for reorganization of the square drawn up after that date, it was not until the 1700s that a satisfactory solution was found.

Under Pope Pius VI, Antinori separated the two statues somewhat and placed an **obelisk**, found in 1781 near the Church of San Rocco and once belonging to the decoration of the Mausoleum of Augustus, between them.

In 1818, during the reign of Pope Pius VIII, Stern transformed the massive basin used as a watering-trough in the Roman Forum (at the time known as the *Campo Vaccino*) into a **fountain** that replaced the one installed under Sixtus V in the 16th century. In the meantime the square - at the time called 'Monte Cavallo' after the horses of the Dioscuri - had assumed a more distinct appearance thanks to the removal of the ruins of the Baths of Constantine and the Temple of Serapias, the demolition of a number of churches, and the raising of Palazzo Rospigliosi and Palazzo della Consulta, which was totally renewed by Fuga in the 1700s.

It was during this period that the **Stables** were built across the square from Palazzo del Quirinale, while on the other side the so-called **Palazzo della Panetteria**, linked to the pontifical residence by Bernini's round turret, was renovated.

Sant'Andrea al Quirinale. The high altar framed by four Corinthian columns supporting the pediment with the statue of Saint Andrew.

SANT'ANDREA AL QUIRINALE

A masterpiece by Gian Lorenzo Bernini, Sant'Andrea al Quirinale was commissioned of the great master in 1658 by Pope Alexander VII with the support of Prince Camillo Pamphili, to replace an earlier 16th-century church used by the adjacent Jesuit Noviciate, today used as offices.

Sant'Andrea al Quirinale. The splendid, richly gilded, gored and coffered ceiling of the elliptical dome.

Underlying the peculiar architectural syntax of Bernini's building are the ellipse and the semicircle. The interior space is in fact elliptical, as is the dome and the lantern topping it; the *prothyrum*, the entrance staircase, and the window that opens in the quadrangular facade are instead all semicircular.

The **interior** was later decorated, to plans by Bernini, by Antonio Raggi, who populated the spaces above the great arched windows, the gilded coffered cupola, and the lantern with figures of *putti* and cherubim arranged in such a manner as to lend theatrical emphasis to the central scene. Borgognone's excellent *Martyrdom of Saint Andrew* on the high altar is preceded by a columned aedicula with the *Glory of Saint Andrew* by Raggi.

FONTANA DI TREVI

The legend runs that a nymph led the exhausted troops of the consul Marcus Vispanius Agrippa to drink at a spring, which in honor of the divine maiden was named Vergine; a while later, in 19 BC, Agrippa directed its waters into a distribution system that he called Acqua Vergine, after the same nymph. Damaged by neglect and time, the aqueduct was restored in the mid-15th century under Pope Nicholas V, who ordered that there be built a fountain supplied by its waters near that *trivium* that lent its name to whole Trevi district.

About three centuries later, in 1732 to be exact, Pope Clement XII decided to replace the original fount with a grander, more majestic construction. The architect Nicola Salvi, taking his inspiration from drawings by Bernini, gave form to a sort of monumental theatrical backdrop against one of the sides of Palazzo Poli, a marvelous union of architecture and sculpture.

The focal point of Salvi's invention is Pietro Bracci's statue of *Oceanus* standing on a shell-shaped chariot pulled by sea-horses led by tritons, the work of Maini. The stately sculptural group moves on a rocky podium enlivened by plants and fabulous creatures of all kinds. In the side niches there instead stand two allegorical statues, by Filippo Valle, of *Salubrity* and *Abundance*; these are surmounted by two low reliefs of the *Virgin Nymph Leading Agrippa's Troops to the Spring* and *Agrippa Ordering Construction of the Aqueduct*, by Bergondi and Grossi, respectively. Topping the structure, supported by Corinthian columns, is an elaborate attic with a dedicatory inscription, the statues of the *Four Seasons*, and, on the balustrade at the summit, the *coat-of-arms of Pope Clement XII* between the two allegorical figures of *Fame*. The complex structure of the fountain was thirty years in the building, and was completed only under Pope Clement XIII.

The Fontana di Trevi against the triumphal arch crowned by the coat-of-arms of Pope Clement XII.

Details of the Fontana di Trevi with Oceanus (left) driving a chariot pulled by two sea-horses, called the 'spirited horse' and the 'placid horse', led by tritons emerging from the waters.

Sant'Isidoro - The original 17th-century structure of the building, ordered built by the Spanish Franciscan monks and later ceded to the Irish order, was completed over the centuries along Borrominian lines. The clearly Baroque interior vaults the Da Sylva Chapel, built to plans by Bernini in 1663 and decorated with elegant sculptures by the master and his son Valentino.

Palazzo Boncompagni - Seat of the United States Embassy, and also known as **Palazzo Margherita** since it was once the residence of the Queen Mother, Palazzo Boncompagni was built by Gaetano Koch in the late 1800s for Prince Boncompagni Ludovisi on the site of Villa Ludovisi. Of the original villa there remains a much-retouched portion, variously attributed to Maderno or Domenichino, standing against the 19th-century building.

VILLA BORGHESE
(p. 172)

Fontana delle Api - This fountain, another of Bernini's creations for the Barberini family (1644), explores the possibilities offered the bee, their family symbol, as a decorative motif. In 1917, the fountain was moved from the nearby Via Sistina to the corner of Piazza Barberini in which it currently stands.

Quadrivium of the Quattro Fontane - The crossing of the Strada Pia and Via Felice was marked, in the late 1500s, by four fountains inserted in the same number of niches and decorated with statues portraying personifications of the *Tiber* and the *Aniene* rivers and *Diana* and *Juno* (in the photo, the *Tiber*).

SAN CARLINO ALLE QUATTRO FONTANE
(p. 170)

Via Ludovisi

Via Crispi

Via Sistina

Vitt. di Veneto

Via del Tritone

Piazza Barberini

Via Barberini

Via del Quirinale

Via delle Quattro Fontane

Via XX Settembre

Via Firenze

Via Napoli

Via Genova

Via Nazionale

Via Friuli

N

Santa Maria della Concezione - The notoriety of this church, built between 1626 and 1630, is due above all to its subterranean chapels in which is located the so-called **Capuchin Cemetery**. The skulls and bones of the friars are composed in such a manner as to form an infinite variety of garlands, festoons, and capitals in a macabre play of decorative virtuosity. The church is also home to such masterpieces of painting as Guido Reni's *Saint Michael Archangel* and Caravaggio's *Saint Francis*, as well as celebrated canvases by Domenichino and Gherardo Delle Notti.

San Nicola da Tolentino - The rigidly Baroque conception of this church is the work of Baratta, who built it in the latter half of the 17th century on a preexisting building erected by the Augustinian friars. The harmonious **facade**, with its rhythmical array of columns, precedes an equally harmonious domed interior containing valuable works by Baciccia and Algardi. The *Gavotti Chapel* was designed and decorated by Pietro da Cortona in collaboration with other 17th-century artists.

Fontana del Tritone - Pope Urban VIII commissioned Bernini to create the Triton Fountain for Piazza Barberini. The artist accomplished the work in 1642-1643, making use of allegorical motifs alluding to the marine gods and exalting the commissioning family by including the symbolic Barberini *bees* among the decorative themes.

PALAZZO BARBERINI AND THE GALLERIA NAZIONALE D'ARTE ANTICA
(p. 170)

Galleria Nazionale d'Arte Antica. Giulio Romano, Heitz Madonna. *16th century.*

PIAZZA BARBERINI AND THE LUDOVISI DISTRICT

*T*he northwestern slopes of the Quirinal hill, between the Servian and the Aurelian walls, were in antiquity distinguished by their lack of urban settlements, since the city developed more toward the Tiber than toward the heights behind. During the classical era, this district was the site of suburban villas surrounded by immense green spaces, among which the so-called Horti Sallustiani. The principal thoroughfare was the axis represented by the Alta Semita, today's Via del Quirinale, and its continuation into Vico di Porta Collina, today Via XX Settembre, that linked up to the Via Salaria. The area preserved its prevalently rural character through the Middle Ages; in early modern times it was a vast expanse of cultivated fields, vineyards, and pastures constellated by isolated cottages and a few country homes belonging to the richest and most prestigious of the noble families of Rome. These gave rise (as in the cases of Palazzo del Quirinale and **Palazzo Barberini**, its ideal extension) to the many villas that from 16th century onward began to spring up and multiply in the area (Villa Ludovisi, Villa Valenti Gonzaga) until they were almost completely wiped out by urbanization in the time of Umberto I.

A great stimulus to the development of this area of the city was also lent by the reorganization of the road network, which began under Pius IV with construction of the Strada Pia that linked the Quirinal and the Vatican and then followed the route of the ancient Vico di Porta Collina to the Via Salaria; further work began in 1585, under Sixtus V, with the construction of Via Felice, an artery linking Trinità dei Monti and the Jubilee basilica of Santa Croce di Gerusalemme. The point of intersection of these two streets - near which in the 17th century there arose one of the masterpieces of Roman Baroque architecture, the church of **San Carlino** - offers one of Rome's most suggestive urban prospects: the crossroads of the **Quattro Fontane**, with lookouts toward each of the four cardinal points and views of the obelisks of Trinità dei Monti, of the Quirinale and of Santa Maria Maggiore.

Beginning in 1870, as part of the development work undertaken when Rome was made capital of Italy, the upper portion of the Trevi neighborhood was completely revolutionized by the construction of the various ministry buildings; the new Ludovisi district took form, around the **Fontana del Tritone**, with the opening of **Via Veneto** with its palaces of the noble families, like **Palazzo Boncompagni**, today the seat of the United States Embassy, great luxury hotels, and elegant villas. Via Veneto, made famous in the years of the Italian economic boom by the director Federico Fellini, who immortalized its resplendent atmosphere in the movie La Dolce Vita, leads to the **Park of Villa Borghese** with the **Casino Borghese**, home of the famous **Galleria**.

Fontana del Tritone. A detail of a bee in the Barberini coat-of-arms.

Palazzo Barberini.
A detail of the 19th-century railing on
Via delle Quattro Fontane.

Filippo Lauri, Celebration at Palazzo Barberini in Honor of Queen Christina of
Sweden. *Museo di Roma. 17th century.*

PALAZZO BARBERINI
AND THE GALLERIA NAZIONALE
D'ARTE ANTICA

In 1625, when Carlo Barberini, brother of Urban VIII, purchased the suburban villa of the Sforzas near the vineyard of Cardinal Grimani to make it his family home, the Barberinis already possessed a lavish residence in Via dei Guibbonari, and had commissioned Maderno to restructure it. The same architect also undertook construction of a new, more sumptuously-appointed palace, suitable for holding refined receptions for foreign ambassadors, in a strategic location on the slopes of the Quirinal hill, in close communication with the summer residence of the popes - of which in a certain sense it could have been considered the direct extension. Maderno, whose designs called for a building on a square plan around a courtyard, died in 1629 leaving the courtyard open and the long sides of the building, which were later transformed into wings, unfinished.

He was succeeded as director of construction by Borromini, who was in turn succeeded by Bernini. The latter architect revolutionized the original plan by inserting between the wings a rather compact building, which despite its mass was considerably lightened by a series of windows with deep splays that created a loggia-like effect on the **facade**. In the interior, two **staircases**, one by Bernini, the other by Borromini, led from the atrium to the main hall, on the decoration of which Pietro da Cortona participated from 1633 onward with the grandiose ceiling painting of the *Triumph of Divine Providence* exalting the glories of the Barberini family.

But the decoration of the halls and the sumptuous rooms of the palace was also entrusted to the precious statues and Roman antiquities that the Barberinis had collected over the years, and to the many paintings that form the nucleus of today's **Galleria Nazionale d'Arte Antica** founded in 1895. The absolute masterpiece of this collection, which in-

cludes works by Filippo Lippi, Perugino, Bronzino, Tintoretto, Guido Reni, and Guercino, among others, and by many foreign masters, is Raphael's *La Fornarina*, in which criticism traditionally sees the portrait of the woman the artist "loved until his death." Particular interest also invests the *Judith and Holophernes* by Caravaggio and the *Narcissus* for many years attributed to the Lombard painter but now believed by criticism to have been painted by one of his pupils.

Besides the picture gallery, the palace also sported a *library* and, above all, many architectural features conceived to support its role as a reception facility. Among these were the famous theater designed by Pietro da Cortona, a spheristerion which was later demolished, and the immense space (no longer existing) in front of the building in which fêtes and carrousels were held, including a celebration organized in honor of Queen Christina of Sweden.

In 1864, modification of the urban layout of the district and the construction of the monumental gate supported by massive telamons radically changed the exterior aspect of the palace, which at the time stood out imposingly against the slope of the hill but today seems to be somewhat suffocated by the structures that surround it.

SAN CARLINO
ALLE QUATTRO FONTANE

Near the Quattro Fontane crossroads, this small church, the dimensions of which are more or less equivalent to those of one of the four pylons that support the dome of Saint Peter's, is one of the jewels of Roman Baroque architecture. Borromini was commissioned to build it and the adjacent convent by the Spanish Trinitarians, who had chosen the site as their seat in the early 1600s; the church was begun in 1638 and terminated, as regards its essential structures, in 1641.

The **facade** took a while longer. The Ticinese architect worked on it from 1664 until his death in 1667; it was completed in accordance with the master's drawing, today in the Albertina in Vienna, by his nephew, who in 1670 also raised the bell tower. The facade is concave at the sides and convex at the center; its wealth of moldings, columns, niches, and statues create a lively and imaginative architectural score.

The curvilinear theme of the exterior of the church is taken up again in the **interior**, but here Borromini also accentuated the vertical development of the structure, where the **elliptical dome** - decorated according to an intricate scheme of cruciform coffering, the hexagonal and octagonal lacunars becoming smaller and smaller as they approach the lantern - exalts the perspective and suggests a space larger than that actually available. The lower church repeats the motifs and forms of the upper church, as does the adjoining **cloister**, with its harmonious and elegant proportions.

In creating this complex masterpiece, Borromini took attention to detail to an extreme: he even designed the confessionals and the wrought-iron rail of the well at the center of the cloister.

San Carlino alle Quattro Fontane. Right, a detail of the curved facade;
bottom right, the interior of the elliptical dome with the lacunars forming various patterns including the crosses symbolizing the Order of the Trinitarians who commissioned Borromini to build the church.

Below left, the small cloister with its well with wrought-iron decoration.

VILLA BORGHESE

The green slope of the Pincio, delimited on the Ludovisi district side by the Aurelian Walls, was chosen in 1608 by Cardinal Scipione Borghese, nephew of Pope Paul V, as the construction site for a suburban villa immersed in an enormous park. The villa was designed by Flavio Ponzio, who nevertheless did not complete the work that was instead terminated by Vasanzio and Rainaldi.

Work on both the villa, which housed the magnificent art collection of the Borghese family, and the enormous surrounding **park** continued into the next centuries in two major stages: one, between 1766 and 1793, conducted by Mario and Antonio Asprucci and another, beginning in 1822, at the hand of Luigi Canina. Canina revamped the garden - which had already been modified from its original Italian style to English - by adding statues and architectural elements of neoclassical inspiration (the Greek and Egyptian **propylaea**, the **Fountain of Aesculapius**, the **Roman Arch**) to those elements already installed in the late 1700s by the Aspruccis (the **Lion Portico**, the **Temple of Aesculapius** on the island at the center of a small lake, and **Piazza di Siena**, on the model of the Roman stadiums, which today hosts one of the most important world equestrian meets).

The recently restored villa, also called the **Casino Borghese**, is home to the **Museo Borghese** (collection of sculptures, marbles, and other finds of the Roman age) and the **Galleria Borghese** (picture gallery). These are two of the most celebrated collections of art in the world; both got their start with the collections of Cardinal Scipione, who besides many paintings also brought together antiquities of different provenance and charged the greatest artists of the time with their restoration. Perhaps the most illustrious was Gian Lorenzo Bernini; for his rich patron,

Museo Borghese. Gian Lorenzo Bernini, Apollo and Daphne *and below, the* Rape of Proserpine.

Galleria Borghese. Above, the tondo of the Virgin with the Child, Young Saint John, and Angels *by Botticelli.*

Museo Borghese, the celebrated Paolina Borghese *by Canova.*

Bernini also sculpted an number of masterpieces of Baroque statuary: *David*, sculpted in 1623-1624, whose head is a self-portrait of the artist, *Apollo and Daphne*, a marble group of the same period but of mythological inspiration, as is the *Rape of Proserpine*, a youthful masterpiece.

Bernini also created other works, in collaboration with his father Pietro, such as *Aeneas and Anchises* and *Truth Unveiled by Time*, an example of that allegory so dear to the Baroque heart. These sculptures are on exhibit in the villa alongside such ancient works as the celebrated *Hermaphrodite*, the *Dancing Silenus*, and many *busts of emperors* that alternate with the *polychrome marble busts* created in the 16th century, following the classical models, by Della Porta.

The collection, further enlarged in the 1700s, was arranged in rooms of the Casino that were specially decorated for the purpose (by artists such as Pacetti and Unterberger) with motifs inspired by the works each was destined to house. In 1807, Prince Camillo Borghese sold his collection to his brother-in-law Napoleon Bonaparte, who carried off many of the works to Paris, where they still form the nucleus of the classical antiquities section of the Louvre. Two years earlier, Camillo's wife Paulina Bonaparte had been portrayed by Canova in the pose of *Venus* in the work also known as **Paolina Borghese**, one of the museum's treasures.

Museo Borghese. David by Bernini and above, a detail of the head.

Like the collection of statuary and antiquities, the collection of canvases that makes up the **Galleria Borghese** was begun by Cardinal Scipione Borghese, who assembled in the rooms of the villa a great number of masterpieces by the greatest painters of the 16th and 17th centuries. Caravaggio is perhaps the best represented, with some of his most interesting and evocative works: the *Boy with a Fruit Basket*, one of the master's first Roman works, the *Little Bacchus*, the *Madonna dei Palafrenieri*, *Saint Jerome*, and the *David* with the head of Goliath that is one of the Lombard painter's last works and in which the slain giant wears his countenance. Alongside the canvases of the great Baroque artist, Cardinal Scipione collected works of enormous value by Raphael (the *Entombment of Christ*, perhaps better known as the *Borghese Deposition*), Titian (*Sacred and Profane Love*), and painters of the Ferrarese school (*Apollo* by Dosso Dossi). Later acquisitions (including the addition of the collection of Olimpia Aldobrandini, wife of Paolo Borghese) brought to the gallery such masterpieces as the *Virgin and Child with Young Saint John, and Angels* by Botticelli, Correggio's *Danaë*, the *Portrait of a Man* by Antonello da Messina, and works by many other Italian and foreign masters (Domenichino, Lorenzo Lotto, Parmigianino, Veronese; Rubens, Cranach).

Galleria Borghese. Caravaggio, Boy with a Fruit Basket and Saint Jerome.

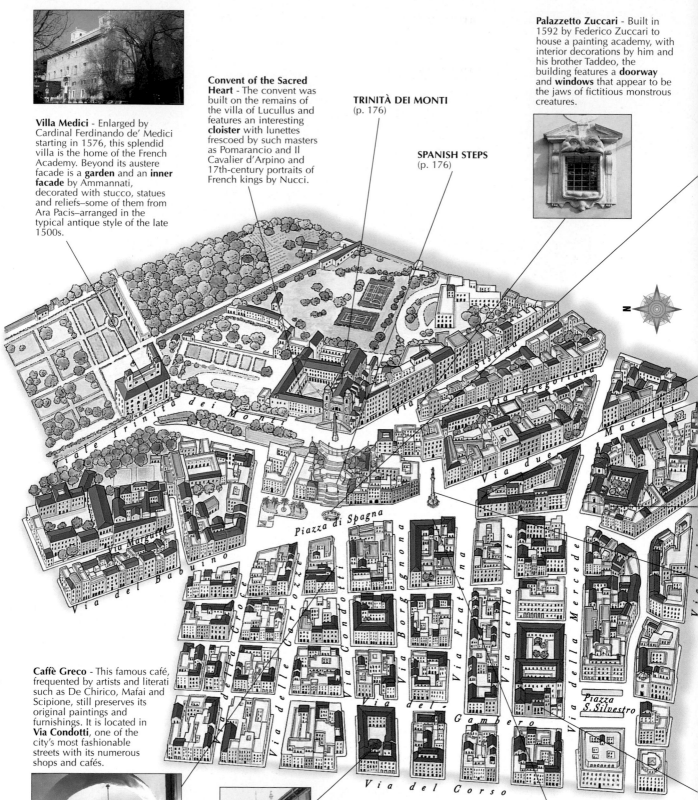

Villa Medici - Enlarged by Cardinal Ferdinando de' Medici starting in 1576, this splendid villa is the home of the French Academy. Beyond its austere facade is a **garden** and an **inner facade** by Ammannati, decorated with stucco, statues and reliefs–some of them from Ara Pacis–arranged in the typical antique style of the late 1500s.

Convent of the Sacred Heart - The convent was built on the remains of the villa of Lucullus and features an interesting **cloister** with lunettes frescoed by such masters as Pomarancio and Il Cavalier d'Arpino and 17th-century portraits of French kings by Nucci.

TRINITÀ DEI MONTI (p. 176)

SPANISH STEPS (p. 176)

Palazzetto Zuccari - Built in 1592 by Federico Zuccari to house a painting academy, with interior decorations by him and his brother Taddeo, the building features a **doorway** and **windows** that appear to be the jaws of fictitious monstrous creatures.

Caffè Greco - This famous café, frequented by artists and literati such as De Chirico, Mafai and Scipione, still preserves its original paintings and furnishings. It is located in **Via Condotti**, one of the city's most fashionable streets with its numerous shops and cafés.

Santissima Trinità degli Spagnoli - This church, with its adjoining convent, was designed in the mid-1700s by Emanuel Rodriquez, who gave it the harmonious concave facade. The interior, with its elliptic plan, contains the *Holy Trinity* by Giaquinto.

Palazzo di Spagna - Built to house the Spanish Embassy to the Vatican, the building, an expression of Roman Baroque, owes its interior decorations to the works of several great masters, including Bernini. His *Damned soul* and *Blessed soul* are among his most intense works.

Fontana della Barcaccia - Commissioned by Pope Urban VIII Barberini, to whom the heraldic bees in the decorations refer, the fountain was perhaps one of the most successful works of Pietro Bernini, who designed it with the help of his son Gian Lorenzo in 1629.

Palazzo di Propaganda Fide - Originally built at the end of the 1500s, the palace was donated in 1626 to the congregation of Propaganda Fide, instituted by Gregory XV in 1622. Bernini was first given the project to enlarge and remodel building, which was then finished by Borromini. Bernini produced the terra cotta facade on the piazza, while Borromini designed the original facade in via di Propaganda. Within the palace is the **church of the Re Magi**, whose original plan by Bernini was altered by Borromini between 1660 and 1666.

SANT'ANDREA DELLE FRATTE
(p. 176)

Column of the Immaculate Conception - The column, moved here in 1856 to recall the dogma of the conception of Mary without original sin proclaimed by Pius IX, came from the monastery of Santa Maria della Concezione in Campo Martius. Surmounting the column is the bronze statue of the *Virgin*, and at its base are the statues of the *prophets Moses, Isaiah, Ezekiel* and *David*.

San Silvestro in Capite - This church, first built in the 8th century with the adjoining convent, the latter being demolished to make way for the central post office, was initially called '*intra duos hortos*' for the gardens and vineyards that surrounded it. It was later

called '*in capite*' because of the precious relic it held: the head of the Baptist. The original church was completely rebuilt in the 13th century, when the soaring and airy Romanesque **campanile**, with five levels of twin coupled-columns, was built. Despite the Baroque restoration of the entire structure, traces of the church's medieval past remain in the fine **doorway** that adorns the rich **facade**, with its pilaster strips giving it a rhythmic effect and the *statues of Saints* that look out on the piazza below, designed between 1595 and 1601 by Francesco da Volterra and Carlo Maderno. The green inner court features numerous *stone fragments*.

PIAZZA DI SPAGNA

*T*he large and elegant area that extends around Piazza di Spagna and its famous Spanish Steps comprises two small sections of the Colonna and Campo Martius precincts, which have come together here through a common experience of urbanization that has developed over the centuries. In antiquity, both areas were within the Campo Martius, constituting the easternmost part and the outer edge of the inhabited area. The areas rose to the verdant heights of the Pincio, then called Collis Hortulorum owing to its wealth of gardens; among these were the famed Horti Luculliani of the villa of Lucullus, where the **Convent of the Sacred Heart** stands today. The area's rural status continued through the Middle Ages, when it was home to numerous vineyards, vegetable gardens and woods. This latter feature is still evident in the name of the church of **Sant'Andrea delle Fratte**, derived from the Latin expression 'de fractis', or the thickets for which the area was known. Other remaining names also trace the area's antique rural status: Via Capo le Case, for example, comes from the Latin 'ad capita domorum', or the limit of the inhabited city, a characteristic that did not change until the 1600s. For the most part, however, the area was only dotted here and there by occasional houses and old religious foundations, among which **San Silvestro in Capite**, built on the ruins of the ancient Temple of the Sun.

In the 1500s, while the western parts of Colonna and Campo Martius underwent a building boom with the addition of new streets, squares and buildings, the areas closer to Pincio witnessed the creation of new convents, such as those of the Carmelites at **San Giuseppe a Capo le Case** and the Discalced Hermits of Spain at **San Idelfonso**. The commanding position and vast gardens at the summit of Pincio convinced Cardinal Ferdinando de' Medici to buy a mansion there in 1576, which he transformed into the sumptuous **Villa Medici**.

Gregory XIII gave impetus to a more far-reaching urbanization in the area, which especially continued with Sixtus V, who designed the strada Felice and undertook a major program of public works between 1585 and 1589. The strada Felice, now called **via Sistina** in its first section, linked the church of **Trinità dei Monti** with the Jubilee basilica of Santa Croce di Gerusalemme, passing around the basilica of Santa Maria Maggiore.

During the 1600s and 1700s, a building boom was initiated by the two foreign communities in the area. The French founded their national church in **Santi Andrea e Claudio dei Borgognoni,** and in the 1800s converted the Villa Medici into the seat of the French Academy, founded by Louis XIV in 1666 as a way to allow young artists to finish their training in Italy. The Spanish established their religious center in the church of **Santissima Trinità degli Spagnoli** and their political center in **Palazzo di Spagna**, which is still the Spanish Embassy to the Vatican. The strong presence of these two nations also influenced the names and nature of the area. What had been known until the 16th century as the 'platea Trinitatis', from the church of Trinità dei Monti that dominates the square, started to be called **Piazza di Spagna**. In the meantime, the area towards Via del Babuino was called Piazza di Francia.

The streets around these squares began to host artists, writers and foreign intellectuals, especially in the houses of **Via Margutta**, where many workshops and artists' studios are still found. And it was in Piazza di Spagna that one of the most famous and scenographic examples of urban embellishment of the Baroque period arose: the **Scalinata di Trinità dei Monti**, or the **Spanish Steps**, are still one of the most popular spots for tourists from all over the world.

THE SPANISH STEPS AND THE CHURCH OF TRINITÀ DEI MONTI

In 1728, Montesquieu, then traveling in Italy, saw the Spanish Steps, completed only several years earlier. Surprisingly, his opinion was negative. "The Scalinata di Trinità dei Monti," he wrote, "is in bad taste. There is no architecture of any kind, and it can barely be seen, except for the first ramp. They should have made it a fine work and put up some columns. Moreover, the work was done so poorly that part of it has collapsed."

Although the historical fact about the partial collapse is true, caused by a movement of the earth beneath the hill, the opinion of the French philosopher on the harmonious stairway is not widely shared. Ordered by Pope Innocent XIII and initiated by architect Francesco De Sanctis in 1723, the Spanish Steps impress the thousands of visitors who come every day to enjoy the monument, now one of the symbols of Rome and of all of Italy.

The ascent to the church of Trinità dei Monti, which was once reached by tree-lined paths, is now made on the sinuous stairs formed by a succession of twelve ramps, which split apart and reconnect in a play of perspectives. The focal points throughout remain the church itself and the **Sallustian Obelisk**, which was once in the *Horti Sallustiani* and then placed here by Antinori in 1789, under Pius VI. The decorations of the stairs include the heraldic eagle of the Conti family, to which Innocent XIII belonged, and the French lily, since the **church of Trinità dei Monti** was French. The church and the adjoining convents were built by King Louis XII of France in 1502 and consecrated some 80 years later by Sixtus V in occasion of the opening of the strada Felice, which passed in front of the church. Restored in the 1800s, the church now has a universally known **facade**, with two characteristic twin belltowers by Maderno, perhaps from a design of Giacomo Della Porta. The **interior**, with a rich collection of art and impressive architecture, has numerous side chapels adorned with paintings by Perin del Vaga, the Zuccari brothers and especially Daniele da Volterra, with his famous and intense *Deposition*.

SANT'ANDREA DELLE FRATTE

In the 12th century, this church was so far beyond the inhabited area that it received the name Sant'Andrea de Hortis, meaning "of the gardens." Later the name was changed to the more prosaic '*de Fractis*' and then 'delle Fratte' (thickets), the name it has kept. Originally belonging to the Scots and donated by Sixtus V to the Minim friars of San Francesco di Paola, the building was entirely rebuilt by Gaspare Guerra for the marquis De Bufalo in the early 1600s and completed by Borromini in the middle of the same century.

It was Borromini who designed the semi-elliptical apse, the drum of the cupola, left incomplete, and the original **campanile**, which can admired in all of its bold architectural conception from via Capo le Case. The tower is a square structure over several levels, surmounted by a fanciful crowning of hermae in the shape of cherubs holding the *cross of St. Andrew* and the *buffalo*, the heraldic symbol of the commissioning family. It is all topped by a metallic crown like that of St. Ives of the Sapienza.

The **interior**, with a single nave and barrel vaults, has among its works two pieces by another genius of Roman Baroque, who was said to be the implacable adversary of Borromini. The two beautiful **angels** are in fact by Bernini, the *Angel with the crown of thorns* and the *Angel with a scroll*. Sculpted by the master between 1668 and 1669 to decorate Ponte Sant'Angelo, they were brought here to save them from the elements. One of the side chapels provides access to the **cloister** of the adjoining convent of the Minim, where lunettes with frescoes depicting the *story of San Francesco di Paola* can be admired.

Trinità dei Monti.
The plaque giving the history of the famous Spanish Steps.

A view of the Sallustian Obelisk.

Above, right, the inscription on the facade of the Palazzo di Propaganda Fide.

Left, the original campanile of Sant'Andrea delle Fratte.

Trinità dei Monti, the church, with its facade and the characteristic twin belltowers, at the top of the Spanish Steps.

N

Santa Maria della Scala - The church, adjoining the Carmelite convent, was begun in the late 16th century to contain the miraculous effigy of the *Madonna della Scala* and completed near the end of the following century. The interior is decorated with precious works of art, including the touching *Beheading of Saint John the Baptist* by Gherardo delle Notti, a *Virgin with Child* by the Cavalier d'Arpino, and the *high altar* with a ciborium by Carlo Rainaldi. The *Death of the Virgin* by Caravaggio, now in the Louvre, was originally painted for this church.

Ponte Sisto - This bridge owes its name to Pope Sixtus IV, who in 1473 charged Baccio Pontelli with building it to link the Regola and Parione districts to Trastevere. The new bridge rose on the site of the *Pons Aurelius*, built in 147 AD and carried away, after lengthy restoration by the prefect Symmachus in the mid-4th century, by the flood of 589.

San Giovanni dei Genovesi - This church was built at the same time as the adjoining **Ospizio dei Genovesi**, built in the late 15th century to care for ill sailors of the nearby port of Ripa Grande. The **cloister** of the hospice, attributed to Baccio Pontelli and dated to about 1481, with its octagonal pillars and its harmonious beamed loggia that frames the ancient well, is perhaps one of Rome's most beautiful. The **church**, rebuilt in the 1700s and the 1800s, is home to the *funeral monument to Meliaduce Cicala*, the Genovese nobleman who founded the charitable institution.

Torre Anguillara - The tower, like the adjacent small palace, dates to the 13th century. It bears witness of the medieval past of the area and offers a fine example of the fortified homes of the powerful Roman families that fought over control here.

Sant'Egidio alla Scala - Formerly administered by the Descalced Carmelite Nuns, this small 17th-century church is home to a fine *Saint Giles* by Pomarancio, and the adjoining convent to the **Museo del Folklore**.

SANTA MARIA IN TRASTEVERE
(p. 182)

Piazza di Santa Maria in Trastevere - The space in front of the basilica of Trastevere, with an octagonal *basin* designed by Carlo Fontana in 1692, at its center, is delimited by an array of beautiful buildings. One of these is the *Palazzo di San Callisto*, once a Benedictine monastery adjoining the church dedicated to the saint; another is the 16th-century *Palazzo Cavalieri* with its elaborate Baroque portal.

SAN CRISOGONO
(p. 183)

Church and Monastery of San Cosimato - The complex, which includes the former Benedictine monastery and the church, was raised in the 10th and 11th centuries and restored in the 13th, to which time dates the **first cloister**. The **second cloister** was built under Sixtus IV. The 14th-century facade of the **church**, attributed to Baccio Pontelli, has a finely-decorated portal and a band of ogival arches in Tuscan red brick. The single-nave interior was remodeled in the 19th century but still conserves its precious 15th-century *frescoes* and parts of the coeval *funeral monument to Cardinal Lorenzo Cybo*, once in Santa Maria del Popolo and here reused to decorate the main altar.

SAN FRANCESCO A RIPA
(p. 183)

Santa Maria della Luce - Despite the competent 18th-century renovation by Valvassori following the episode of the prodigious light emanated by an image of the Madonna, this small building still exhibits traces of its medieval past in its beautiful Romanesque bell tower. The interior, which in its spatial organization reflects the most harmonious of late Baroque stylistic canons, was decorated by the painters Giovanni and Sebastiano Conca.

San Benedetto in Piscinula - This church was built in the 11th and 12th centuries over the *Cell of Saint Benedict*, a portion of the home of the saint's father in which Benedict is said to have spent the early years of his life. With the exception of the neoclassical facade, the building clearly exhibits its medieval origin, from the Romanesque bell tower downward to certain of the *capitals* on the columns of the center aisle, the *Chapel of the Madonna* that was once decorated with mosaics, the 14th-century paintings, and the beautiful *Cosmatesque floors.*

Piazza Mastai - This square, in the heart of the Mastai Quarter, was commissioned in the late 19th century by Pope Pius IX to provide space for the *Manifattura Tabacchi*, a neoclassical building designed by Antonio Sarti, and the homes of the tobacco workers. It was designed by Andrea Busiri Vici, also the author of the *fountain* at the center of the square.

SANTA CECILIA IN TRASTEVERE (p. 180)

SANTA MARIA DELL'ORTO (p. 181)

Former Apostolic Hospice of San Michele a Ripa Grande - This enormous complex, today the seat of the Ministry of Cultural and Environmental Resources, that with its more than 300 meters of facade dominated the port of Ripa Grande, was founded in the early 17th century by Monsignor Tommaso Odaleschi. The primitive nucleus, built by De Rossi and Fontana, rose near Porta Portese; a woolen mill, a reformatory, barracks for the port customs officers, the church of the Madonna del Buon Viaggio, a hospice for the aged, the church of San Michele, and other minor buildings were later added to the original boarding facility.

Porta Portese - Opened by order of Innocent X in Urban VIII's city walls to replace the *Porta Portuensis* in the Aurelian Walls, this gate is today the starting point for the Sunday **market**, with its stalls lining Via Portuense, at which it is reputedly possible to find anything one desires.

TRASTEVERE

*I*n the republican age, the right bank of the Tiber, known as Trastevere from the Latin trans Tiberim ('beyond the Tiber'), was occupied by commercial settlements connected with the activities of the river port on the opposite bank. Only later, when villas began to be built in what are now the preeminent portions of the neighborhood, did the district take on a residential character; it also acquired a few public buildings, such as Augustus' **Naumachia**, of which there remain traces near San Cosimato. The rest of the area was populated by communities of foreigners, above all Oriental peoples, who were responsible for the diffusion of many cults of which traces are visible in the **Syrian Sanctuary** built in the sacred wood of the goddess Furrina in the first century AD. The Jews were also many in number, and this fact explains the rapid spread in this area of the city of the Christian religion and the creation, in the 4th and 5th centuries at the dawn of the Middle Ages, of the various tituli on which there later rose basilicas and churches of great importance, such as **Santa Maria in Trastevere**, **Santa Cecilia**, and **San Crisogono**.

Many bridges linked the district to part of the city on the left bank of the Tiber. There were the two from the Isola Tiberina, the Pons Fabricius and the Pons Cestius, and a short distance away the Pons Aemilius, today known as Ponte Rotto. The bridges led directly to the Portus Tiberinus facilities, the Forum Boarium, and the Forum Holitorium. Further up the river, instead, Trastevere was linked to the Campus Martius by the Pons Aurelius - rebuilt as **Ponte Sisto** under Sixtus IV - and another bridge built by Agrippa, now lost. Downriver, near Ripa Grande, was the **Pons Sublicius**; it is best remembered for the episode of Horatius Cocles who singlehandedly repulsed Porsenna's Etruscan forces at this crossing. Lastly, there was the fourth-century Marble Bridge (or Bridge of Theodosius) that linked the district with the Aventine and the Emporium.

Although the population decreased in the Middle Ages, the ethnic composition of the area remained unchanged; the Jewish component was strong until 1555, when Pope Paul IV relegated the Jewish community to the Ghetto; there were also many synagogues, none of which has survived. Between the year 1000 and the 13th century, development in the area was characterized by a sharp upswing in civil and religious architecture: Trastevere thus acquired new churches and monasteries like **San Cosimato**, **San Benedetto in Piscinula**, and **San Francesco a Ripa**, and many of the older churches were restored and enlarged. With the temporary transfer of the papal see to Avignon, the development activity was suspended.

Building resumed on a large scale only in the late 15th century, and in particular under Sixtus IV, with the construction of the roads along the banks of the Tiber - among which the Via Santa, later rebuilt by Julius II as Via della Lungara - and new streets like Via dei Pettinari. Following the expansion of the **Ripa Grande river port**, the area behind it also became the object of development, with the church of **Santa Maria dell'Orto** and above all the church and hospice of **San Giovanni dei Genovesi**, built especially for caring for sailors who were ill or in need of assistance. Important construction work was also conducted under Paul V in the 17th century: Trajan's Aqueduct was restored to use and renovation of the area behind the port began.

In the following century, construction activity extended to the area immediately backing on the Tiber, where the immense complex of the **Apostolic Hospice of San Michele a Ripa Grande** rose up a piece at a time. The last of the great urban development projects of papal Rome was that conducted by Pope Pius IX around **Piazza Mastai**. Later, the decline in port activity, the improvement of the banks of the Tiber with the raising of walls to protect against the frequent floods, and the creation of Viale Trastevere brought other changes to the area, but all this notwithstanding Trastevere has never lost its unique character and its unmistakable atmosphere.

Santa Cecilia in Trastevere. The facade on the courtyard, with its garden, and the fine Romanesque bell tower.

Below, the ciborium in the church of Santa Cecilia in Trastevere and a detail of its decoration.

SANTA CECILIA IN TRASTEVERE

This basilica in Trastevere is dedicated to the young martyr Cecilia, who according to tradition lived here with her husband Valerian, sainted as well. Despite its having been remodeled many times over the centuries, the complex has preserved all its ancient charm with its series of courtyards and other structures in the shade of a superb Romanesque **bell tower** crowned by unmistakable pinnacles, its still-inhabited enclosed convent, with its marvelous cloister, and the innumerable masterpieces of art preserved within its walls. The church was built on the site of the *titulus Caeciliae* before Pope Paschal I's reign in the fifth century, and was in large part rebuilt in about 1110. Other remodeling followed; not the least important was the work that in the 19th century 'imprisoned' the ancient columns of the nave, which threatened to crumble, in pillars.

In the 1700s, Ferdinando Fuga created the theatrical **entrance** that leads to a large garden **courtyard** with at its center a sizeable marble basin used in Roman times as a fountain. The courtyard is overlooked, as well as by the bell tower, by the Baroque facade of the church, which is preceded by a charming **portico** decorated with an elegant mosaic frieze dating to the 12th century. Under the arches, alongside numerous medieval finds, is the *monument to Cardinal Sfondrati*, designed by Girolamo Rainaldi (or by Stefano Maderno), commemorating the prelate who engineered the finding of the body of Saint Cecilia. The interior, preceded by an **atrium** with the *monument to Cardinal Forteguerri* by Mino da Fiesole, is in 18th-century style with a wide **nave**, the ceiling of which was frescoed by Conca with the *Apotheosis of Saint Cecilia*.

Off the aisles, which are embellished with valuable paintings including Guido Reni's *Saint Valerian and Saint Cecilia*, there open a number of interesting chapels. The name of the harmonious *Calidario Chapel*, in late Renaissance style with stuccowork decoration and paintings of scenes from the life of the martyr, recalls the room that in Roman times was used for steam bathing and in which, as tradition narrates, Cecilia's persecutors left her for three days in an attempt to suffocate her - but from which she escaped unscathed. The 15th-century *Ponziani Chapel* is decorated with beautiful coeval frescoes and a Cosmatiwork altar facing; the *Reliquary Chapel* was designed by Luigi Vanvitelli, also the author of the altarpiece and the fresco in the vault.

But the portion of the basilica that more than any other preserves works of intense artistic inspiration is the **apse** with its facing **presbytery**. Here, as though projected against the luminous, 9th-century Byzantine mosaics of the vault of

the apse, portraying the *Blessing Christ with Saints Paul, Cecilia, Paschal I* (shown with a square halo because he was still alive when the work was created), *Peter, Valerian, and Agatha* and the allegory of the *Mystical Lamb*, there dominates Arnolfo di Cambio's **altar canopy**: created in 1293, this elegant masterpiece by the Tuscan artist is like an embroidery in marble constellated with the gracious figures of angels, saints, prophets, and the evangelists. The ciborium in turn contains another outstanding sculpture: the **statue of Saint Cecilia** sculpted by Stefano Maderno, who used as his model the body of the young martyr, found intact during the excavations in the Catacombs of San Callisto on the Via Appia ordered in 1599 by Cardinal Sfondrati. The saint is portrayed as she lay, with her face turned aside and her hands showing the one three and the other one finger to symbolize the dogma of the Trinity she would not abandon even at the moment of her death.

The left aisle leads to the 13th-century cloister, which opens into the **nuns' choir** room with its fine **Last Judgment** by Pietro Cavallini, a medieval fresco more or less coeval with Arnolfo di Cambio's canopy. Although it has reached us in a fragmentary state, it is still an intensely dramatic work showing *Christ* between the beseeching *Virgin* and *Saint John the Baptist*; the group is surrounded by the *Apostles* and around the whole is a *Choir of Angels* and fragments of celestial and infernal visions with the ranks of the blessed and the reprobates.

Interior of Santa Cecilia in Trastevere. Details of the Last Judgment by Pietro Cavallini (13th cent.) and of the portraits of Saints Paschal, Paul, and Cecilia in the Byzantine mosaic in the apse (9th cent.)

SANTA MARIA DELL'ORTO

This church, specially built by an unknown architect of Bramante's circle to house a *Virgin with Child* detached from the wall of a garden (hence the name of the church), was begun in 1495 and completed halfway through the following century by Guidetto Guidetti. Its construction was financed by the contributions of many Roman craftsmen's congregations, among which the quaint and now-defunct 'Universities' of the grocers, the poulterers, and the vermicelli-makers, as is testified in the adjacent **oratory**.

Although the 16th-century facade begun by Vignola and completed by Francesco da Volterra is still intact, the Renaissance **interior** is mostly masked by the vivacious Baroque decoration that frames Zuccari's precious 16th-century paintings in the apse and Baglione's frescoes on the walls of the presbytery and in some of the side chapels.

The Renaissance facade of the church of Santa Maria dell'Orto.

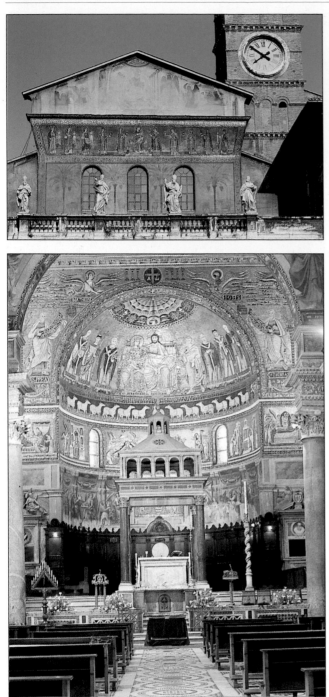

SANTA MARIA IN TRASTEVERE

Traditionally, this church is considered the first to have been opened for worship in Rome and in any case the first to be dedicated to the Virgin Mary. The *titulus Calisti* was founded in the third century by Pope Calixtus I and dedicated to him after he was sainted. It rose on the site on which, according to the chronicles of the times, the earth erupted oil in 38 BC, an event later construed as a miraculous annunciation of the birth of Christ. The *Fons Olei* (Fount of Oil) is still marked by a plaque set near the presbytery of the church.

On the site, Pope Julius I had a basilica-like structure built; the final form is, however, the result of later alterations dating to the pontificate of Innocent II, who between 1130 and 1143 had the building restructured using materials taken from the Baths of Caracalla; nevertheless, neither the original basilica plan nor the placement of the twenty-two ancient granite columns that separate the aisles were modified.

In 1702, Clement XI charged Carlo Fontana with rebuilding the **portico**, which, with its rich collection of epigraphs, marbles, and Roman and Christian reliefs, stands against the beautiful **facade** with its curious horizontal concave molding surmounted by a tympanum and a 13th-century *mosaic* band (perhaps retouched by Pietro Cavallini) portraying the *Virgin Enthroned with Two Donors* and two *Processions of Women*. Alongside rises the massive Romanesque **bell tower**, culminating in a 17th-century aedicula.

At the rear of the **nave**, with its elaborate coffered *wooden ceiling* designed by Domenichino (who also painted the center canvas of the *Assumption of the Virgin*), is the beautiful **apse** decorated with elegant gold-ground *mosaics* from two different eras. Those of the triumphal arch and the vault are from the 1100s; those of the lower register, divided into panels, date to the end of the following century. The first series, created following the death of Innocent II in 1143, portrays on the arch the *Symbols of the Evangelists* and the *Prophets Jeremiah and Isaiah* and in the half-dome of the apse *Christ Crowing the Virgin* with to the left and right a series of figures of saints and popes involved in the various phases of construction of the church. Immediately below, the strip depicting the *Mystical Lamb* surrounded by twelve sheep, symbols of the Apostles, concludes the older series of mosaics. The panels depicting *Scenes from the Life of the Virgin* were instead created in 1291 by Pietro Cavallini for Cardinal Bertoldo Stefaneschi, who is shown as a donor in the medallion of the *Virgin and Child with Saints Peter and Paul*.

The additions in modern times were many: the *Altemps Chapel*, built for Cardinal Marco Sittico Altemps by Marti-

Santa Maria in Trastevere. Above, the upper portion of the facade and the Romanesque-style bell tower.

Center, the interior with the vault of the apse and the triumphal arch, both decorated with mosaics, with at the center the marble ciborium.

Below, a detail of the mosaic, on the facade, with the Virgin Enthroned *(13th cent.).*

Interior of Santa Maria in Trastevere. Twelfth-century bishop's throne.

no Longhi the Elder in 1585, contains the Byzantine-style encaustic of the *Madonna della Clemenza*; the *Avila Chapel* dates to the following century and was designed by Antonio Gherardi, who employed his genius in creating exuberant trompe-l'oeil effects above all in the imaginative small dome that appears to be supported by four flying angels; the tiny *Baptistery Chapel*, by Filippo Raguzzini, is instead a true masterpiece of the rococo, dated 1741.

plan, with its three aisles divided by twenty-two ancient granite columns, its beautiful Cosmatesque floor, and the **apse**, the vault of which is still refulgent with the splendid mosaic, by Pietro Cavallini's school, of the *Virgin and Child with Saint Crysogonus and Saint James*.
Bernini is instead the author of the **Chapel of the Holy Sacrament** at the end of the right aisle, and his pupils of the sculptures decorating it.

SAN CRISOGONO

This third largest of the medieval basilicas in Trastevere was built on the 5th-century *titulus Chrysogoni* in 1123-1129 by order of Cardinal Giovanni da Crema, who had the original basilica filled in. Portions of the structure can still be seen below today's church, together with some of the frescoes that decorated its walls and apse.
Despite the transformation of the structure in the 17th century, the 12th-century plan suffered no major modifications. In 1620-1626, Giovanni Battista Soria directed the renovation of the building promoted by Cardinal Scipione Borghese.
On the exterior, he rebuilt the **portico**, using the same granite columns used in the Middle Ages, but he left substantially intact the mighty **bell tower**, built in 1124, adding only the spire.
Soria's hand in the interior was also rather restrained. He retained the 13th-century medieval basilica

SAN FRANCESCO A RIPA

Once the property, together with the adjoining 10th-century **monastery**, of the Benedictines who various times offered hospitality to Saint Francis, the church was acquired in 1229 by the Friars Minor, who also occupied the monastery and in the 1250s promoted various renovation actions.
Saint Francis' presence is attested to by a copy (the original is in the Pinacoteca Vaticana) of the *effigy of the saint*, attributed to Fra' Margaritone d'Arezzo, in the Chapel of Relics.
In the simple three-aisled church, rebuilt by Mattia De Rossi in the late 1600s, the Paluzzi Albertoni Chapel is home to a masterpiece of Baroque sculpture, the statue of **Blessed Ludovica Albertoni**, a powerful late work by Bernini that in certain ways is superior to his *Saint Theresa* in Santa Maria della Vittoria.

Interior of Santa Maria in Trastevere. The apse mosaic of the Presentation in the Temple *from the series* Scenes from the Life of the Virgin *(13th cent.).*

San Crisogono. The facade with the 17th-century portico and the massive Romanesque bell tower.

Interior of San Francesco a Ripa. The death of the Blessed Ludovica Albertoni as portrayed by Bernini in a late work (1675).

Villa Celimontana - The land on which the villa stands with its adjoining public **park**, was bought by the Mattei family in the second half of the 1500s, to which period the **Casino**, by Jacopo Del Duca, dates. The Egyptian **obelisk** from the time of Rameses II that stands in the park was once preserved in the convent of Santa Maria in Aracoeli and was donated to Ciriaco Mattei in 1584 by the Roman senate.

Santi Giovanni e Paolo - The brief return by the emperor Julian the Apostate to the ancient pagan religion and to the persecution of Christians culminated in 362 with the murder of the two officials of the imperial guard, Giovanni (John) and Paolo (Paul), to whom the church is dedicated. It was built in 398, by the Roman senator and saint Pammachius and his father Bizante, on the site of the martyrs' torture and death, but was soon thereafter damaged during the 5th-century barbarian incursions. After being sacked for the nth time in 1084 by the Normans, Pope Paschal II had the church restored at the same time that the adjoining convent and the beautiful **bell tower** were being built. The tower was completed in the 12th century together with the **portico** that replaced the original narthex.

After renovations in the 1700s and 1800s, mid-20th century restoration revealed what remained of the early structures of the church: for instance, the lovely marble *five-lighted windows* of the 4th-century facade and the beautiful 13th-century *portal* with its Cosmati-work inlays and an eagle sculpted in the architrave.

The interior, with a *plaque* halfway along the nave marking the site of the martyrdom of John and Paul, persists in its 18th-century guise. Traces of the past are instead clearly visible in the intricate labyrinth of the **foundations**, which incorporate the remains of five buildings raised between the 1st and the 4th centuries for a total of about 20 rooms.

La Vignola - This 16th-century summerhouse with its airy portico was originally on the slopes of the 'Piccolo Aventino'; it was moved to its present location when the Passeggiata Archeologica was created.

Arch of Dolabella - Built by the consuls Publius Cornelius Dolabella and Gaius Junius Silanus, this first-century arch may represent the reconstruction of the early Porta Celimontana in the Servian Walls, over which Nero's aqueduct ran in imperial times.

San Gregorio Magno and the Three Oratories - Today's complex structure rises on the site of the monastery of Saint Andrew the Apostle founded by Saint Gregory the Great in 575. The **facade** by Giovanni Battista Soria, on the model of that of San Luigi dei Francesi, stands at the summit of a wide staircase. In the large courtyard are three oratories, or chapels, that were renovated in the early 17th century by Cardinal Baronio. That of **Sant'Andrea**, probably the original church founded by Saint Gregory; conserves two famous frescoes: the *Flagellation of Saint Andrew* by Domenichino and *Saint Andrew Led to Martyrdom* by Guido Reni. The oratory of **Santa Barbara**, or Oratory of the Triclinium, is also part of the original construction and owes its name to the ancient stone table on which it is said Saint Gregory offered food to twelve poor people who were later joined by a shining angel. The last oratory, dedicated to Saint Gregory's mother **Santa Silvia**, was built by Baronio; in the apse is Guido Reni's *Concert of Angels*.

N

Piazzale Numa Pompilio

Santa Maria in Domnica - The first church, raised in the 7th century on the remains of one of the barracks of the ancient Celian military complex, was rebuilt a couple of centuries later under Pope Paschal I. It then remained unaltered until 1513, when Cardinal Giovanni de' Medici, the future Pope Leo X, had it restored by Sansovino, who is undoubtedly the author of the elegant five-arch portico; tradition ascribes the elegant design of the **portico** to Raphael. Although documentation proving authorship does not exist, the Raphaelesque matrix is clearly visible in both this and much of the other work conducted in the 1500s.

Fontana della Navicella - This fountain takes its name from the marble model of an ancient Roman ship found in the nearby *Castra Peregrina* (the barracks of the provincial guard). It was set on a base during the reign of Leo X, but was not adapted to its present function until 1931, on occasion of the widening of the street on which it stands. The model was probably a votive offering to Isis by one of the Egyptian mariners serving with the Roman fleet, who venerated the goddess as their protectress. Other sources hold it to be a reproduction of the ship of Aesculapius.

Santo Stefano Rotondo - As the name itself suggests, this is one of Rome's three early-Christian circular-plan structures (together with the Baptistery of San Giovanni in Laterano and the church of Santa Costanza), all built during the first two centuries of Christendom and directly derived from analogous Roman constructions, typically those of the city's bath complexes. The building, completed in the 5th century and consecrated by Pope Simplicius, was originally composed of three concentric aisles divided by columns and intersected by the arms of a Greek cross structure. The early church began to undergo changes under Pope Innocent II (1300s) when a **portico** with columns taken from ancient monuments was added; a couple of centuries later, a transversal **colonnade** was built.

The 34 columns of the exterior ambulacrum were encased in the perimeter wall, along which in the late 1500s Pomarancio and Tempesta painted the *Martyrology*: thirty-four dramatic frescoes that show, with what is often explicit bluntness, the tortures to which the same number of saints were subjected.

The central portion of the church, separated from the exterior ambulacrum by twenty-two marble columns with Corinthian capitals, has a high **drum** in which a series of cambered windows, some of which with two lights, were opened during the 15th-century restorations.

San Sisto Vecchio - This medieval church was totally rebuilt in the 1700s by Raguzzini, who left only the soaring 12th-century **bell tower** intact. The church was granted in 1219 to Saint Dominic, who established his first monastery here; off the cloister, on what is traditionally considered the site of the saint's cell, is the **chapel** dedicated to him. In the interior of the church, among the flights of Raguzzini's architectural fancy, are traces of the building's medieval past in the 14th-century cycle of *frescoes* in the apse.

THE CAELIAN HILL

*O*riginally, the Caelian hill was called the Colle Querquetulano, on account of the vast oak (quercus in Latin) forests that covered its slopes in ancient times. It took its present name early in history - before the inhabitants of Albalonga, led by Tullius Hostilius, moved here after the destruction of their city - when the height was inhabited by the Etruscans, whose chief, Caelius Vibenna, had aided Romulus in the war against the Sabines. Recalling the first name of the hill was the Porta Querquetulana in the Servian Walls, from which the ancient Via Tuscolana started out. The other gates that opened on the hill were Porta Celimontana, on the remains of which the **Arch of Dolabella** was built, and Porta Capena, the starting point of the **Via Appia Antica**. The area was dotted with opulent patrician homes until Tiberius' time, when a fire swept the hill. The proverbially generous emperor indemnified the owners of the homes so fully that they were able to rebuild even more sumptuous villas - and the incident earned for the hill the name of Mons Augustus.

It was also home to some notable religious buildings, such as the temple of Hercules Victor and that of Minerva Capta; the most important, however, was the **Temple of the Divus Claudius**, built by Agrippina in memory of her husband. The structure was of colossal size (with a perimeter of 800 meters) and was unbelievably opulent in both its decoration and building materials. There remain some traces, near the church of San Giovanni e Paolo, of the enormous podium and the superstructures it supported.

Claudius' successor Nero instead made the hill the site of a great market, the Macellum Magnum, with a circular-plan domed building that according to some historians supplied the model for the early Christian church of **Santo Stefano Rotondo**, built nearby in about the 5th century. In the imperial age, this was the site of the Castra Peregrina, the barracks for the police forces detailed to the arrest and surveillance of prisoners. It was to two soldiers of this imperial guard, who were martyred under Julian the Apostate in 362 because they refused to make sacrifice to Jupiter, that the church of **Santi Giovanni e Paolo**, built on the site of their dwelling on the hill, was dedicated. Another house, belonging to Pope Gregory I, gave rise in the 4th century to another important Caelian church, **San Gregorio Magno**, dedicated to the sainted pope. It was from the adjoining convent that in 506 the monk Augustine set out for England on his mission of evangelization. The founding of **Santa Maria in Domnica** instead dates to the time of Paschal I. The church has a beautiful portal surmounted by an aedicula by Master Jacopo and his son Cosma, who between the 12th and 13th centuries founded the famous Cosmati school of Roman decorators and architects who for two centuries created refined works of inlaid marble and stone.

Otherwise, during the entire Middle Ages and the Renaissance the hill retained its agrestic character: it was scarcely populated and remained so even later, despite 19th-century speculation that threatened the harmonious rural atmosphere. The constitution of the enormous garden of **Villa Celimontana** as a public park put an end to such operations, even though work conducted in 1931 to widen Via della Navicella, on which the **Fontana della Navicella** stands, partially changed the look of the area.

Porta San Sebastiano - Originally called Porta Appia, the gate was built by Aurelius in connection with the consular Appian Way, with an opening of two arches and with cylindrical towers on each side. Honorius had the towers raised a further two storeys and strengthened with a robust quadrangular base. With only one of the two arches remaining, the exterior was restored with marble taken from the burial monuments lining the first section of the road. The gate, which is the best preserved of the Aurelian walls, houses the **Museum of the Roman Walls**.

Porta Latina - Flanked by a medieval tower, this gate is built of travertine and represents one the best preserved sections of the Aurelian Walls.

San Giovanni a Porta Latina - Probably founded around the 5th century, the church has undergone significant changes over the course of the centuries. It nevertheless still maintains much of its medieval appearance, with the facade featuring marble and granite columns and a beautiful 12th-century Romanesque *campanile*. The interior, with marble columns of varying dimensions separating the nave and aisles, contains a **cycle of frescoes** from the 12th century with *Scenes from the Old and New Testament*.

Jewish Catacombs - Together with those of the Villa Torlonia, these catacombs constitute the largest underground cemetery of the Roman Jewish community in the Imperial age.

Pagus Triopius - This vast estate belonging to Herodes Atticus, writer and friend of Marcus Aurelius, contains the remains of the **Tomb of Annia Regilla**, the wife of Atticus, and the **Grotto of the nymph Egeria**. According to tradition, the beautiful creature fell in love with Numa Pompilius, the second king of Rome, and inspired him to create the laws with which to govern his populace. Also found on the estate are the ruins of the **Temple of Ceres and Faustina**.

Arch of Drusus - The arch was erected between 211 and 216 to allow for the passage of the *Aqua Antoniniana*, the branch of the aqueduct that fed the nearby Baths of Caracalla, above the Appian Way. Honorius made it part of the defensive system of the adjoining Porta San Sebastiano, maintaining the fine columns in ancient yellow marble which can still be admired.

BASILICA DI SAN SEBASTIANO
(p. 188)

Via Appia

San Giovanni in Oleo - This small 5th-century oratory, completely rebuilt under Julius II by Baldassarre Peruzzi and later renovated by Borromini in 1658, was erected on the spot where St. John the Evangelist was martyred. Its name is derived from the cauldron of boiling oil in which the saint was said to have been immersed and from which he came out unharmed.

Via Ardeatina

CATACOMBS OF DOMITILLA
(p. 189)

Tomba di Priscilla - The tomb, built by the freeman Domitian Abascanthus for his wife Priscilla, was an enormous cylindrical mound covered in travertine and decorated with niches and statues. The Caetani erected a guard tower on the tomb in the 13th century, the remains of which are still visible. The **Catacombs of Priscilla** are located on the Via Salaria.

CATACOMBS OF ST. CALIXTUS
(p. 189)

CATACOMBS OF ST. SEBASTIAN
(p. 188)

Church of 'Domine quo vadis?' - Known in the Middle Ages as Santa Maria in Palmis, or del Passo, the church was built in the 9th century and again rebuilt between the 1500s and 1600s on the site where, according to tradition, Christ appeared to St. Peter as he was fleeing Rome; upon being asked the fateful question *"Domine, quo vadis?"* (Lord, whither goest thou?), Christ answered '*Romam iterum crucifigi*' (To Rome, to be crucified again). With that, the Apostle returned to Rome to face his martyrdom. The stone on which Jesus left his imprint (thus the medieval name of the church) was preserved here before being moved to the basilica of St. Sebastian.

THE CONSULAR ROADS

The Romans were the greatest road builders of antiquity. The most tangible sign of Roman expansion, the road network expanded apace with their territorial conquests and allowed for relatively easy linkages with the capital. First laid out during the Republican age and then lengthened during the Imperial age, the so-called 'consular roads' radiated from the center of Rome. They began, or converged, in the Roman Forum at the *Miliarum aureum*, a column erected by Augustus with the distances between Rome and the most important cities of the Empire inscribed on it. The first of the Roman roads was the **Appia Antica** (Appian Way), begun in 312 BC by the censor Appius Claudius. The road left Rome through the ancient Porta Capena in the Servian walls (and later through the Porta San Sebastiano in the Aurelian walls), and ran almost 400 kilometers to the city of Brindisi (Brundusium), is southern Italy. Running north, instead, was the **Flaminia** road, built between 223 and 219 BC by the censor Gaius Flaminius and linking the city with Rimini. The road, passing through the Aurelian walls at the Porta Flaminia (now the Porta del Popolo), crossed the Tiber at Ponte Milivio (*Pons Milvius*). This was also the point of departure for another north running road, the **Cassia**, built between 117 and 107 BC by censor Lucius Cassius Longinus to link Rome with central Etruria. The Cassia was also linked with the **Aurelia**, opened in 241 by censor Gaius Aurelius. Leaving Rome from the Porta Aurelia (now Porta San Pancrazio), the road connected Rome to the Tyrrhenian coast. Extended during the Imperial age to Arles, in France, the Aurelia rejoined the Cassia near present day La Spezia, and was throughout the Middle Ages the main link with France, taking on the name 'Francigena' and becoming the route used by pilgrims reaching Rome from northern Europe.

The Tomb of Cecilia Metella - Symbol of the Appian Way, this tomb, remaining nearly intact with the addition of the crenellated tower installed by the Caetani family in 1302 when it was made the keep for their adjacent castle, is the best preserved piece of the entire archaeological park. The tomb was erected around 50 BC for Cecilia Metella, the daughter of the counsel Quintus Metellus Creticus and the wife of the son of Crassus, a member of the first triumvirate with Caesar and Pompey. At one time the tumulus, at 20 meters in diameter, had a conical covering which was subsequently demolished. Still intact is the frieze with bucrania–heads of oxen garlanded with flowers–which gave rise to the area being called *Capo di Bove*. Next to the picturesque remains of the 14th-century **Caetani Castle** are the ruins of the antique Gothic church of **San Nicola a Capo di Bove**, a rare example of this style of architectural in Rome.

Pignatelli

Circus of Maxentius - Better preserved than the Circus Maximus, the Circus Maxentius still has the remains of the towers on the west side, the *carceres* from where the horses exited and the tiers of seats which accommodated some 10,000 spectators. Located along the 'spina' was the obelisk of Domitian, which Bernini brought to Piazza Navona to decorate the Fontana dei Fiumi.

The Mausoleum of Romulus - The structure, built by Maxentius for his young son Romulus, consisted of a large area enclosed by a portico, with a cylindrical building rising at the center. Inside, placed within the central pilaster, were the niches for the cinerary urns.

*T*he Appian Way was the most famous of the Roman consular roads, known since antiquity as Regina Viarum, or the queen of roads. This section of the old Appian Way, just beyond the walls of the city, is still lined with antique tombs, churches and catacombs. Today they are protected in an archaeological park, which begins at **Porta San Sebastiano** and continues for nine kilometers, at times through open countryside with cluster pines and cultivated fields. The road was opened in 312 BC by censor Appius Claudius, after whom it is named, and originally connected Rome with the Alban Hills. It was then lengthened by Appius to Capua and then, in 190 BC, to Brindisi. Still used during the Middle Ages, the road fell into decay in later times until it was repaired by Pius VI in the 18th century. The idea of transforming it into an archaeological park dates from the late 1800s, a job which is still in progress. With the dead buried outside of the city walls by law, the construction of the **Aurelian walls** led to a progressive build up along this section of the Appian Way, as in the suburban tracts of the other consular roads, with sepulchers and mausoleums. Some of these displayed much pomp and monumental greatness, as in the **Tomb of Annia Regilla** and the **Tomb of Cecilia Metella**, which became incorporated into the **Castello dei Caetani** during in the Middle Ages. The beauty and peace of the area also induced the construction of sacred buildings and princely homes. In the early 4th century the **Imperial Palace** of ancient Rome was built near the road, with the **Circus of Maxentius** and the **Mausoleum of Romulus**, the family mausoleum dedicated by Maxentius to his young son.

With the rise of Christianity, the Appian Way began hosting not only the tombs of pagans, but also those of the followers of the new religion. By the end of the 2nd century the first collective burial grounds arose; for practical reasons and local tradition, they were placed underground, often in pre-existing quarries of the locally abundant pozzolana or tufa. Thus began the **catacombs** (probably derived from the word cumba, or ditch), true hypogea or underground cemeteries that spread for kilometers through a network of subterranean galleries into which numerous tombs were dug. At least until the 4th century, they were used only as a burial grounds, where the cult of the dead was celebrated with liturgical commemorations and the so-called refrigeria, a sort of ritual banquet in honor of the defunct person. Starting from the 6th century and through the 12th century, the catacombs became sanctuaries dedicated to the worship and commemoration of the martyrs, so much so that they were called memoriae, or 'places of remembrance'. During this long period the shape of the catacombs changed, with the construction of small underground basilicas with stairways connecting them to the churches built above ground. These underground rooms were particularly important during the Barbarian invasions, when they were used to hide the precious relics of saints and martyrs.

On the Appian Way, the so-called **Catacombs of St. Calixtus** represent a rather ancient phenomenon, as they were mentioned as early as the beginning of the 3rd century, when Pope Zephyrinus entrusted their care to his deacon Calixtus. When the latter became Pope, he enlarged them to make them the official burial grounds of the Roman Church. Numerous popes were inhumed here, such as Sixtus II, martyred in 258 during the persecutions of Emperor Valerian. During the same persecutions the bodies of the Apostles Peter and Paul were temporarily kept in the nearby **Catacombs of St. Sebastian**, which took on the suggestive name of Memoria Apostolorum ad catacumbas. Only afterwards were the catacombs and the **basilica** above them dedicated to **St. Sebastian**, as among the numerous relics placed there were those of the centurion of the imperial guard, martyred by Diocletian at the Palatine Stadium. From the 9th century, due to new foreign invasions, all of the relics began to be placed in the city's basilicas and churches, and the catacombs steadily lost their importance until they were forgotten. Interest for this legacy of the beginnings of Christian life rose again in the 16th century, when Antonio Bosio, ante litteram scholar and archaeologist, retraced the entrances to some 30 catacombs during explorations of the consular roads, including the Appian. But it was not until the 1800s, on the basis of the information provided by Bosio, that they were systematically explored and reopened to the faithful and to lovers of antiquity.

BASILICA DI SAN SEBASTIANO

Built as the *Basilica Apostolorum* where the bodies of Saints Peter and Paul were once kept temporarily, the church, one of the seven pilgrimage churches of Rome, was dedicated to St. Sebastian in the middle of the 4th century. The saint's relics had been placed in the crypt below. In the early 1600s, Cardinal Scipione Borghese asked Flaminio Ponzio to rebuild the church, which was later completed by Vesanzio, giving it an elegant **facade** with a portico and an **interior** with a single nave and a fine wooden ceiling. The church contains the **Chapel of the Relics**, with the original stone bearing the footprints of Christ from *Domine, quo vadis?* The other chapel, dedicated to St. Sebastian, holds one of the arrows shot into the saint and is built above his crypt. There is also a *statue of the saint* by Giorgetti, a pupil of Bernini.

CATACOMBS OF ST. SEBASTIAN

Dug out of an ancient stone quarry, the catacombs of St. Sebastian were initially a pagan burial grounds before being used by Christians. They were actually composed of three **Mausoleums**, built in the 2nd century and covered with earth a century later to create an open flat area, the so-called **Triclia**, with a portico where the *refrigeria*, or liturgical banquets, were held and where the relics of Saints Peter and Paul, brought here temporarily in 258, were worshipped. The central focus of the intricate labyrinth of galleries is the **Crypt of St. Sebastian**, where the martyr who gave his name to the entire burial grounds was entombed. The numerous rooms of the catacombs have extremely interesting frescoes. Worthy of note among them is the fresco in the **Cubiculum of Jonah**, with a cycle depicting the famous biblical figure, and the *Miracle of the demoniac of Gerasa*, preserved in one of the three mausoleums. The subterranean grounds also contain the remains of the *Basilica Apostolorum*.

Basilica of St. Sebastian: the facade and two views of the interior.

Below, a detail of the wooden ceiling with an image of the martyr St. Sebastian.

*The Catacombs of Calixtus,
the painting of the Good Shepherd in the Crypt of Lucina
and a view of the Crypt of St. Cecilia.*

*Catacombs of Domitilla, the basilica of the Saints Nereus
and Achilleus and a section of the galleries.*

CATACOMBS OF ST. CALIXTUS

These vast catacombs, spreading out over four levels with some 20 kilometers of galleries, display an immense number of *cubicula* and *hypogea* decorated with frescoes in the preserved areas. The most ancient nucleus are the **Papal Crypt**, where the popes who were martyred and sanctified in the first centuries of Christianity were buried; the **Crypt of St. Cecilia**, where the body of the young martyr was found; the **Crypt of Lucina**; and the **Cubicula of the Sacraments**, with 3rd-century frescoes representing a wide range of religious objects. Dating from the 4th century are the **Crypts of Saints Gaius and Eusebius**, with the *sarcophagi* of the two popes.

CATACOMBS OF DOMITILLA

The catacombs, also called the Catacombs of Saints Nereus and Achilleus, are among the largest in Rome. According to tradition, they were built from the simple household sepulcher that belonged to Domitilla, the wife and niece of Flavius Clement and put to death by Domitian. Inside of the catacombs are the remains of the **Basilica dei Santi Nereo e Achilleo**: behind the apse is a cubiculum containing the fresco of *The defunct venerable invoking St. Petronilla*. Near the basilica is the very ancient *Cemetery of the Flavians*.
In another area of the catacombs is the so-called 'Good Shepherd', which takes its name from a sculpture and which preserves 2nd-century AD paintings in the vault. Found in a later area are fine depictions of the grain market and scenes of everyday work (3rd-4th century).

INDEX

Sites possessing museums or galleries are underlined

VATICAN, 10